the financial diaries

The Financial Diaries

*How American Families Cope in
a World of Uncertainty*

Jonathan Morduch
& Rachel Schneider

Princeton University Press
Princeton and Oxford

Requests for permission to reproduce material from this work should be sent to
Permissions, Princeton University Press

Published by Princeton University Press, 41 William Street,
Princeton, New Jersey 08540
In the United Kingdom: Princeton University Press, 6 Oxford
Street, Woodstock, Oxfordshire OX20 1TR

press.princeton.edu

Jacket design by Faceout Studio
Jacket image courtesy of Shutterstock

ISBN 978-0-691-17298-9

Library of Congress Control Number: 2016955128

British Library Cataloging-in-Publication Data is available

This book has been composed in Glypha LT Std and Sabon Next LT Pro

Printed on acid-free paper. ∞
Printed in the United States of America

1 3 5 7 9 10 8 6 4 2

For Amy, Leon, Sam, and Joe
For Ben, Isabel, and Ezra

Contents

Acknowledgments

The idea behind the U.S. Financial Diaries project was not initially ours. Instead, we got lucky. The Citi Foundation and Ford Foundation felt it was the right moment to take a fresh look at the finances of American households, and they approached us with the idea. We were honored and not a little daunted. The foundations provided us with an initial planning grant in 2009 and, later joined by the Omidyar Network, saw the project through with a helpful mix of patience and impatience. They pushed us to move quickly given the urgency of families' struggles, but they also allowed us the time needed to get the research right. While they offered insights and advice along the way, they imposed no restrictions on our conclusions or analyses. No doubt, they disagreed—and may still disagree—with some of what we have written, but they never asked us to do anything other than describe the data accurately and tell the families' stories as we heard them. We are deeply grateful to Frank DeGiovanni and Amy Brown at the Ford Foundation; Brandee McHale, Graham MacMillan, and Daria Sheehan at the Citi Foundation; and Chris Bishko and Tilman Ehrbeck at the Omidyar Network.

We are proud and humbled when we think about the families who shared their lives with us. This project required far more of participants than a typical research survey, both in terms of hours and openness. The families' willingness to share both their highs and their lows, to answer probing questions not only about what they were doing but about why and how they got there, has shaped all of the ideas in this book.

The U.S. Financial Diaries project benefited greatly from earlier experiences with financial diaries, particularly the work of Stuart Rutherford, Orlanda Ruthven, and Daryl Collins. Daryl and her colleagues at Bankable Frontier Associates were critical to the development of the U.S. Financial Diaries project, working with us to adapt the international methodology to the U.S. context. We greatly value Daryl's partnership.

For much of the project, Tim Ogden led the team's operations day to day. He was integral to the development and communication of our findings, not only as a reader and an advisor but also as a roll-up-his-sleeves editor and creator. His contributions can be seen on every page of this book.

The fieldwork was ably led by Nancy Castillo, who threw herself wholeheartedly into the project in its early years. She crossed the country consulting with experts, researched possible sites, developed and executed our initial project plan, and then recruited and managed the team of field researchers. The data analysis was conducted primarily by Anthony Hannagan and Julie Siwicki. Their ability to toggle between fine-grained views of individual households and big-picture technical analyses was essential to telling the families' stories, both in the specifics and in the broad picture.

Like the families, the dozen field researchers who collected the data at the center of the project invested far more than the gift of their time. The trust they established with the families during the year of data collection made the project possible. We are grateful to Alex Bibb, Mayra Cerda, Karen Durgans, Luzdary Giraldo, Naishia Jackson, Fredy Llanos, Mithu Maniruzzaman, Olivia Montgomery, Karla Reyes, Joyce Roberson, Kyle Schoolar, and Julie Siwicki.

We were also ably assisted in ways large and small by Alicia Brindisi, Megan Carver, Deidre Ciliento, James Davis, Shannon Deere, Kate Marshall Dole, Cheryl Durgans, Maria Enache, Liz Engle, Stephen Juneau, Charlene Kim, Aishwarya Kumar, Mithu Maniruzzaman, Zac McDermott, Kristen McNeill, Andrea Parra, Spencer Perry, Caroline Preston, James Schintz, Zachary Seaverns, Viral Tarpara, and Caiying (Lisa) Xu. Barbara Kiviat, Jean Lee, Rourke O'Brien, and Angela Profeta helped build and revise surveys and protocols to ensure that our questions would connect to broader conversations. Caitlin

Weaver, JoAnne Williams, and Vivian Yela expertly managed budgets and administration.

Many people and organizations helped. Local partners in each research site made introductions to families, gave field researchers office space and encouragement, and provided opportunities to share findings. We have not listed these partners individually in order to preserve the anonymity of the research sites, but their dedication and hospitality were essential to the project's success.

We benefited from regular conversation with the community of researchers, policy wonks, and practitioners who are advancing ideas about how to improve household economic security. We are indebted to these fellow travelers. Some of their work is described in the book, but we could have written about many more. We especially thank the U.S. Financial Diaries Advisory Board: Oren Bar-Gill, Michael S. Barr, Ray Boshara, Janis Bowdler, Alan P. Branson, John Caskey, Jose Cisernos, J. Michael Collins, Sheldon Danziger, Randy Dotemoto, Kathryn Edin, Amelia Erwitt, Gina Harman, David John, Jeffrey Liebman, Cathie Mahon, Justin Maxson, Sendhil Mullainathan, Manuel Orozco, Leigh Phillips, William M. Rogers III, David Rothstein, Ellen Seidman, Luz Urrutia, and Sudhir Venkatesh.

The Aspen Institute's Financial Security Program launched a yearlong inquiry into income volatility at just the right time for us. We are especially grateful to the participants in their convenings, who helped us crystalize key arguments that appear in this book, sometimes even while hiking. We also appreciate the chance to try out ideas at the CFED Assets Learning Conference, EMERGE, and Money2020, and at events sponsored by the Federal Reserve, Consumer Financial Protection Bureau, Federal Deposit Insurance Corporation, Roosevelt Institute, University of Wisconsin, Yale, Princeton, the World Bank, and other institutions. At each of these events, we found our ideas prodded and strengthened.

We were fortunate to have readers who commented on all or part of the draft manuscript with gentleness and good humor, and in many cases a sharp red pen: Ray Boshara, Ajay Chaudry, Frank DeGiovanni, Tilman Ehrbeck, Quinten Farmer, Tim Flacke, Joel ben Izzy, Melissa Koide, Susan Lambert, Rob Levy, Signe-Mary McKernan, Ida Rademacher, Caroline Ratcliffe, Luke Shaefer, Daria Sheehan, Michael

Sherraden, Viviana Zelizer, and James Ziliak. Ellen Seidman and Jennifer Tescher were especially kind to closely read an early draft of the full book.

Ted Weinstein, our agent, saw the potential for the book and helped us frame the overarching story. We have been wonderfully supported by Princeton University Press, especially Seth Ditchik, Joe Jackson, and Peter Dougherty. Jennifer Backer, Kathleen Cioffi, Tim Harper, Jessica Loudis, Caroline Preston, and Laura Starita helped turn the drafts into a polished book.

Jonathan Morduch is grateful for support from colleagues at the Financial Access Initiative at New York University, especially Tim Ogden, and at the NYU Wagner Graduate School of Public Service. I'm also grateful for temporary intellectual homes provided during stints at the Institute for Economic Research at Hitotsubashi University in Tokyo; Toynbee Hall in London; the Consumer Financial Protection Bureau in Washington, D.C.; and the Institute for Advanced Study in Princeton, where I was the 2016–17 Roger W. Ferguson Jr. and Annette L. Nazareth member. My wife, Amy Borovoy, and our sons, Leon, Sam, and Joe, accompanied me through every spike and dip, and, with good humor, made everything much smoother.

Rachel Schneider is grateful to the staff and board of directors of the Center for Financial Services Innovation (CFSI), especially Jennifer Tescher, not only for your encouragement and many contributions to the U.S. Financial Diaries project but for a decade of work together to advance the financial health of struggling American families. My parents, Alan and Sherie Schneider, imbued our family life with both gratitude for our good fortune and awareness of the combination of luck and hard work that created it—in ways that led me to care about household financial security in the first place—while the love and support of my husband, Benjamin Marks, and our children, Isabel and Ezra, renew my gratitude for my good fortune every day.

The Financial Diaries

Introduction

A Hidden Inequality

An October Day

The afternoon was perfect—75 degrees and clear, not too hot and not too cold. But Becky Moore was complaining about the weather. This was the kind of weather she said was "killer" on her husband Jeremy's paycheck. Jeremy, 38, worked full-time as a mechanic, repairing long-haul trucks on the evening shift at a service center on the interstate north of their Ohio town, earning a commission for each truck he fixed. Their children were still at school when Jeremy—usually dressed in a pair of Levi's, a western shirt, and steel-toed boots—pulled his pickup out of the driveway to get to work by 2:00 PM. The children, and sometimes Becky, were fast asleep by the time Jeremy got back after midnight.

Jeremy's biggest paychecks came during the hot weeks of summer, when the tar bubbles on the roads and the pavement is too hot to walk on with bare feet. The heat burns out truck tires, and Jeremy spent most of his summer shifts patching them. Icy chills weaken batteries and alternators, and the winter months brought big paychecks too. But during the fall and spring, Jeremy's take-home pay could be as low as $600 for two weeks of full-time work. The mechanics on the day shift kept busier, and Jeremy complained that there often wasn't much left to do when he arrived at 2. Some mild-weather days, Jeremy had only one truck to work on during his entire eight-hour shift. For Becky, 34, the uncertainty of that weighed heavily, and it was only October. "I'm thinking that two weeks from now it will be crap," she said, imagining Jeremy's next paycheck.

For Jeremy, having a full-time job did not mean having a steady income. Like many of their friends, and a third of Ohio adults, neither Jeremy nor Becky has more than a high school diploma. But finishing high school used to be enough to land a solid factory job in southwest Ohio, one that came with guaranteed pay, benefits, and a pension.[1] General Motors had built cars in Norwood, about an hour away, since 1923, and for decades Norwood proudly turned out Camaros and Firebirds, America's muscle cars. When Jeremy was twelve, though, GM shut the Norwood plant along with ten others across the country, citing high costs and foreign competition. It's now more than a decade since Procter and Gamble closed the local plants that made Tide detergent, Crisco shortening, Crest toothpaste, Secret deodorant, and Head & Shoulders shampoo. This is not just an Ohio story. In August 1987, the month the last Camaro rolled off the Norwood line, about 18 percent of Americans nationwide worked in manufacturing. Since then, the percentage has been halved, as has the rate of union membership.[2] Office jobs and clerical jobs have given way to automation too, part of America's shift toward a service economy.

Fixing trucks on commission means that Jeremy, and not just his employer, bears the risks of weather, slow days, and business ups and downs. In the heat of July, Jeremy took home $3,400 after taxes—in March he took home about half that, $1,800. Now, October was threatening to be as bad as March.

Becky stood at the kitchen table, dressed in jeans, a T-shirt, and flip-flops, folding laundry in neat stacks as she talked. Her time was tight with Jeremy working the evening shift since she had to manage the household by herself. "It's hard on me mentally because I'm doing the sports, meals, school. So I have to do everything. And," Becky paused with a tight smile, "it's hard on him."

While the kids were at school, Becky also volunteered at a local animal shelter and sometimes worked cleaning neighbors' houses.

Most of the family budgeting fell to her, and her large green wallet was stuffed with receipts. Given the uncertainties of Jeremy's paychecks, Becky wasn't sure whether to pay her mortgage yet. The payment was not due for three weeks, but Becky already had the money in hand. Still, she was wavering. "I want to make sure I have enough money on hand, and I don't know what my husband will bring home this paycheck." She started talking herself into writing the check: "I just want to get it done." But then she decided to wait. Becky knew her bank account was almost empty. If she spent her remaining cash on the mortgage and Jeremy's next paycheck turned out to be as small as she feared, she would have to borrow from her older sister to make ends meet. Becky had borrowed $200 from her not long before when Jeremy's paycheck was short and they had needed gas for their minivan. "That right there was $75 alone," she said.

"I'm blessed with a sister with a guaranteed paycheck," Becky boasted, with a look that betrayed some envy. Her sister is unmarried and can usually help when money is tight. Becky pays off the debt by cleaning and doing yardwork for her. Becky knows that many others have to turn to payday lenders and other loan companies whose business models depend on trapping customers in cycles of debt. "Oh Lord no," she exclaimed when asked about those options. "I've seen so many people get in trouble."

The Long Arc

The story often told about financial success in America is that slow and steady saving over a lifetime, combined with consistent hard work and a little luck, will ensure financial security, a comfortable retirement, and better opportunities for one's children. But that is not Becky and Jeremy Moore's experience. The 2016 elections brought to the fore how frustrated so many Americans are about the fact that this is no longer, or never was, their experience either.

The often-told story is rooted in a world in which the norm is to gain education, move to better jobs, reach peak income in middle age, and then retire. Researchers call this basic arc the "life cycle," and it captures the life stages for which teachers and financial educators try to prepare students. The idea underpins nearly all advice on managing wealth and how families should save and invest over time. It is the backbone of the life-cycle theory of saving, a framework so fundamental to economics that in 1985 the Nobel Memorial Prize in Economics was awarded to Franco Modigliani, the MIT professor who elaborated its consequences for families' financial choices.[3] The advice to young families like that of Becky and Jeremy is to prepare for major life events early on: to start saving for a down payment on a house and to begin steadily saving for retirement. Later, as earnings rise, people should pay down their mortgages and set aside more for retirement. In this world, slow, steady, disciplined adherence to a budget and savings plan promises to conquer financial challenges. In the past fifty years, mastering the stages of the life cycle has become synonymous with being financially literate in America. And helping families achieve life-cycle goals drives hundreds of billions of dollars of government support for housing, education, and retirement.

Assuming that everyone can follow this trajectory is dangerous. Becky and Jeremy don't have the luxury to focus much on long-term plans. Without basic economic stability, their choices are often difficult, and they're forced to make them frequently. Short-term imperatives undermine long-term goals. Saving and borrowing need to be recalibrated with the spikes and dips of their income. The consequences of bad decisions can compound, and quickly. Stress and anxiety make it all harder.[4] Seeing that, it's hard not to question basic assumptions about financial literacy and what governments and businesses should be doing to serve working families.

As we will see through the stories and data in this book, even if Becky and Jeremy were expert financial planners trained in the life-cycle model, they still would have found it nearly impossible to follow its prescriptions. In the past, Jeremy would contribute part of each paycheck to a 401(k) retirement plan, hoping he could keep it invested. Each time Jeremy switched jobs, however, he pulled all their money from the retirement plan, even though that meant extra taxes and penalties for early withdrawal. They simply needed the money sooner than at age sixty-five. Becky and Jeremy are in a position that's increasingly common in America. Why are so many families forced to make such costly—and some might say self-destructive—choices? Why do so many families feel so financially insecure?

Becky and Jeremy

Becky lives in the same house she grew up in, a modest white bungalow in a row of similar houses, each with a square of grass in front and a cement driveway running up the side. A garden crowded with yellow flowers and a few knocked-over clay pots is tucked next to the front door. Children's pink and purple bicycles lean against the side of the house, next to an abandoned basketball and a Frisbee. Two chairs crowd the porch, where Becky chats with neighbors or just watches cars drive by.

Becky and Jeremy bought the house from Becky's mother soon after they married fifteen years earlier. The oldest of their four children is now in middle school, and Becky has placed wall hangings in the living room to remind the kids about the big things in life. One says "Family," another, "Belief."

The Moores' town could be any from a 1960s sitcom: it's nearly 90 percent white, neither very rich nor very poor. It feels safe. Both the bustle and the urban poverty of Cincinnati are an hour's drive away. The neighbors have known Becky or her mother for decades. From a distance, everything about Becky and Jeremy and their family suggests an archetypal middle-class American life.

But Becky and Jeremy's struggles indicate that things haven't worked out the way they should. When Becky is asked about their situation, she reveals how thin their margin is:

- If the main earner in her household stopped working, how many months does she think her household could manage without borrowing money? Zero.
- At what age does she believe she'll be able to retire and not have to work if she doesn't want to? Never.
- When her children are her age, does she think they'll have as much opportunity as she did? No.

- Does she believe her family's financial well-being depends on events within her control? Mostly not.

When asked if she'd rather be a little richer or have a steadier, more stable financial life, Becky doesn't hesitate: she wants more stability.

Out of Control

Becky isn't alone. In 2014, the Pew Charitable Trusts asked more than 7,000 Americans the same question, and, like Becky, 92 percent of respondents chose stability over mobility.[5] The researchers were struck by the response and weren't sure what the answers meant. The American Dream has historically been about rags-to-riches mobility, about moving up the income ladder. Although the survey set up stability and mobility as competing goals, there's no reason why this should be an either-or proposition: the daydream about mobility *is* the daydream of the fatter paycheck that makes it easy to save and pay bills. But if most people saw moving up the income ladder as the ticket to financial stability, their answers would favor mobility. Seeing the clear preference for stability over mobility implies a fundamental shift in America.

The lopsided response to the question signaled that there was a bigger, more complicated story about economic insecurity. Participants in a focus group revealed that they had opted for stability over mobility simply because they had given up on ever moving ahead. From where they stood, what they really wanted was greater control over their financial situations. Their expectations were ratcheted down to what they thought was possible. Why, though, do so many Americans feel out of control?

That question leads to other questions that also lack complete answers: when we read about families with middle-class incomes just scraping by, it is hard not to wonder why they don't budget better and save more. Why are so many poor families unable to get on a better path? Why do families continue to build mountains of debt that they then sink beneath? Why does financial education do so little to improve financial outcomes?

Part of the story is surely connected to widening inequalities of income and wealth—the frustration of seeing a small part of the population rocket ahead while the rest struggle to keep their place—but inequality alone cannot account for problems that have to do with saving, debt, and budgeting. The available explanations for those problems tend to come down to failures of personal responsibility, lack of knowledge, or insufficient willpower. Yet those explanations don't reveal why Becky and Jeremy are struggling. Like so many others, they work hard. Becky aced a standard test for financial literacy, and she never goes shopping without a handful of coupons. Nor are their challenges a short-lived result of the Great Recession.

We have both spent our careers concerned with the finances of low-income families—Jonathan Morduch as an academic economist and Rachel Schneider as an expert on financial services—but in recent years we have found ourselves less and less able to answer basic questions about American households today. Normally we would turn to government reports and surveys for perspective, but they offer only high-altitude views. Even the most detailed national surveys are usually only collected once a year, and they seldom follow the same families over time. When researchers track families, they usually do so with a year's gap between surveys. We suspected, though, that a vital part of the action was happening from week to week and getting lost in the annual sums. Moreover, surveys only showed what families were earning, spending, or investing, not what they were wrestling with during the year, what they were going without, or, most important, why they were making the choices they did. The only way we knew of to find the missing pieces was to spend time with Becky and Jeremy and households like theirs.

One of us (Morduch) had previously been part of a research project designed to understand the financial lives of families, though in a very different context. That project took place in the slums of Delhi and Dhaka, and the townships outside of Johannesburg, places far removed from communities in the United States. Most of the families involved in that study lived on less than two dollars a day per person, a sum so small that it is hard to imagine how they survived through the year, much less moved forward economically. To understand how they did, the research team developed an approach based on "financial diaries" that gave a day-by-day picture of financial choices made over the course of a year.[6]

The goal was to take a sustained look inside families' lives by tracking everything they earned, spent, borrowed, saved, and shared in careful detail over time. We have adapted that same approach for this book. The resulting "diaries" are not diaries in the usual sense—the data were recorded by our team of researchers during conversations with the families—but, like traditional diaries, they capture the personal, sometimes intimate records of daily experiences, mundane and profound, week after week.

Year-to-Year Instability: The Tightrope

When we started this project, most evidence on the insecurity of American families was drawn from a single research project, the Panel Study of Income Dynamics (PSID), run by the University of Michigan.[7] The power of the PSID lies in its extraordinary longevity. Starting in the late 1960s, researchers began following the same households year after year. As the years went on, the survey included data on the respondents' children, who were also followed, and then their grandchildren. The data that emerged challenged fundamental assumptions about how Americans earn and spend. By turning attention away from the life-cycle arc, with its implications for managing long-term wealth, researchers began to realize why so many people were finding the commonsense advice spun from the life-cycle arc impossible to follow.

The evidence supporting the slow rise and fall of income as depicted by the life-cycle arc came from plotting the earnings of different people, arranged from youngest to oldest, in a given year. This kind of "age-earning profile" is constructed using a snapshot of all earners at a moment in time, grouped by age and education. According to national data for 2013, for example, men like Jeremy in their late twenties and early thirties who did not attend college earned about $37,000 a year on average. The same data show that men in their late fifties with a similar education earned around $50,000 on average. And, turning to older men, similarly educated retirees earned several thousand dollars less. This same kind of up-and-down arc of annual earnings holds for other groups as well. (Average income for men with college degrees, for example, peaked above $80,000 in 2013.) No matter the level of schooling, an arc emerges from cross-sectional snapshots of the average earnings of people at different ages.[8]

These averages, though, can mislead. One problem is that the age-earning profiles conflate the effect of age and the effect of birth year: men who were thirty in 2013 were born in 1983, while men who were sixty-five in 2013 were born in 1948. The earning differences between the two groups likely involve more than their age differences. The averages also make it impossible to see variation within the groups. The PSID instead allowed a view of the changing incomes of the *same* people over time, and the new pictures it provided often diverged widely from conclusions drawn from the cross-sections underpinning the life-cycle arc.[9]

Finding "a striking degree of economic turbulence," the Michigan-based researchers saw that for many families the pattern of income was hardly a smooth upward glide.[10] Incomes were volatile, sometimes rising or falling sharply from one year to the next. A report described economic and social trajectories as "disparate and chaotic" relative to the life-cycle arc.[11] Most of the poor weren't poor forever. And people who weren't poor most of the time sometimes had stints of poverty. Even the rich took their share of hits. The turbulence showed that economic life in postwar America was far from static. Some families were experiencing mobility, moving up or down the income ladder in permanent ways. But many families were simply getting knocked around.[12]

The patterns were dutifully reported in academic papers, reports, and books. By 2015, the PSID had been the basis of a remarkable amount of analysis, filling 2,601 academic studies, 68 books, and 492 book chapters. Yet the thousands of figures and tables did little to shift the popular narrative about what it takes to be financially successful in America: the image of a slow and steady upward progression over a lifetime was hard to dislodge in favor of an image of turbulence. We found when talking to families, however, that the kind of year-to-year income volatility revealed in the PSID was usually a critical context for their stories.

The PSID highlights major misfortunes, the kinds of large swings that show up in annual data: jobs lost and marriages unraveled, illnesses and disabilities. These are the kinds of catastrophic losses that transform lives, and they are one part of the stories in this book. The Yale political scientist Jacob Hacker calls the challenges revealed by the PSID "the new insecurity," writing that incomes have been "rising and falling much more sharply from year to year than they did a generation ago. Indeed, the *instability* of families' incomes has risen faster than the *inequality* of families' incomes."[13] The economic journalist Peter Gosselin likens the instability to balancing on a high wire without much of a safety net.[14] His book *High Wire: The Precarious Financial Lives of American Families* was published in 2008, just as the recession hammered the nation, wiping out wealth and housing investments. The recession reminded Americans that we can no longer take for granted the promise of stability, security, and continual progress.

The word "precarious" now arises often when Americans talk about their financial lives. It captures a heightened sense of anxiety, a feeling of walking a tightrope with a fear that the next misstep or piece of bad luck could be the one that knocks a family off course, perhaps irretrievably. The sense of precariousness has led to the creation of a new word, "precarity," to describe the condition of living a precarious existence. Related conversations are active all around the world, and especially in Europe, where precarity has become *precariedad*, *precariedade*, *précarité*, *precarietà*, and *prekarität* in Spanish, Portuguese, French, Italian, and German, respectively. Alongside fast-food workers, janitors, and maids with contingent jobs and variable hours, the European idea of precarity is often applied to web designers, freelance journalists, and other professionals making a living without the stability of 9-to-5 days and forty-hour weeks. In Japan, the word is applied to "freeters"—a phrase formed from the German *frei arbeiters*, free workers—young people who are unable to secure steady full-time work and find themselves forced into unemployment or strings of part-time jobs.[15]

As more data accumulate, views of Americans' growing insecurity are coming into focus.[16] Using an updated version of the PSID, researchers found a 30 percent increase in year-to-year income volatility between 1971 and 2008.[17] A 2015 update by the Pew Charitable Trusts found that, on average, nearly half of households had a gain or loss of income by 25 percent or more from one year to the next.[18] The insecurity is not a product of the 2007–9 recession. Instead, the Pew team found that this level of volatility emerged in the 1980s and has persisted through several economic cycles.

Moreover, the probability of large financial losses has increased over time.[19] Some households bounce back from their losses, but others don't. Looking back to households whose income dropped by more than 25 percent in 1994, a third had failed to regain that ground a decade later.[20] The year-to-year income volatility seen in the PSID cannot be dismissed simply as "noise" or statistical outliers around the arc of the life cycle from youth to retirement. For many families, the noise *is* the story.

The PSID findings have helped researchers see how ideas about America have been stuck in the past. Ways of thinking that were adopted at a time when middle-class jobs came with steady paychecks and benefits no longer make as much sense in today's economy. The income swings revealed by the PSID are big, and, not surprisingly, the proposed solutions are big as well. Experts have proposed rescuing families from the tightrope by strengthening the safety net, patching America's retirement system, creating new laws with stronger workplace protections, rethinking trade policy, and reforming financing for housing and education. For families, proposed solutions center on building big reserves of savings for emergencies.

Many of the families we met in the Diaries project have experienced the year-to-year instability documented in the PSID. But their diaries also show how ideas of "precariousness" and precarity are incomplete and sometimes misleading, and they point to fundamentally new ways of tackling economic instability.

Month-to-Month Instability: The Rocky Road

After spending a year with Becky and Jeremy Moore and the other Financial Diaries households, it became clear that they face challenges beyond the big ones that show up in the year-to-year data of the PSID. During our year of data collection, spanning 2012–13, the Moores, for example, lived in the same house, drove the same cars, had the same jobs, remained married, and were basically healthy. Yet they felt financially insecure. The tightrope metaphor captures only part of their situation. The families we met are not balancing on a high-wire so much as driving on a very rocky road, hitting bumps and potholes, getting slowed down, knocked off course, and sometimes stopped entirely. Things are already out of control. Families are dealing with today's hazards while also trying to prepare for whatever might be waiting around the bend.

The PSID allowed researchers to take a big step into people's lives by viewing events year by year.[21] The Financial Diaries get even closer. By following Becky's cash flows (in addition to her overall income and wealth), we zoom in from a year to a month, a week, and, in some cases, a day. The Diaries allowed us to create a moving picture of her life—one that reveals the costs of instability.

In getting to know families over a year, we collected data on more than income, spending, and wealth. We also tracked households' situations, and we documented why they made the choices they did. When Jeremy changed jobs, we learned why. We watched as Becky tried to save money by not purchasing a prescribed medicine, and we saw how Becky and Jeremy stretched to give their children a "normal" Christmas.

Unless you track Becky's occasional earnings from cleaning houses and Jeremy's biweekly paychecks week by week, the extent of their financial instability is hard to see. Of course, Becky and Jeremy would benefit from higher incomes, but if those incomes came with the same uncertainties as today, the Moores would still face basic challenges. The Financial Diaries reveal that a fundamental financial challenge for them and so many other American families—regardless of their income level—is coping with moments when expenses must be paid but income is not yet in hand. The Diaries make salient the critical distinction between not having money at the right time versus *never* having the money, or in more academic terms, illiquidity versus insolvency. Too often illiquidity is mistaken for insolvency (or, not having money at the right time is mistaken for never having money). One consequence is that it becomes much harder to recognize the fundamental problems created by uncertainty, and to identify solutions. The Diaries reveal the volatility in sharp relief. They also show the strategies that families create to limit the impact of volatility, sometimes at high cost. In doing so, the data and stories challenge common assumptions about how a large segment of American households earns, spends, borrows, saves, shares, and plans.

The stories show how families often must navigate toward seemingly contradictory goals. Families work hard to stabilize their month-to-month spending while also needing moments when they can spend in large spikes. They seek ways to maintain the strict discipline of saving while simultaneously permitting flexibility in case of emergencies. They save actively but do not build balances that last over time. They grasp for middle-class lives but sometimes find themselves in periods of poverty. By following their dilemmas, and seeing their responses, we can begin to discover ways to address America's hidden inequality—an inequality in exposure to risk and in access to dependable ways to cope.

How the Financial Diaries Work

Our main aim was to see families through a lens that extended beyond measuring yearly income, spending, and wealth. The key shift was to follow cash flows. By watching the movement of money in and out of households, we aimed to see exactly where and when families got tripped up or succeeded. To do that, we designed surveys to record every dollar each household earned and spent. The surveys also tracked all funds saved and borrowed, any donations made to charity or friends, gifts given or received, and government transfers. To the extent possible, we noted every financial exchange, whether it was paid electronically or in cash, even if it was simply a gift of time (as when Becky cleaned her sister's home) or if it was paid in kind (such as preparing a meal for a sick friend). We also captured the time of each transaction and where it occurred.

Our team of ten researchers lived in the Ohio, Kentucky, California, Mississippi, and New York communities where the studies took place. Researchers often met families in their homes, sitting in the living room or at the kitchen table; other times, they met at a local library or restaurant. It sometimes took months to build trust and fill in gaps in the stories we heard. Some details were too painful or embarrassing for participants to reveal at first. Sometimes life was just too hectic to keep track of everything. But we were ultimately able to see parts of a household's economic life that sometimes even close friends and relatives could not. We occasionally made discoveries that even members of the household were unaware of. From the 235 households surveyed in the final sample, we collected records of just under 300,000 cash flows over the course of 2012 and 2013, including everything from buying a pack of gum at the local convenience store to making a down payment on a newly purchased car.[22]

One thing we could not figure out was how to be invisible in family members' lives. We knew that our presence surely had an effect on the people we got to know, at least some of the time. Some were happy to see us go at the end of the year; the meetings could be tedious for households and researchers alike, since we insisted, as professionally as possible, on noting all relevant specifics of every financial transaction. Others wished we could stay longer. Meeting with researchers had helped them stay focused on their finances, and some were motivated simply by the chance to have outsiders get a close-up sense of the challenges they faced every day. In the end, we simply accepted that participating in the study had consequences for the households. In the final interview, researchers asked members of each household how they thought their lives had changed as a result of their involvement in the project. About a quarter said the experience was neutral, while the rest said that it had affected some of their choices. Sometimes we distracted them from precious family time or took up time that would otherwise have been used for chores. But most said that our presence helped them pay more attention to their finances and see things as part of a bigger picture. For them, we likely saw a better version of what might have happened had we not been there. In light of that admission, we were struck even more by the crises, moments of regret, and persistent struggles that we observed.

The intensive nature of the Diaries meant that forming a nationally representative sample was impossible. Instead, we aimed for the richest, most complete stories we could glean from a select group of

households. We had long conversations about the kinds of households to include in the study, debating whether to aim for a broad
sample that reflected a wide variety of communities, or whether we
should spend a lot of time in only a few. In the end, the sample was
restricted to households with at least one working member, but otherwise the households were diverse—they included recent immigrants, members of families that had been in the United States for
generations, single mothers, grandparents, agricultural workers, sales-
people, office workers, and traditional nuclear families. Participants
were Hispanic, non-Hispanic white, South Asian, and African American. None of the households was among the richest or the poorest
in their communities. Focusing on working households came with
certain restrictions, though. Others, for instance, are better placed
to speak to particular issues faced by retirees or those who survive
largely on public assistance.

For our research, we settled on four sites: communities in southwest Ohio and northern Kentucky; the San Jose, California, region;
eastern Mississippi; and, closer to home for us, Queens and Brooklyn
in New York City. The choice of locations shaped our window. The
towns where we worked in Mississippi are several hours removed
from the well-photographed hamlets and "wrong side of the tracks"
neighborhoods of the high-poverty Mississippi River Delta. Our site
was to the east, closer to the Alabama border, where the region still
boasts a range of manufacturing jobs and benefits from its proxim-
ity to Mississippi State University in Starkville. Similarly, the site we
chose in San Jose abuts Silicon Valley's technology corridor, differ-
entiating it from inner-city Los Angeles or the heart of the agricultural Central Valley, two California sites with persistently high rates
of poverty. In Ohio and Kentucky, we worked in and around Cincinnati, where factory jobs have steadily given way to positions in the
retail and service sectors. The communities in New York reflect the
city's diversity: we spent time with African American families with
generations of history in the United States, and with recent immigrants from Ecuador, Colombia, India, and Bangladesh. None of the
sites we chose was thriving, but all had opportunities.

We knew that understanding the struggles of poverty and near-
poverty would be an important part of the story. With that in mind,

we subdivided the households into income groups based on the U.S. Bureau of the Census's Supplemental Poverty Measure (SPM), which adjusts for, among other things, regional variation in cost of living— that is, the fact that Becky's dollars go a lot further in her Ohio town than they would in Brooklyn or San Jose.[23] Just under a quarter (23 percent) of households were poor; they had resources during the year that placed them below the SPM poverty line. We grouped another 31 percent as "near-poor": above the SPM poverty line but below 150 percent of the line. Twenty percent had income during the year that placed them a notch above that; we label them as "low-income" and include households with annual resources between 150 percent and 200 percent of the SPM line. And the remaining 26 percent are labeled "moderate income"; they earned at least twice the amount defined by the SPM line.[24] Twice the local poverty line tends to be close to the median household income in many areas—for example, the poverty line in the Cincinnati metro area for a family with two adults and two children was $23,415 in 2012, while the median household income was just above $54,000—so our sample includes both poor families and families safely in the middle class.[25]

Local organizations put us in contact with families, and those families introduced us to other families. More than 400 households initially agreed to take part in the Diaries, but not all stuck with it. The project required intense commitment from very busy people.[26] Some dropped out as soon as they realized how deep the questions would go; others simply left when participating in the U.S. Financial Diaries no longer fit with their other obligations. In the end, the members of 235 households opened their lives to us for a full twelve months.[27] They entrusted us with their stories—and sometimes their secrets— and we have aimed to be as accurate as possible in sharing the truths revealed within them. To maintain their confidentiality, we have changed names and identifying details in this book.

"At first it seemed to be kind of a hassle," Taisha Blake, a nurse's aide from Cincinnati, complained about the project. "I have to write down all that I spend and set out these blocks of time to meet." Gradually, though, she shifted her view: "But then, to know that maybe, just maybe, things that I'm going through financially could help someone else not have to experience that payday loan cycle, maybe my experience could help someone else, that's what kept me going."

The Price of Steadiness

The last time we met with Becky, on a visit to Ohio after the formal record keeping of the Financial Diaries was complete, her mood had lightened. Jeremy had found a new job. His old position was closer to home, but he was fed up working the evening shift with all the uncertainties, volatility, and family disruption that came with it. After he gave notice, his boss had tried to keep Jeremy by offering him daytime hours. But Jeremy had grown so frustrated that he worked his final two weeks, collected his last paycheck, and left.

Jeremy was still a mechanic fixing the trailers of 18-wheel trucks, but he was no longer on commission. Now he was working hourly and getting overtime: $17.50 an hour before taxes, paid weekly. He was guaranteed a minimum of forty hours a week. The yearly pay *was lower* than that of his old job, and Jeremy now had to commute up to forty-five minutes each way. But Becky and Jeremy felt that they were in a better situation; the newfound stability had lifted a weight from their shoulders.

When a longer commute for less pay for the same work is a step up, it's time to fundamentally rethink our understanding of the challenges facing working Americans.

Worlds of Uncertainty

Chapter 1

Earning

Janice

Seven nights a week, the buses rumble more than three hours from Alabama into Mississippi to deposit gamblers in the sprawling parking lot of the Pearl River Resort. By about 9:30, the gamblers, mostly from Birmingham and Tuscaloosa, slowly file out of the buses and head inside, some to the blackjack and poker tables, others to the blinking and beeping slot machines.

Double Diamond Haywire!
Triple-Double Red White & Blue.
The Best Things in Life.

The slot machines hunch shoulder to shoulder in rows across the casino's carpeted floor, and the gamblers, many beyond retirement age, scatter among them. Most of the players sit by themselves, some in wheelchairs or with walkers beside them. Some puff on cigarettes. Some nurse drinks. All steadily, quietly feed the noisy machines.

Pearl River bills itself as "Vegas with Sweet Tea," a family-friendly destination on the Choctaw reservation in central Mississippi with water slides, a spa, two golf courses, a high-end steakhouse, and more than a thousand rooms. But the clear centerpiece at Pearl River is gambling. Running twenty-four-hour slots and table games has turned the Mississippi Band of Choctaw Indians into one of the state's biggest employers.

Janice Evans works the night shift, beginning at 8:00 in the evening and clocking out at 4:00 AM. She has been dealing cards at Pearl River for close to twenty years, since starting in her mid-thirties. A single, African American mother with a high school degree, Janice was searching for a steady job. There weren't a lot of options.

One day she noticed an ad for classes on how to become a card dealer at the casino and signed up. "Anyone could do it," she told us matter-of-factly. Janice's quiet manner and kind smile are nothing like the depictions of card dealers in James Bond movies, outfitted in bow ties and reeling off practiced patter. But Janice's customers, too, are more sweet tea than Vegas, and they settle in at her card table for long, low-key evenings.

On this night in Mississippi, Janice stands at her table in her Pearl River casino dealer uniform: black slacks, black shoes, and a black shirt open at the neck, adorned with a simple gold stripe. Her hair is parted on the side, straightened and falling to her shoulders in bleached wisps. Her red nail polish, with two nails painted deep purple and appliquéd with small stars and hearts, is starting to chip.

Janice quietly roots for the people at her table, encouraging winning hands with a smile. A hint of a grimace crosses her face when a hand is a tough loser, more so when a regular is having a bad run. The gamblers know she likes to see them win, and they appreciate it, even though they know they're expected to tip her more if they do.

Janice is guaranteed $8.35 an hour, but in a good week she can double that in tips. Customers share their winnings with Janice by adding chips to her "toke" box—shorthand for tokens of gratitude. At the end of each shift, the tokes are collected and counted, and the equivalent in dollars is added to Janice's next paycheck. When gamblers are on a lucky streak, the tokes pile up. The more gamblers, the more lucky streaks, and the more tips. Janice does well when the tables are full, especially during the hot summer months when the air-conditioned comfort draws crowds. Fall, especially, can be slow.

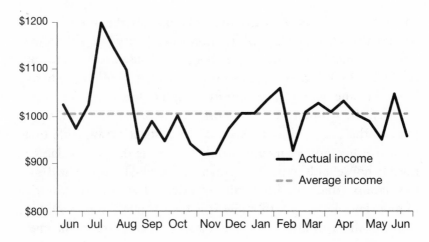

Figure 1.1. Janice's biweekly paychecks, June 2012–June 2013. The dashed line gives her average paycheck value over the period. Paychecks are net of taxes and medical insurance premiums. August and April are three-paycheck months.

Janice gets a paycheck every two weeks. The money isn't great, but she is proud of working her way up, and the benefits, especially health insurance, are good. Over the course of the year, Janice takes home just over $26,000 from her job at the casino.[1]

The yearly total means that Janice averages about $2,200 each month, or just over $1,000 each biweekly paycheck. But as Figure 1.1 shows, the size of those paychecks varied widely. Over the course of the year, her highest was $1,200; her lowest, $900. As a percent of the average of $1,000, that's a nearly 30 percent swing between those two paychecks.

Just before the study began, Janice's son, Marcus, was laid off from his maintenance job after his employer lost a contract. He and his three-year-old daughter moved in with Janice. Without income, Marcus now qualified for food stamps, an average of about $125 a month. But there were big swings here, too. At one point the local social services agency mistook Janice's income for Marcus's and canceled his food stamps. It took two months to get them back. And while Marcus also qualified for unemployment benefits, several months passed before his checks began to arrive. In a way, that was a blessing because they started in the fall, a season when Janice's paychecks were low. But while the benefits helped boost the household's net income to about $33,000, they added to the monthly volatility: the household's income swung 70 percent from high to low months.

Given the nature of Janice's work in a seasonal, low-skill, tipped job and the unreliability of Marcus's benefits, it's reasonable to assume that her family's income would be among the more volatile of the 235 households in the U.S. Financial Diaries. It's not. The degree of volatility Janice and her family experienced was on par with that of most families we got to know. It is hard enough to provide for a family of three on just $33,000; doing so with an unsteady income is even harder.

Constants

Work, family, and church are the constants in Janice's life. And worry. There are always worries. At fifty-five, she worries about her health. Her doctor has told her to lose weight. She wishes she could do more for her church and for her friends. Her home always needs something.

Janice's parents still live in the area. Her father leads a small Pentecostal church in town, and her mother makes sure Janice attends every Sunday. Janice notes proudly that she is part of the "first family," and church members always provide a good meal after worship services. The membership numbers about fifty, including children, and everybody knows everybody. If you miss church, Janice said with a laugh, "you're gonna hear it."

Going to church helps assuage Janice's nagging ambivalence about working in a casino. She doesn't gamble herself, but she still worries that her role as a dealer enables others. "If I didn't go to church, I couldn't do the job," Janice said. "It keeps me grounded." She repeated the thought, as if to reinforce the power of the protection she receives: "It keeps me grounded." Contributing to the church is important to Janice. Like the rest of her finances, though, her ability to tithe—give 10 percent of her income to the church—depends on how many people come to the casino and how much they leave in tips.

Most of the year, Janice can pay all the bills on time, but barely. During the most difficult stretch, from September to November, she had to cut back on food purchases. Four years before we got to know her, during a particularly bad dip, she turned to payday loans. It's easy to find payday and other "short-term" or "small-dollar" lenders in Janice's town (and nationally there are more "small-dollar" credit storefronts than McDonald's or Starbucks).[2] Borrowers head to Cash Inc. on the commercial strip, Car Title Loans on a nearby street, Cash Xpress and Express Check Advance near the highway entrance, and a dozen national lenders available by telephone. CashNetUSA runs an ad in Janice's regional Yellow Pages that boasts of its "Easy five-minute application; Cash next business day; 4 out of 5 applications approved; nothing to fax, no paperwork."[3] Janice borrowed from a payday lender for a couple of cycles, but she knew she had to get out of the trap. "You borrow $60 and you pay back $75. If you borrow $200, you pay back $250," she recounted. "But what if you then don't have the $250?"

When Janice wrote the last check in her checkbook, she didn't order another box. The local payday lenders require that, as security, borrowers hand over a signed check in the amount of the loan, dated for the next payday. If she didn't have any checks, Janice figured, she couldn't be tempted by the payday lender's quick money. Since then, Janice pays bills by money order and uses only a debit card to make purchases. Giving up her checkbook creates headaches, but it avoids the payday loan trap: "It's like an addiction if you have a checking account," she said.

When we sat down with her after church one Sunday afternoon in October, Janice told us she wouldn't be getting many tips that night. When fall arrives, children go back to school and parents who gamble in the summer hold onto their money for school supplies and clothes for the kids. Janice knew that they're "doing what they're supposed to," but it was a blow to her paycheck. Perhaps even more significantly, it was football season, and that meant instead of playing cards many gamblers were watching games on weekends. "Southern people love their football," Janice said. During the fall, Friday nights are high school football games, Saturdays are for college football, and Sundays are for the NFL.

Janice's tips also depend on whether it's an odd-numbered or even-numbered year. In odd-numbered years, the University of Alabama and LSU football teams head to Starkville, just over an hour's drive north of the resort, to play Mississippi State. Fans often visit the casino on their way home from the games. "Oh Lord from Zion!" Janice exclaimed. "They're going to stop at the casino, and they're going to be drunk, and they're going to play a lot." But the year we got to know Janice was an even-numbered one; both games were away, and her paychecks suffered.

On this particular Sunday, though, Janice didn't mind that many of her regulars would be home in front of the TV instead of at her card table. "You know Monday they got to go to work. That makes me so happy. Because I know if they go home, they're going to go to work. People need to work." Still, she worried about how she would get through the fall. Janice has lived with a volatile income for years, and she knew what was coming. By Christmas, money would be tight, not only for Janice but for others in her family, and they'd all struggle to come up with the extra needed for Christmas gifts. To save money, they draw names for Christmas presents so everyone doesn't have to buy gifts for everyone else. The previous year, Janice had drawn her aunt's name and gave her dishwashing detergent, toilet tissue, and other "useful things like that."

A Bundle of Worries

Janice, her son, and granddaughter share a single-wide trailer on a dirt road ten minutes from the center of town, about two miles from where she grew up. She's been there for almost thirty years. She owns the land where her trailer rests, plus another plot down the road (her monthly mortgage payment is about $400). The trailer is decorated with homey touches. Velvet curtains hang above a velvet-covered couch on the long wall of the sitting area. They form a cozy space with a television and coffee table, squeezed in beside the kitchen. On the adjoining wall is her favorite possession, a reproduction of an oil painting of magnolia blossoms, framed in thick gold-painted wood, flanked by two wall-mounted brass lamps.

In some ways, much has changed since Janice was a child. During the "Freedom Summer" of 1964, the year Janice was seven, hundreds of political organizers from across the country flooded to her part of central Mississippi to register voters and integrate schools. In June of that year, the Ku Klux Klan and local police murdered three of the activists after ambushing them along a county road fifteen miles from where Janice's casino now stands.[4] The killings of James Chaney, Andrew Goodman, and Michael Schwerner became part of the story of Janice's childhood, just as they became part of the story of America's struggle for civil rights, leading up to Martin Luther King's march in Selma and the passage of the Voting Rights Act of 1965.

In 1969, when Janice was in seventh grade, her school district, along with a few others nearby, became the first in the area to integrate, some fifteen years after the Supreme Court's ruling in *Brown v. Board of Education* that school segregation was unconstitutional.[5] "We didn't know we were trailblazers," Janice said with a laugh. "We were just going to school." Her parents were not "crazy about it, but they were more *worried* than they were anything else," she recalled. "But they knew times were changing." The teenage boys worked out their frustrations playing sports, Janice remembers, but the girls would sometimes fight, white girls versus black girls.

Racial divisions persist today. Black students have held reunions over the years, but it wasn't until 2015, forty years after Janice's graduation, that all of the students, regardless of race, met for a joint high school reunion. And, for all intents and purposes, this year's graduating class will still have largely segregated class reunions. While the county population is split nearly evenly between black and white, the schools aren't. The public schools are largely black, the private schools almost all white. Local churches are de facto segregated as well. The local White Pages lists more than forty churches in Janice's town of seven thousand, but it is difficult to find a local church that, as they say in Mississippi, is "blended."

The racial divide—and its consequences for education, housing, income, wealth, and jobs—is in large measure responsible for the situation that Janice finds herself in. But it is not all that preoccupies her.

To understand Janice's everyday worries, we have to zoom in closer. When we do, her week-to-week finances loom large. As Figure 1.1 shows,

Janice's paychecks rose and fell with the seasons; Marcus's benefits were somewhat erratic, sometimes cushioning a low paycheck, sometimes amplifying a large paycheck. Some of these ups and downs were predictable—Janice knew that the football schedule was not in her favor so the fall would be especially bad—but much was not. Certainly Janice had no way of predicting the exact amounts of her paychecks and no way of knowing what was going to happen with Marcus's benefits. The volatility and unpredictability of her income is not the only challenge that Janice faces—and perhaps not the most fundamental—but it is a large part of her bundle of worries, and one that has been very hard for anyone outside her household to fully see or understand.

Spikes and Dips

There are some obvious causes of the swings in monthly income. At tax time, more than half of American households receive a refund, causing their income to spike. Twice a year, people who are paid every two weeks receive three paychecks in a month.[6] But neither explains the total amount of volatility we saw from month to month. In our analysis, we removed tax refunds from the calculations in order to isolate spikes and dips that reflected income from earnings.[7]

There are several ways to measure the remaining income volatility. One is to calculate the swing between the highest month and the lowest month as a percentage of average household income. Janice's monthly swing was about 70 percent (30 percent when looking only at biweekly paychecks as noted above). The average swing for households with comparable annual income to hers was actually higher, at 116 percent. For poorer households it was higher still, as high as 126 percent (meaning that if average monthly income was $1,000, families saw at least one month with income of, for instance, $1,730 and one month with income of $470).

A second measure of variability is the CV or coefficient of variation. CV takes a measure of the variability of monthly income (the standard deviation for a household during the year) and expresses that measure as a fraction of the household's mean monthly income. The advantage is that the CV can compare the volatility of households with different levels of average income. The disadvantage is that CV measures aren't intuitive. Comparing the CVs of different people's income provides context: a person who earns a $50,000 annual salary, paid every two weeks (and so having two months a year with three paychecks), with a $500 year-end bonus would be 0.18. Janice had a CV of about 0.21. The median for the entire U.S. Financial Diaries sample was about 0.34, nearly double that of our imagined salaried worker with a steady job.

Figure 1.2 shows a third way to measure income volatility: by counting the months when income is a certain amount above or below the average.[8] We chose to look at variations of 25 percent above or 25 percent below the average. This benchmark is consistent with other researchers' measurements of year-to-year volatility, enabling us to compare what we were seeing with other research. It's also easy to imagine how a spike or dip of that magnitude could affect a household's spending and ability to plan. Counting spikes and dips gives a more conservative view than tracking the size of swings—which can be exaggerated by a few outlier months while most of the year is steady. Its advantage over the CV calculation is mostly in its simplicity.

The numbers of spikes and dips are striking. Households in the Diaries sample experienced, on average, 2.2 months with spikes and 2.4 months with dips in income over the year. Put another way, for about five months a year, household incomes weren't even close to average. Across the whole sample, virtually no one—just 2 percent—got through the year without any spikes or dips in income.

As is often the case, the averages don't tell the whole story. There was substantial variation within our sample. When we split the sample in half by level of volatility, the higher-volatility group had an average of 6.6 months where income was either spiking or dipping, while the lower-volatility group had an average of 2.5 months.

Income level only roughly predicts which households faced high or low volatility. While poorer households generally had more volatility (as you can see in Figure 1.2), even the best-off families we followed saw a surprising amount of income volatility. This "moderate-income"

Size of spikes & dips as a percentage of income

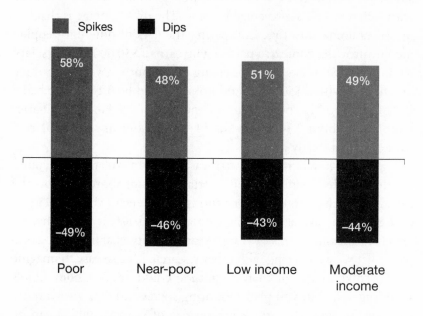

Number of spikes & dips by income level

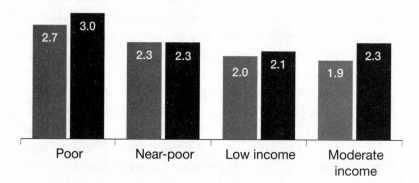

Figure 1.2. Income volatility in the U.S. Financial Diaries. Here are two ways to look at income volatility. On top we calculate the size of income spikes and dips by comparing them to the households' monthly average income; below we look at the number of months when income was 25 percent above or below average.

group earned more than two times the poverty threshold and included households around the local median income in their region. These middle-class households experienced, on average, 1.9 spikes and 2.3 dips during the year, which meant that even they spent a third of the year with earnings far from average. Many of these households also fell into the high-volatility group: moderate-income households made up 26 percent of our sample and 22 percent of high-volatility households.

For all families in the sample, the spikes and dips are often large in size: the average spike in income was in fact 52 percent above the household's average monthly income. The dips, similarly, were substantial hits to income: the average dip was 46 percent below average.

For households below the poverty line, it was worse.[9] Poor households in the Diaries project faced, on average, 2.7 spikes and 3.0 dips over the year. In total, then, they spent nearly half the year with income far from average. Their poverty was deeply bound up with the instability of their income. The poorest families struggle even more than Janice and Marcus, whose household income is well above the supplemental poverty threshold (their total annual income is 177 percent of the poverty threshold). It's not just that the poor earn less, it's that income volatility compounds their struggles.

135 Million Transactions

Our early work documenting household income volatility helped inspire another research group. The newly formed JPMorgan Chase Institute (JPMCI) had access to a very different set of data: as one of America's largest banks, Chase processes many of the financial transactions of its 27 million customers. The researchers at JPMCI created a sample of 100,000 randomly chosen account holders, with a total of 135 million transactions.[10] The sample includes only people who banked intensively with Chase products: they had Chase checking accounts and Chase credit cards, deposited at least $500 every month into an account, and made at least five payments or other withdrawals each month. Their data thus includes a much smaller percentage of people at the lower end of the income distribution, like Janice, and misses any income that doesn't flow through a Chase account, but it is a far larger number of households than we were able to track in the U.S. Financial Diaries.[11]

The Chase researchers examined whether their customers were also subject to significant month-to-month income volatility. Like us, they found that income held fairly steady for just a minority. In the total sample, 55 percent saw a month-to-month change in total income of 30 percent or more. As in our data, the ups and downs were most pronounced for the poorest, but volatility extended across the income distribution. There was no meaningful difference in the prevalence, amount, or range of income volatility among households with annual income between $23,000 and $100,000.[12] Chase's data show that within-year income volatility affects a broad cross-section of American households.

A National View

Neither the Diaries data nor the Chase data are nationally representative. Five years after the recession of 2007–9, though, the Federal Reserve launched a new national survey, the Survey of Household Economics and Decisionmaking (SHED), to monitor how families were coping in the recession's aftermath. The survey was relatively brief (half of respondents completed the questions in nineteen minutes or less), but it covered a lot of ground. Of the ninety-nine questions, one was a simple query, in part inspired by our initial results, that zeroed in on income volatility: "Which one of the following best describes how your household's income changes from month to month, if at all?" The answers aren't detailed, but they provide a useful check on the broad patterns, and it comes from a nationally representative sample of 5,642 people.[13]

In the Fed's data, the reported incidence of income volatility was lower than in either our sample or the Chase study (see Figure 1.3).[14] Two-thirds of the respondents reported that their income was "roughly the same" each month. In other words, many people reported that they were free from worry about large month-to-month spikes and dips of income. But 20 percent of respondents reported that they experienced

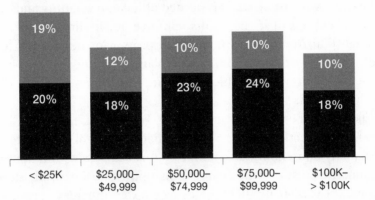

■ Income often varies month to month
■ Some unusually high or low months

Figure 1.3. Income volatility in the Federal Reserve's Survey of Household Economics and Decisionmaking (SHED), 2015. About a third of all respondents reported volatile monthly incomes.

"some unusually high or low months." Another 12 percent saw even more volatility, reporting that their income "often varies quite a bit from one month to the next."

As with the U.S. Financial Diaries findings, the challenges were greater for the poorest. Among households earning less than $25,000 for the year, almost 20 percent experienced extreme income volatility. For households earning at least $50,000, that figure was 10 percent.

The differences among the three studies are worth noting. The Diaries and Chase analyses track income flows, while the Federal Reserve survey measures people's perceptions of their income volatility. In the Diaries study, we also asked participants how easy or difficult it was for them to estimate their future earnings. People expressed greater confidence in their ability to predict their future incomes than their measured volatility would have led us to expect. Of course, predictability and volatility are different things. Janice can predict her income fairly well. She knows she'll earn more in the summer and less in the fall. She knows she'll get a boost in the years when Alabama and LSU come to town. Her income is predictable but still volatile. As Janice's story suggests, while predictability may make it easier to cope with volatility, it still doesn't make it easy.

Overall, while more study is needed of income volatility and people's perceptions of it, the results reinforce our finding of a hidden inequality in American earnings. A disproportionate share of low- and moderate-income families faces volatility. Meanwhile, better-off households not only earn more, they are much more likely to have steady earnings.[15]

Taken together, the Diaries and the Federal Reserve and Chase data reveal something new about the financial lives of families today. First, many households face significant unsteadiness within the year. Second, the cause is not infrequent disruptions to a basically steady income. Instead, many households face a very different reality: the base condition is unsteady. The spikes and dips in income make for a bumpy path for many households, especially, as we will see in the next two chapters, when those income fluctuations are exacerbated by spikes and dips in expenses. The road is rockiest for those at the bottom of the income distribution, as we will explore in greater detail in chapter 3 and chapter 7. But month-to-month ups and downs aren't limited to the poor or even the near-poor: instability is increasingly part of middle-class life too.

The All-Important Paycheck

We considered a number of possible causes of the unsteadiness of incomes. One obvious source was job loss, particularly since we gathered data at a time when unemployment remained relatively high. Another possibility was people moving into and out of the household—families today are less stable than they once were. If someone with a job moves into, or out of, the household, that contributes to volatility. Just over a quarter of our households saw members join or leave during the study. Perhaps households were engaged in more self-employment, earning a little extra income when they needed it, which could increase or decrease volatility (depending on whether they were creating a spike by working "overtime" or buffering a dip to cover for lost hours at a job). Many of the households qualify for public benefits such as food stamps and public health insurance. The process of applying for benefits, and regularly recertifying one's eligibility, is much more time-consuming and uncertain than many realize. Perhaps people went on and off of these benefits more often than we had assumed.

To pull apart which of these factors was the biggest contributor to volatility for our households, we calculated the CV of all income within the sample. Then we smoothed out different kinds of income, essentially removing the volatility from a particular source, to see which variables had the biggest effect on the overall CV. If we treat all income that wasn't earned from a job (such as food stamps or unemployment benefits) as if it were the same each month, more than four-fifths of the volatility within the sample remains. Self-employment was an even smaller factor: treating all self-employment income as though it is constant decreases the CV by only 15 percent. If the majority of volatility is coming from sources other than benefits or self-employment, that still leaves the question of whether volatility was driven primarily by changes within a job (up-and-down income from the same job, like Janice's) or from changing jobs (losing, getting, or switching jobs). Job changing explains a third of the CV, but nearly half of overall income volatility was due to changes in income from the same job.[16] Many households could not count on their jobs to provide a steady income from one month to the next.

Our analysis matched that of the Chase research team. Nearly all of the income volatility experienced by the households in their study (86 percent) could be explained by variation in pay for a given job, not from job loss or job changes. About a quarter of the volatility from wages was due to months when workers paid weekly received five checks (instead of four) or workers paid biweekly received three (instead of two). But about three-quarters of the volatility could be attributed to fluctuations from one paycheck to the next.[17]

The Great Job Shift

In 2006, political scientist Jacob Hacker described what he called the "Great Risk Shift" in a book by the same name. Over the half century following World War II, governments and businesses gradually shifted financial risks from their ledgers onto the shoulders of individuals and families. Hacker's insight, which we'll explore in greater detail in chapter 2, is important to understanding the finances of American families and the instability we see in the Diaries. Our data revealed not only evidence of the shift in risk that Hacker describes, but also the impact of a parallel transformation, one occurring in the labor market. We've taken to calling it the Great Job Shift.

Since the 1970s, steady work that pays a predictable and living wage has become increasingly difficult to find. This shift has left many more families vulnerable to income volatility. While there are many factors, as with so many other features of modern life, the Great Job Shift is a story mostly about how technology has shifted power, in this case from workers to employers. And it is a story of how that power has shifted risk from employers onto workers.

A well-known example of this trend is the decline of manufacturing jobs in the United States, once a source of reliably middle-class, often unionized, work. While economists debate the relative importance of automation and globalization in this decline, no one disputes the numbers. In 1960, about a quarter of U.S. workers were employed in manufacturing. Now the share is less than 10 percent.[18] As Figure 1.4 shows, jobs in production, crafts, and repair, as well as clerical, administrative, and some sales jobs, are shrinking.[19] In contrast, jobs in the service sector—food service, home health assistance, personal care, and private police jobs, as well as professional, technical, and managerial jobs—are growing.[20]

The shift away from manufacturing jobs can be seen in our Ohio and Kentucky sites, but the changing nature of work plays out in the New York, Mississippi, and California sites as well. For the families we met, the broad economic trend has real human consequences. Professionals and managers are seeing new opportunities, but those jobs are less available to less educated workers. The options available without a college degree are generally in the service sector, such as Janice's job dealing cards or Becky's work cleaning houses. But these jobs offer less stability.

As manufacturing jobs have declined, so too has the clout of unions. Some experts, including former labor secretary Robert Reich, place most of the blame for unions' problems on politics and the introduction

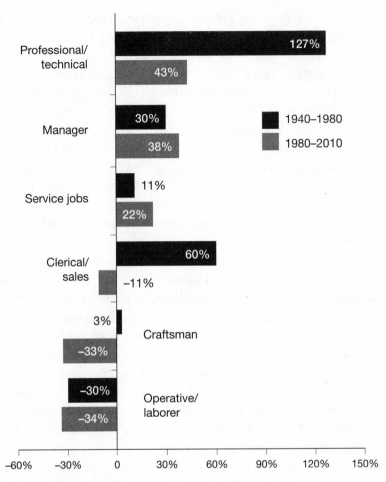

Percentage growth of job types as a portion of the labor force

Figure 1.4. Changes in employment in the United States. Jobs that typically had steady wages and long-term security have been shrinking in recent decades while jobs associated with more variability have grown. Data from Lawrence Katz and Robert Margo, "Technical Change and the Relative Demand for Skilled Labor: The United States in Historical Perspective," via David H. Autor, "Why Are There Still So Many Jobs? The History and Future of Workplace Automation," *Journal of Economic Perspectives* 29, no. 3 (Summer 2015): 3–30.

of right-to-work laws and other limits on union influence in many states.[21] But union membership is also declining because the kinds of jobs and sectors that were once unionized are shrinking. According to the Bureau of Labor Statistics, 20 percent of workers were union members in 1983, compared with 11 percent in 2014, and many of those are in the public sector. Union jobs make up just 7 percent of private sector workers today.[22] Even within job categories, union membership has fallen: 21 percent of workers in installation, maintenance, and repair occupations were unionized in 2000, compared with just 15 percent in 2014.[23] Without unions, workers lack the ability to bargain collectively for higher wages and other attributes of quality work like being able to count on a stable number of hours each week.

Meanwhile, technology has provided employers in all sectors with a host of new means to rapidly measure and adapt quickly to market conditions. These changes, which boost companies' efficiency and profitability, have consequences for how companies use workers. As early as the 1950s, for example, Japanese manufacturers such as Toyota began using a "just-in-time" system to scale production up or down quickly based on market demand.[24] The approach requires not only the technology to measure and understand shifting needs but the ability to rapidly change how much is being produced. That ability is not just technical; it means that workers absorb a portion of the ups and downs in demand by working overtime or reducing their hours. Just-in-time manufacturing has also meant a growing reliance on temporary workers. Even Toyota, which has a reputation for treating employees very well, employs temporary workers to fill gaps, sometimes for years. Last year, the U.S. Department of Commerce estimated that about 8 to 10 percent of production jobs in manufacturing were temporary.[25]

Technology-enabled rapid adjustment has spread to many other sectors of the U.S. economy, too. In fact, it's often easier for service sector firms to rapidly adjust workers' hours, since there's no production line to worry about. Many large employers now have the technology to estimate precisely how many workers they'll need, down to the day and time. This can lead to dramatic swings in the number of hours that employees work, depending on the season, month, week, and even the day. Smaller employers may not have all the same technological tools at their disposal, but they employ similar practices. Workers are sent home early if sales are slow. Their shifts are sometimes canceled with no warning, and, when things are busy, they're called in with little or no advance notice.[26]

Elaine Sullivan, a middle-aged woman from California who was part of the study, lived the Great Job Shift. For more than fifteen years she worked as a cafeteria manager at an elementary school. Not only was her job unionized, but she was the local union representative. She was laid off in 2008 and was unable to find another job in the school system—in part, she believes, because of her role in the union. It took her a year and a half to find a new job. She started working hourly on the front lines of a quick-serve restaurant. It took her another year and a half to work her way up to a managerial position. She told us she pursued the promotion not just because of the higher pay but because managers don't get told to go home early. There's a catch, though: now, instead of being the union representative for her coworkers, she is the one who tells others that their shifts are being cut when traffic to the restaurant is slow. She doesn't like having to do it, but there is a strict algorithm the company uses to determine staffing levels based on hourly sales. If she lets "unneeded" workers stay on the clock, she gets an email from corporate headquarters within twenty-four hours asking for an explanation.

The rapid translation of rising and falling sales into worker salaries isn't unique to the restaurant industry. Using data collected directly from firms, economists at the Federal Reserve and Harvard Business School found that volatility in publicly traded firms' sales growth rates and profit-to-sales ratios has increased dramatically since 1970—and that the increased volatility is reflected directly in the wages of workers within the year. In other words, firms seem to be reacting more quickly to changes in the business environment by increasing or cutting what they are paying their existing workers (not by layoffs or new hires). This connection is most pronounced in the service sector and for low-wage workers.[27]

Indeed, the Great Job Shift has not affected all workers equally. Using data from the U.S. Census Bureau and national unemployment insurance records, Michael Strain of the American Enterprise

Institute found that business downturns had bigger effects on the earnings of low-wage workers than of high-wage workers.[28] More than half (58.5 percent) of the U.S. workforce was paid hourly in 2015.[29] Low-skill, hourly positions are the easiest for companies to quickly scale up and down.[30]

One recent national study by Susan Lambert, Peter Fugiel, and Julia Henly of the University of Chicago found that about 60 percent of "early career" workers, those between ages twenty-six and thirty-two, commonly had variable work hours.[31] For these workers with unsteady hours, fluctuations averaged almost 50 percent.[32] The fluctuations were greatest for part-time workers, but they were notable for full-time workers, too. Schedules were not just volatile but unpredictable, even a week in advance. Lambert, Fugiel, and Henly's findings are in line with the experience of the households we met, for whom changes within jobs was the largest source of volatility.

Tipped workers are also subject to more income volatility than are salaried workers. Janice's work at the casino shows the instability of a living earned through tips and commissions. Tipping is often seen as part of a well-functioning business—after all, when we tip, we reward hard work and good service. But the system of tipping also opens the door to inequality and uncertainty, and it can leave workers vulnerable to mistreatment and harassment by managers and customers. One of the origins of tipping in nineteenth-century America lies in the refusal of white business owners to pay newly freed, black workers a wage, and there are still documented differences in tips received by servers today based on their race.[33] Even when not guilty of these deep harms, tipping can be capricious, leaving the income of servers subject to factors outside of their control (a customer's mood, how quickly the kitchen fills food orders—or, as in Janice's case, if college football games will be played at home or away). Basing wages on tips places risk on workers' shoulders. When a hotel can't fill its rooms, maids share the loss too. Janice has to pay for groceries, diapers, and gas no matter how many gamblers emerge from the Tuscaloosa bus. Jeremy Moore, when he was working as a mechanic on commission, was in a similar position.

Because women and people of color are employed in tipped, low-wage, and hourly jobs in high numbers, they tend to be disproportionately affected by the volatile schedules and incomes resulting from the Great Job Shift. Nearly half of the women who work in the retail and restaurant industry, for example, are women of color.[34] About 40 percent of tipped workers are people of color, versus 32 percent of the general workforce.[35] In the summer of 2016, more than a quarter of black and Latino part-time workers were classified as "involuntarily part-time" (which means always pushing for more hours) by the Bureau of Labor Statistics, in comparison to only one in six among part-time white workers.[36]

Another group especially vulnerable to income volatility is contingent workers, sometimes called freelancers, and known in regulatory terms as independent contractors. Estimates of the number of people working independently vary. According to a Government Accountability Office report, the figure ranges from less than 5 percent of American workers to more than a third, depending on how contingent work is defined. The Freelancers Union, an advocacy group that represents independent contractors, embraces the broader definition, reporting that more than a third of American workers, nearly 53 million, performed some freelance work in 2014. According to IRS data, the number of people filing 1099-MISC forms—indicative of receiving income from work that is not formal employment—has risen steadily since 1989 and at a faster pace than the number of people filing W-2s.[37]

Contingent workers aren't employees—and don't have employee protections or benefits, particularly unemployment insurance, which dampens income volatility when a job is lost. If companies are passing on volatility to their employees, they pass it on even more to contingent workers. In addition, contingent workers don't have the same recourse if they are not paid fully or promptly for their work. According to the Freelancers Union, roughly a third of those they count among contingent workers, over nineteen million people, have experienced this sort of wage theft.[38]

Freelance work is a mixed bag when it comes to volatility. Promoters of the "gig economy"—the term used to describe freelance work enabled by technology platforms like AirBnB, Uber, and TaskRabbit—often argue that it can reduce financial instability. When workers' income dips in their regular jobs, the argument goes, they can fill the gap with short-term gigs. While that may be true in theory, how it works in practice is much less clear. Being a freelancer can be a symptom of instability as much as an answer to it, and not everyone has equal access to opportunities to supplement or smooth their income. Data from the Federal Reserve indicate that while 11 percent of adults earned freelance income in 2015, those with higher levels of education were more likely to have income from informal work. The indication is that participating in the gig economy requires either a base of capital (a vehicle, a room to rent) or technology skills—both of which are associated with higher levels of education—and less vulnerability to income volatility, since higher levels of education are correlated with salaried and non-tipped jobs.[39] The JP Morgan Chase Institute found that labor platforms like Uber and TaskRabbit sometimes supplemented income dips, while capital platforms like AirBnB were more often used to supplement relatively steady wage income.[40]

Of course, there are other factors too. Age is one: the young are more likely to participate in technology-enabled freelance work. Another is geography (there is very little demand for Uber drivers in the small town where Becky and Jeremy live). Overall, it seems there's little evidence so far that the gig economy reduces income volatility by providing additional earning opportunities, rather than increasing the risk of volatility relative to traditional jobs.

While volatility in earnings within jobs is the biggest contributor to income volatility, between-job volatility was also important. That can mean losing a job and gaining a new one or having multiple jobs at the same time. Nationwide, according to the Bureau of Labor Statistics, 6.5 million workers wanted full-time jobs in 2015, or more hours from their part-time jobs, but couldn't find them.[41] Among Diaries families, 38 percent of working adults had two, three, or four jobs during the year (some simultaneously, some sequentially). The other 62 percent were like Jeremy Moore, employed in a single job that accounted for their total earnings. But many of these adults were nonetheless part of households where someone else was working too: in most households where an adult had just a single income source, another working-age member also held a job. So while less than half of working adults worked more than one job, roughly two-thirds of entire households did. Even if these multiple jobs added up to a living wage, the multiple jobs did little to dampen overall volatility. When there is a second earner in a household, their wages reduce household volatility only about 5 percent on average.[42]

Stability's Benefits

The dispassionate economist would look at income volatility and say it's not necessarily a problem in and of itself. People should just save and borrow as necessary to cope with the spikes and dips in income. But to do that kind of saving and borrowing, you have to have access to affordable, quality financial services designed for those purposes. Many people don't. But even when families have tools to cope with their financial ups and downs (be it by saving, borrowing, or earning more), volatility brings costs.[43]

At the most basic level, volatility, when combined with illiquidity, can require households to expend a large amount of a scarce resource: attention. Sendhil Mullainathan and Eldar Shafir, in their book *Scarcity*, survey decades of research in psychology and economics in order to illustrate how limited a resource attention is and the problems that arise when people can't pay enough attention. The most important point is that attention is zero-sum. That means that each moment of focus a household with a volatile income spends figuring out their budget is stolen from making other important financial decisions and choices, or from activities like parenting or community engagement.[44] That's a cost that all of society bears, not just these households and their families and neighbors. Henly and Lambert followed up on their research about the prevalence of unpredictable schedules and found that, independent of non-standard hours (nights and weekends), unpredictability increased stress and conflict at home.[45] Some of these costs are obvious once people see the havoc an unpredictable schedule and volatile income can wreak. A 2014 *New York Times* profile of a Starbucks barista so clearly demonstrated the serious negative consequences of her frequently changing work schedule (especially on her ability to find quality child care), and how common irregular and volatile schedules were for Starbucks workers, that the company announced changes to its scheduling policies within forty-eight hours.[46]

But there are also costs and harms that are harder to see—and they can be long-term, even intergenerational ones. Studies suggest that people who experience income volatility tend to be more risk averse, which can limit their willingness to invest in their own or their children's future.[47] There's evidence that children from households with volatile incomes perform poorly in school. Teenagers, in particular, were more likely to face suspension or expulsion or to drop out.[48] James Heckman, winner of the Nobel Prize in 2000 for his scholarship about early childhood education and lifetime outcomes, has noted how short-term income shortfalls can rapidly cascade into decreased investment in children's education.[49]

Volatility wreaks havoc with all the standard advice on how to manage finances. How do you create a realistic budget—and stick to it—if for half the year your income isn't close to average? In the moments that income unexpectedly dips, as Janice knows, it can be tempting to choose a quick fix like a payday or auto title loan that can end up being extremely costly and amplifying future volatility problems. Even when households don't turn to predatory products, a drop in income can—and does, for many of the households we followed—lead to missed bills, late fees, utility disconnections, evictions, or damaged credit.[50] With a greater number of families choosing insurance plans with high deductibles to hold down the total cost of medical insurance, an income dip can lead to delaying or doing without medical care.[51] Even the inability to buy groceries in bulk, because of an actual income dip or the risk of one, can materially increase the total amount families pay for household goods.[52]

Income volatility can also interfere with the existing social safety net. Some welfare programs require beneficiaries to work a certain number of hours each week, assuming that the number of hours worked is under the control of the employee, rather than the employer.[53] Qualification for programs like food stamps and health insurance subsidies is based on an average monthly income threshold. But of course volatile incomes mean that families bounce in and out of eligibility.[54] Bouncing in and out of Medicaid ineligibility causes interruptions in care for chronic conditions, particularly in places where the doctors who accept Medicaid and private insurance don't overlap.[55] There can also be severe penalties for "fraud" in these programs, receiving benefits when your income is too high. But households subject to volatile incomes may not, themselves, know when or whether they will cross thresholds of eligibility. For instance, as of 2016, the Pennsylvania Medicaid Application asks whether anyone in the household has a hard time predicting their income, but in the very next question requires applicants to do exactly that—for the next twenty-four months—in order to establish eligibility.

"Stop worrying so much"

Janice's father's church is down a narrow road, on the left just before the pavement ends and the road turns into a patchy mix of asphalt and pebbles. It's small, not like the large stone churches on the main street of town. The building sits in the middle of a grass-covered plot with no driveway or parking lot. Two car-sized rectangles of gravel mark parking spots, but on Sundays, when church members arrive in suits and dresses, cars spread across the lawn.

The church has a single-story brick façade, and in the past year, members erected a small portico above the main door, supported by four white columns, making the entrance a bit grander. Janice's father usually moves about as he preaches. Sometimes the sermons are "shouting sermons" in the Pentecostal tradition, but on this day it's a teaching sermon, anchored in Jeremiah 7:21–23, a call to repentance: "Walk ye in all the ways that I have commanded you." As Janice's father has aged, services have become shorter. Now they usually end after two hours, not like past days when he preached all morning and sometimes into the afternoon.

Janice worries about the ups and downs of her finances, but she mostly keeps her concerns to herself and doesn't trouble her parents. Janice's father is sympathetic to her struggles; he senses the stress created by car payments and utility bills in the months when Janice's paychecks are short. "He knows I'm on my own without a husband. He came to me and said, 'It's good you pay your tithe. But you are not supposed to lose things because you pay your tithe. Pay your car note first?" Even when Janice can't afford the 10 percent tithe for the church, she makes sure to put something in the collection plate on Sundays.

One Sunday, Janice's father called a prayer line. The members stood to receive prayers, forming a line down the center aisle. Each person waited his or her turn to receive a prayer to heal illness or ease other struggles. Janice's father placed his palm on the head of the person at the front of the line, offered a prayer, and gave a gentle shove backward.

Janice was having a particularly stressful week. "I was *worried*. It was going rough," she remembered later. When Janice got to the front of the line, her father paused. "He was standing right in front of me. And he had his hand on top of my head." Instead of offering a prayer, he lowered his voice so only Janice could hear. "Stop worrying so much," he whispered. "It will be all right."

In that moment, Janice felt a weight lift. "And, really, the worry just went away. It just went away. And I don't think I worried about nothing since." Janice paused for a moment as she reconsidered. "You know, every now and then something bad goes through my head. But now I don't hold it and worry about it like I did. Now I don't do that." She took a few more moments to think about her life. "I'm not a very important person. I just do what I do, and go home. I try to be a good person. It gets difficult sometimes, but I try to be a good person."

Chapter 2

Spending

Sarah and Sam

The preschool girls bounced around the gym, chatting, laughing, and occasionally breaking into dance. Teenagers quieted and herded them into a corner to wait for their names to be called. When their names were announced over the PA system, the kids ran onto the floor and high-fived the teacher who stood in the middle of the gym, handing out certificates of achievement. Every girl was awarded one. Parents, perched on the wooden bleachers, smiled and clapped.

Sarah Johnson sat off to the side, filming the scene. She started this program a few years earlier, after searching unsuccessfully for a weekend performing arts program for her own preschool daughter, Amy. The ones she found were either too expensive or too far away. So Sarah won approval from the local public high school, where she worked, to use its facilities. She then recruited high school girls from the drama, chorus, and cheerleading squads to serve as teachers. The program met every Saturday morning during the school year and more frequently during summer months. In just three years, its enrollment had grown to include more than one hundred children.

Sarah, who wore black-framed glasses and had her dark brown hair pulled back in a loose ponytail, turned the camera on herself and described the program. The idea was to use the video to recruit more children the following year. She spoke into the camera with ease, as if talking to a friend or neighbor. The ceremony, the finale of this year's program, was a satisfying moment for her.

Sarah and her husband, Sam, live in a town near the Ohio River, not far from Cincinnati. They share a three-story house with Amy and two children from their previous marriages, Mathew and Anne. The town's main avenue is busy with coffee shops, ice cream parlors, diners, and hair salons, but after a few blocks the bustle fades. Starting in the 1970s, the area began to shed manufacturing jobs, and the town's population declined by a third. These days, more than half of the children at local schools qualify for free or reduced-price lunch. Though Sarah worries about drugs and crime from Cincinnati, she likes her neighborhood. It is a short drive to the city but feels like a small town. It is the kind of place, she said, where "everyone knows everyone, and everyone knows what you're doing before you've finished doing it."

But Sarah and Sam Johnson have struggles that are invisible to others. In the year of our study, they together earned roughly $65,000 before taxes, a notch above the Cincinnati median income and the national median.[1] Neither Sarah nor Sam held a college degree at that point, but both worked in jobs that used their skills and energy. In her position as an administrative assistant, Sarah spent thirty-five hours a week helping manage the middle school's budget, tracking more than forty-five accounts. Sam, a low-key, friendly guy, worked forty-five-hour weeks selling medical equipment on commission.

These jobs didn't quite cover their expenses, however, so they supplemented their earnings with part-time work. During the school year, Sarah assisted the school district's athletic director by selling concessions at sports events for $15 a game. One summer month, she also worked at a restaurant on nights and weekends. Sam coached a middle school sports team and worked weekends at a call center. On top of this, Sarah, who was working toward her bachelor's degree at the local college, received student loans. In our year with her, she

more and more difficult to strive for mobility without sacrificing stability in the short term.[5]

One Thing after Another

In a typical month, the Johnsons' household expenses totaled roughly
$4,800. The majority of that money—about three-quarters, in most
months—went to predictable, routine expenses like insurance, mortgage payments, and food. Health and car insurance payments totaled
about $500. Their monthly mortgage payment was $500, but occasionally Sarah skipped paying it when she was short and made up for
it later.[6] But what really kept Sarah juggling was the other quarter of
their expenses, the ones that were irregular. Most of those were medical. Sarah relied on free samples from their clinic or put off filling
full prescriptions when the family needed medicine, but she knew
she could only cut back so much. Sarah and Sam both had health
coverage through their employers, but his was a low-premium, high-
deductible policy and costs rose when he required care. In the previous five years, medical bills had piled up: $2,800 for surgery for
Sam; $1,000 for MRIs for Sarah; $700 for an emergency room visit
for Mathew; and the largest bill, $3,800, from a company that offers a
credit card for health expenses. During the year we spent with them,
Sarah and Sam made no progress paying down their debt. Near-term
needs always exerted a stronger pull.

We started tracking the Johnsons' weekly finances in June. That
turned out to be an important month for the family. Anne and
Mathew both graduated high school, Mathew in the top 5 percent of
his class. Sarah and Sam were determined to celebrate; they threw a
graduation party for the kids, spending $600.

The month before, Sarah had been late on their mortgage, so in
June she paid an extra $150. Then they learned Anne had decided
to marry her sweetheart—the following week. An ROTC member
in high school, he'd decided to enlist in the military full-time. The
ceremony was small and informal, but Sam and Sarah still needed to
pay for a gift and refreshments. With all those extra expenses in June,
Sarah had to skip paying the electric bill.

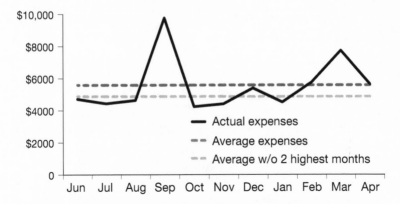

Figure 2.1. The Johnsons' monthly spending, June 2012–April 2013. The Johnsons had two big spending spikes during the year: when a leaking pipe caused significant damage to their home and after they received their tax refund. The spending spikes are large enough to significantly alter their average monthly spending.

At that point, she'd missed a few months, and in early July she received a disconnection notice. She needed around $300 to get the power turned back on. Mathew loaned her $200 from his graduation gifts, and Sam borrowed the rest against his next paycheck.

Things didn't get any better in August and September. A water pipe in their home sprung a major leak, requiring $1,400 in repairs. The water damage aggravated Amy's asthma, which required a trip to the doctor and the pharmacy. The Johnsons pulled up rugs, replaced furniture, and bought an air purifier. Infuriatingly, the leak caused a substantial bump in their water bill. Attracted to the dampness, silverfish swarmed the house. As if that weren't enough, the leak occurred just as one of their cars finally broke down. They bought another to replace it for $3,000, financed by an auto loan. The Johnsons did get one financial break: in September, Sarah's $4,000 student loan check arrived. She used part of that money to cover the home repairs and to catch up on utility bills, skipping other bills that didn't seem as urgent. To cope, the family spent less on food and tried to keep their spending low during October and November, slowly catching up on old bills.

But in December, they were hit again. The used car they'd purchased at the end of the summer started giving them trouble. The transmission needed to be replaced, to the tune of $868. Christmas gifts came to $1,000; Sarah's mother loaned them most of it, $900. In February, Sarah's next student loan check arrived. The $3,600 was less than she expected, but it allowed her to catch up on some bills, including $863 for the family's cell phone plan, which had been building up for months because of partially paid bills. In March, their tax refund of $3,171 gave the Johnsons some additional breathing room—but not enough to make a serious dent in their debt.

Spikes and Dips of Spending

The Johnsons' year shows the danger of assuming that most households spend roughly the same amount each month, punctuated perhaps by a bump caused by a summer vacation or the odd doctor's visit. That might seem a reasonable assumption; after all, rents and mortgage payments don't change from month to month, and utility bills, groceries, and transportation tend to be pretty predictable if not completely stable.

So when we first looked at the families' spikes and dips in spending, we thought we'd made a mistake. We were surprised to see that spending was nearly as variable as income.[7] (Spikes occur when monthly spending is higher than average by at least 25 percent, dips when monthly spending falls 25 percent or more below average.) Households experienced about five months of the year when their spending was at least 25 percent above or below their average monthly spending. We found an average of 2.2 spending spikes over the year and 2.6 spending dips. So much for smooth and steady spending interrupted by the occasional shock or emergency.

We devoted an extra two months to looking for possible data problems, but the results stood firm: the number of spending spikes and dips was similar to the number of income spikes and dips.[8] Federal Reserve data show that only a little more than half of Americans report steady month-to-month spending while 44 percent say their spending bounces up and down from month to month.[9] The Johnsons were unlucky but not so unusual.

The Johnsons, like most of our households, experienced two clear spending spikes during the year, in September and March, but life conspired to prevent any spending dips. Whenever there was money on hand, Sarah devoted a chunk of it to catching up.

Mismatch, Ripples, and Expected Emergencies

One explanation for volatile spending is that households are living paycheck to paycheck, spending everything they earn in the month that they earn it. If this kind of extreme illiquidity holds, we would expect to see the spikes and dips of income line up with the spikes and dips of spending. That would indicate that households have no choice but to spend when they have cash on hand with little ability to put aside some cash for when they need it later.

When we looked at how the spikes and dips in income and spending lined up, the patterns were partially consistent with this explanation: looking across households, in about 30 percent of months in which spending spiked, income also spiked. Those big income months were matched with big spending months.[10] But the spikes of income and spending more often did not match. In the other 70 percent of months when spending spiked, there was no corresponding income spike. In fact, income was below average in about a third of the months in which spending spiked. These moments of mismatch were often difficult to manage.

Another cause of expense spikes is that volatility begets volatility; ups and downs one month can contribute to volatility the next. We came to think of this as "ripple-effect volatility." For example, because Sarah missed a few $500 monthly mortgage payments in the winter when she was short on cash, she paid $650 per month during the summer. She did the same with other bills. Among the Diaries households, this kind of volatility was common. Only 20 percent of families hardly ever missed a bill, paying all or almost all of their bills in roughly the same amount during the same time of each month, for eleven or twelve of the Diaries months. Among the other 80 percent, half of the households tended to skip the same one or two bills each month, creating a spending spike when they finally caught up. The other half were like the Johnsons, playing a juggling game in which they chose different bills to skip in different months.[11] Ripple-effect volatility operates like credit: Sarah essentially managed her ups and downs by "borrowing" in the form of late payments. As a result, she often paid late fees and penalties. Her spending spikes were, in part, the result of how she managed her money—once she was in a cycle of volatility, it was hard to smooth it out.

Sarah and Sam also experienced a third type of spending volatility, which can arise independently of income. This is driven by factors beyond families' immediate control: the house needs repairs, the kids need clothes for school, or Christmas requires gifts. Some of these costs are infrequent while others are urgent, but either way, taken together these kinds of expenses are fairly common.

These expenses are so ordinary that it's difficult to characterize them as true emergencies. The word "emergency" implies suddenness, unpredictability, and, hopefully, rarity. The phrase "economic shock," which economists prefer, has the same connotation. But, if you own a house or car, at some point it will need repair. This is especially true if you start out with a lower-cost, lower-quality home or car. The size and timing of repairs are unpredictable, but the fact of their eventual occurrence is not. Calling this emergency spending isn't exactly right because it masks just how common this type of spending really is.[12]

Often, as in the case of the Johnsons, this type of spending by Financial Diaries households was related to health care. Of the 235 households, about one-quarter sent a family member to the emergency room during the study year. Ten percent had a member who was hospitalized. Other types of expenses added up, too. Of the poorest Diaries households, a third were threatened with or experienced disconnection of utilities or cable, repossession of an asset, or eviction during the year. That was so even for a quarter of better-off households like Sam and Sarah's. Ten percent of families experienced a vehicle breakdown, requiring an average of about $700 in up-front repair costs. Half of the households faced car repairs of more than $100 in at least one month. A quarter owed over $100 for housing repairs in at least one month.

Spending patterns defied other binary distinctions, too. Expenses that budgeting experts might define as fixed rather than variable were not paid as consistently as we expected: rent was generally paid in the same amount each month but not always at the same time, while groceries were purchased at a regular interval but with highly variable costs. We also were tempted to categorize expenses as either urgent or optional. Our data analysis would have benefited from being able to discern a clear pattern in optional spending relative to more urgent spending. However, figuring out which expenses households viewed as urgent and absolutely mandatory was harder than we had imagined. Even health care costs, for example, were often treated as optional. Thirty-three percent of households went without medications during the study, and 22 percent went without some other care.

The national data from the Federal Reserve's SHED survey, which we discussed in chapter 1, also revealed ups and downs in spending. Like the Johnsons, just over one in five households in that survey reported that, in the prior twelve months, they had unexpected medical expenses for which they paid out of pocket (i.e., expenses not covered by health insurance). The costs were not small, averaging nearly $2,800 during the year. And, at the time of the Fed survey, nearly half of households still hadn't paid their bills or were carrying debt related to the health problem.

What's more, nearly half of uninsured households in the Fed's survey said they didn't seek medical care during the previous year because of financial issues, including 45 percent of households with income over $40,000. More striking was that households *with* health insurance, like the Johnsons, also skipped health care they needed, including 16 percent with income above $40,000.[13]

That said, few of the months with expense spikes were caused by just one big catastrophe. Instead, months when spending exceeded 25 percent of the average were more likely to be caused by a pile-up of unusually high spending on two or more things at once.[14]

The Great Risk Shift and the Erosion of Slack

Sam and Sarah were clawing their way into the middle class. After starting her adult life at a financial disadvantage, as a single mother without a college degree, Sarah had scrambled, juggled, and scraped to move forward. Sam leveraged his personality into a series of sales jobs that paid decently, particularly given that he, too, had only a high school degree. Despite their hard work, though, their grip on the middle rungs of the ladder was tenuous. Each spending shock threatened to knock them off.

There was a time when Sam and Sarah would have had help in facing some of their largest costs and financial risks. As we noted in the first chapter, in *The Great Risk Shift*, Jacob Hacker describes how risks have "increasingly shifted from the broad shoulders of government and corporations onto the backs of American workers and their families."[15] Hacker traced the trend to a gradual unwinding of the social contract formed among government, employers, and workers in the 1930s. By the 1970s, that compact was fissuring. In a bid to boost profitability, employers that had once provided their workers with pensions and comprehensive health insurance and folded the costs of risk management into their business plans had begun to shift more of those costs onto workers. Defined benefit pensions were traded for 401(k) plans. Health insurance costs shifted so that companies paid less and workers paid more. Between 2003 and 2013, health insurance premiums for employer-provided health benefits rose by 73 percent—and workers' share of that increase was 93 percent. Deductibles more than doubled.[16] In Hacker's telling, these shifts mean that families bear a great deal more risk than they once did.

Based on the Diaries families' experience, we would go a step further. Because those risks so often come to pass, families not only bear more *risk* of possible costs; they bear more *costs*, too. And when incomes don't keep pace, households' slack erodes. They have insufficient cushion between what they earn and what they spend. Households are therefore hit with a double whammy: they have to shoulder the extra costs and are then less prepared for other challenges.

Health Care

The shifting of health care costs onto workers was a big part of Sam and Sarah's story. When we first met them, they were carrying $6,600 in medical debt. In an earlier era, much of those costs might have been borne by their employers through more comprehensive health coverage. During the year we followed them, they spent approximately

$5,500 more on medical care (including insurance premiums). Because of chronic medical issues in their family, that figure is above the national average. But costs have been rising. According to the Pew Charitable Trusts, in 2014 the median U.S. household (with two earners and two children) spent about $2,500 on health care, twice what they did in 1996.[17] The Johnsons lived these numbers. They sometimes assumed even more risk in order to cut costs in the short term: at one point, Sam went without insurance for several months because adding him to Sarah's plan would have cost $5,000 for the year.

Housing

Housing costs are also squeezing middle- and lower-income families. For the poorest third of households, housing expenses have increased more than 50 percent since the mid-1990s and for the middle third, about 25 percent. In 2015, low- and middle-income families spent an average of 34 percent of their earnings on housing.

Back in 2009, the Johnsons decided to trade one form of housing risk for another, swapping rising rents and difficulty finding suitable apartments for repairs, maintenance, and a mortgage. At the time, Sam, Sarah, and their children shared a one-and-a-half-bedroom rental above a garage. Desperate for more space, Sarah spent a year searching for alternatives, but she couldn't find any four-bedroom rentals, let alone one they could afford.

Then she noticed a house that had long stood empty, a three-story box covered in gray siding with a front lawn about the length and width of a Ping-Pong table. The house was for sale, but buying didn't seem like an option. Even if they could have found the money for a down payment, their low credit scores would have priced them out of a mortgage. But Sarah was out of options, and she figured she had nothing to lose by calling the real estate agent to ask if the owner might be willing to rent.

The home's sellers were three business partners who had planned to flip the house for a quick profit. The 2008 housing bubble had just burst, though, and buyers were scarce. One of the partners called Sarah back. He was happy to rent to her. But then he asked how she felt about eventually buying the property. The owner wasn't an ordinary real estate investor. He was a pastor at a church a few towns away, and he had made a religious commitment to help one hundred people take a step forward in their lives. The man suggested that Sam and Sarah could be among the hundred. He proposed a deal he thought would be mutually beneficial: the couple could rent the house, on the condition that after a year they would purchase it. During that time, $200 of their rent every month would go into escrow as savings toward the down payment. In addition, he agreed to match, dollar for dollar, everything they spent on repairs to the house.

It needed a lot of repairs. The electric wiring was a mess, the kitchen was missing a functioning sink, and the downstairs bathroom didn't work. Sarah and Sam ended up spending $17,000 on those repairs, including tearing out the drywall in the exterior walls so they could install proper insulation and replacing the electric wiring. After eighteen months of labor, they purchased the house, taking out a mortgage for $76,000.

Home ownership is usually considered a force for stability and mobility. That's why so many American families aspire to it, even after the housing market collapse and the Great Recession. Once you own a house, you don't have to worry about rising rent or capricious landlords. Once you own a house, you're building wealth.

Whether that's true, though, depends on the house. The home Sam and Sarah bought wasn't the kind that would add stability; it was just a different source of risk. Whether it would help them build wealth remained to be seen. While U.S. home prices have recovered most of the ground lost since the housing bubble, that's not true for houses worth $100,000 or less. Home values in that range have remained stagnant.[18] In other words, the Johnsons were shouldering more risk with less chance for reward.

Higher Education

Just as a home is often considered a signifier of middle-class life, so too is a college degree. But costs are also rising there. According to the U.S. Department of Education, the cost of getting a bachelor's degree from a public institution increased 34 percent in real terms between 2003 and 2014. The reason? State governments have systematically cut funding for public universities, shifting more of the cost to families.[19] According to the College Board, college costs are rising four times faster than income and two and a half times faster than federal Pell grants.[20] While Hacker didn't focus on the cost of higher education in his analysis, it certainly fits the Great Risk Shift model. As the gap between wages for high school graduates and those with a college degree continues to grow, a university education is becoming an increasingly important form of wage insurance. Families now have to choose between the risk of forgoing a college degree and the risk of taking on increasing amounts of debt to pay for future wage and job security.

The Johnsons were living these numbers, too. Sarah joked that since she would be forty when she graduated college, she'd be paying down her loans the rest of her life. She wished she could do more to help Mathew with his education costs; he would also be graduating with five-figure loans.

Retirement

The same narrative applies to retirement plans. Few businesses now offer pensions that guarantee a fixed payment for life. Instead, most retirement plans help workers set aside their own money, sometimes with the benefit of a matching employer contribution. Workers bear the risk that they will fail to save enough and the risk that the value of their nest egg will rise and fall with the stock market. And that's if employers offer any sort of retirement plan. Sam's didn't. In the past, both Sarah and Sam cashed out their 401(k) retirement accounts when they changed employers.

After several years working in the school system, Sarah qualified for the state's public school teacher pension plan. If she stayed for the next fifteen years, she would have the kind of retirement pension inaccessible to most American households. As Sarah considered the sorts of jobs she might get once she finished her degree, she recognized she would probably have to make a trade-off. A position in the private sector would probably pay more, but she'd be shouldering greater retirement risk.

Stagnant Wages

Compounding the problem of rising costs is the fact that for years wages have been nearly stagnant. From 1980 until 2015, the cumu-

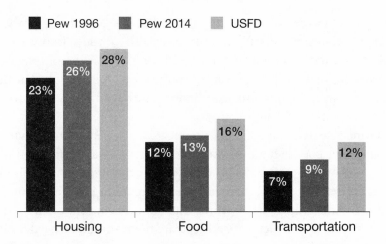

Figure 2.2. The rising cost of living. Pew researchers have found that American house-holds are spending an increasing amount of their incomes, in part because they are spending more on necessities like housing, food, and transportation. The shares of spending in these categories for USFD households are presented for comparison to national figures.

lative increase in hourly wages for middle-income workers has been just 6 percent once accounting for inflation. All of the gains came in the late 1990s. Other than a surge in wages in those years, wages have been relatively flat again until 2015 (and even then, rural wages still didn't budge). Lower-income workers have seen a 5 percent *decline* over that time period.[21] Median household income increased by just 2 percent between 2004 and 2014.[22]

This is the source of the middle-class squeeze: as costs rise and wages stagnate, families have less financial slack, while the trends that Hacker documented have continued piling more risk onto their shoulders. That, in turn, increases their vulnerability.

"Freedom, my friends"

Suze Orman, the popular financial advisor, tells her audience that the only solution for financial trouble is to make radical cuts to spending. "That's not punishment," she declares. "On the contrary, it is freedom, my friends. Figure out how to live on less, find ways to save more, and you'll be emancipated from the shackles of financial stress. Isn't that all the motivation you need?"[23] As we looked at the Johnsons' financial picture, we wondered if they might benefit from some of Orman's advice.

Orman instructs her audience to create worksheets that list where their money goes. Her sample worksheet starts with a row for monthly mortgage or rent payments and works its way through monthly phone bills, coffee at Starbucks, haircuts, manicures, and charitable contributions. After filling in the worksheet, families are told to circle the "wants" (weekly manicures) and separate them from true needs (paying electricity bills).

Then the tough love begins. Orman tells the families to start slicing everywhere possible, cutting out the wants, changing driving habits, and saving money on insurance by choosing plans with high deductibles while building up an emergency saving reserve.[24] Feeling guilty about not providing fully for your family? Unable to make the needed cuts? Orman tells parents that they're being indulgent and destructive: "When you make the commitment to spend less, you will have more money to put toward what your family needs: lasting financial security."[25] Her advice leans on homespun wisdom to live within your means, not be showy, and keep an eye on long-term goals. No matter how hard they are to follow, her tips fit within a deeply American belief system which holds that financial security is a matter of personal responsibility.[26]

When we fed the Johnsons' income and spending data into Orman's online Expense Tracker, Orman's "Get Honest" report screamed that the Johnsons were in the "RED ZONE—the place where you have no money to pay the bills, you have no savings left, and you are most likely living off of your credit cards (if you have any credit left)." If you are in the "RED ZONE," the report continued, "Chances are ... you are also behind on your payments and you don't know what to do." The report showed that the Johnsons spend more than average on cell phones, Internet, cable, utilities, car repairs, groceries, and eating out. It implored that they immediately cut "nonessentials," including their second car.

Yet when we stepped back from the spreadsheets to examine the bigger picture, it was harder to accuse the Johnsons, or families like them, of simply overspending. Sam and Sarah both work multiple jobs and have a young child at home; the second car is essential to making it all work. If they could afford a better vehicle, they might face fewer repair expenses, but they wouldn't be able to cover the monthly car payments. The Johnsons could trim their spending, but it's difficult to see how they might slice off a sizable chunk.

Moreover, they didn't want to have to sacrifice their middle-class lifestyle or their ambitions of economic mobility.[27] They desperately needed an emergency savings fund of the sort Orman advises (and, at the same time, were underprepared for retirement), but things weren't steady enough for them to build and maintain a buffer. When life is unsteady, as we describe in the next chapter, buffers take a back seat to immediate needs. The paradox is that the very people who need a buffer of savings are often the ones who have the hardest time creating it.

Forward and Backward

Sarah kept an accounting calculator on her desk, the kind with a scroll of paper that prints sums. When she talked finances, she'd often punch in numbers. Her calculations revealed the middle-class bind we've described. Orman prudently advises her listeners to cut spending, but the Johnsons were focused on a different solution: increasing their income. Their dilemma comes back to the fact that they didn't want to sacrifice upward mobility for short-term stability.

Throughout the Diaries year, Sarah mostly managed to keep the lights on at home, but credit card and medical debt loomed. Eventually, the issuer of their health care credit card, making its own assessment that the Johnsons would never catch up, wrote off the entire $3,800 balance. Instead of feeling relieved, Sarah was disappointed. She would have preferred to repay the debt and have the credit card available for future medical costs.

When we checked in with Sarah a few years after our data collection had concluded, she had just graduated from college with a bachelor's in counseling and a minor in organizational leadership. She was about to start a master's. And that wasn't her only good news. Buoyed by her success with the performing arts program, she ran for a seat on the local school board—and won.

Her son Mathew was still attending school full-time, with ambitions of becoming a math teacher. He was living at home and working nights as a server so he could borrow less for college. Sarah was proud of him, and relieved: "He's doing really good," she said.

A few months earlier, though, Mathew had broken his wrist after slipping on an icy sidewalk. Confident he was covered under his father's insurance, Sarah and Sam rushed him to the emergency room. It was the right decision; he needed immediate treatment. But Mathew's father hadn't kept up with the insurance payments, and in the aftermath of the episode Sarah and Sam owed the hospital much more than they could afford to pay. Sarah wrote a long hardship letter to the hospital proposing a payment plan, a strategy that had worked in the past. She followed up with a phone call to the collections department, confident that she could get her bills under control with a bit of understanding. She was shocked when the woman in the collections department told her to file for bankruptcy instead.

"I kinda gave up," Sarah said, seeing no option left but to declare bankruptcy. She didn't understand why the hospital wouldn't just work with her. "I'm frustrated as hell about it."

Chapter 3

Smoothing and Spiking

Becky and Jeremy

"I'm a couponer," declared Becky Moore, the mother of four from southwest Ohio. As proof of her seriousness, Becky gestured toward a binder brimming with coupons clipped from the local newspaper. When we first met, this was one of the things Becky most wanted to tell us. Her words were part prideful declaration, part confession; Becky and a friend clipped, organized, and traded coupons, alternating between shopping at the Walmart and a local supermarket depending on which had the best discounts that week. They bought in bulk if there was an especially good deal.

Becky, though, sometimes wondered if her cost-cutting might not be entirely healthy. She had so much toothpaste, shampoo, body wash, and razors stockpiled that she hadn't needed to purchase more in the year we spent with her. "I don't need eight tubes of toothpaste now," she said, "but that's what I have, and I won't have to buy any for six months. And if I see another great deal on toothpaste and I can get it dirt cheap, I will." It wasn't just toiletries. She also had a buffer of canned goods in the pantry and frozen food in the freezer.

Becky's parents divorced when she was young, and she remained particularly close to her mother. "Without realizing it," Becky said, "she taught me things." Not least were financial matters—the need to shop carefully and plan for the future. Becky and Jeremy had little slack in their budget, yet they systematically made provisions to cope with their financial ups and downs, mainly through "saving" by shopping. In the months when Jeremy earned big paychecks, Becky stocked up the cabinets, the fridge, and the freezer. When Jeremy's paychecks were small, she could cut back her spending and still put food on the table and refill the soap dish by drawing from what she had stored away. The row of unopened shampoo bottles neatly lined up on the bathroom shelf and the dozens of pork chops in the freezer attested to her mother's effectiveness as a teacher. As economists term it, Becky was actively "smoothing" the family's consumption—making sure her family had what they needed each day despite the ups and downs of Jeremy's paychecks.[1]

But while Becky put aside household goods for the future, she and Jeremy had far less success with the obvious way to smooth their consumption: building up a financial stockpile in a savings account. During most of the study year, while Jeremy fixed trucks on commission, they could predict reasonably accurately how his paychecks would rise and fall with the seasons. They knew in principle to save during the months with bigger paychecks, but in practice they had little success. Eventually, they simply closed their savings account. "It's tough for us. I don't know why," Becky conceded. "The discipline for us to not dip into that rainy-day fund—for entertainment or something fun—is too much." So Becky instead built up a rainy-day fund composed of toiletries, frozen pork chops, and boxed cereal and thus avoided the temptation to spend on something fun; you can't buy movie tickets with eight tubes of toothpaste.

Coping

More and more Americans are like Becky and Jeremy Moore, Janice Evans, and Sarah and Sam Johnson: they're not poor, but they are financially insecure. The Federal Reserve estimates that about

Figure 3.1. Coping mechanisms. Families who have reliable coping tools can weather volatility without an impact on consumption. Families who face income or spending volatility but do not have adequate coping mechanisms will struggle.

one-third of Americans—approximately 76 million adults—are "just getting by" or struggling to get by. That includes a quarter of middle-class Americans and 10 percent of those with incomes above $100,000 each year. Those with more modest incomes—in particular single parents, adults without college degrees, and racial and ethnic minorities—are more likely to face financial struggle, but insecurity is found at all income levels.[2]

One way to describe people's prospects for financial security is to consider a two-by-two box (see Figure 3.1), with one side representing the inherent steadiness of income and expenses and the other reflecting how well households can cope. Coping captures how easily people can command resources when needed, spend when they want, and consume as they need to. Being financially "okay" could mean something as simple as being able to pay bills in full, on time, and without stress, or it could mean putting enough away for an early retirement or being able to pay for college. The Consumer Financial Protection Bureau ran a national survey on how Americans define financial well-being and boiled down the results to a "sense of security and freedom of choice, in the present and in the future."[3] Like many others we met, Becky and Jeremy find themselves in the lower left corner of the two-by-two box, feeling neither secure nor as though they have much freedom to choose.

To gain financial stability, Becky and Jeremy could pursue three complementary strategies. The first is to focus on reducing the underlying volatility of their income and spending. Achieving a less volatile income is difficult, however, as fewer and fewer jobs pay steady wages. The introduction described Jeremy's attempt to secure more stability by switching from a job working on commission to one with guaranteed hourly pay. For many people, though, that sort of move isn't possible. Even for those who have the option, switching jobs can come with difficult trade-offs: Jeremy had to accept a far longer commute; others might have to make even bigger changes.

Steadying spending needs is hard as well. Emergencies are often unavoidable, and as we described in chapter 2, the costs of health care, education, housing, and other major budget items have risen faster than wages, eroding families' room to maneuver. Moreover, cost-cutting can amplify ups and downs; Sam and Sarah Johnson, for example, saved money by buying a bargain used car, but they were hit later with extra repair bills. The deal they got on their house similarly resulted in large, unexpected costs later.

Earning more is an obvious second approach. Having more income creates the chance to build a savings cushion. That is Sarah and Sam's long-term game plan, though trying to move up the income ladder brought its own pressures, extra expenses, and instability in the short term. Stagnating or slowly rising wages in the U.S. labor market mean many families find it difficult to address volatility by simply earning more.[4] Similarly, accumulating greater wealth would help, but wealth inequality tends to fall along the same lines as other inequalities: compared to other groups, minority, less educated, and lower-wage workers start out with less wealth and accumulate less over time.[5]

If households lack good options to earn more or to reduce the underlying volatility, they need a third approach: they need to find dependable ways to cope with existing ups and downs—that is, to smooth consumption. For Becky and Jeremy smoothing consumption meant trying to build up savings, and, when that failed, it meant borrowing and shopping strategically. Their goal was not to achieve perfectly smooth spending in a plain English sense but instead to insulate important spending choices from the volatility of income. In fact, as we describe later in the chapter, families' attempts to "smooth" are usually accompanied by—and complicated by—the need to sometimes do the exact opposite: to put together big lumpy amounts, like for Christmas gifts or for a car down payment. The overarching goal is to get hold of the right money at the right time. In other words, it is about managing liquidity.

Safety net programs—such as unemployment insurance, food stamps, Medicaid, housing assistance, Temporary Assistance for Needy Families (TANF), and the earned income tax credit (EITC)—help some poor and near-poor families smooth consumption. But America's safety net has, in practice, shrunk dramatically. Today, about a quarter of poor families with children are covered by TANF, for example, down from about 70 percent twenty years ago.[6] Moreover, as Janice and Marcus Evans found, safety net programs are not always reliable and steady, even if you do qualify. And, of course, many families whose income exceeds eligibility for these programs struggle with volatility, too.

Coping with ups and downs thus increasingly means finding workable financial strategies of one's own. Often, families rely on formal financial services, like savings accounts, credit cards, and insurance policies. Yet formal services are not always enough. The problem is not a straightforward lack of access—93 percent of American households own bank accounts.[7] But some financial products are complicated or not designed in ways that make it easy for people to be successful. Others cause more problems than they solve. The many financial products that are safe, affordable, and convenient are more likely to be targeted to the needs of higher-income, higher-wealth families, leaving a gap

between what existing products provide and what economically insecure families need. So, as the next chapters show, families look for
other ways to cope, too—stockpiling canned goods, for instance, or
borrowing from family, paying bills late, and sharing with friends.

Smoothing

Becky and Jeremy's attempts to smooth consumption turned out to
be far from perfect (see Figure 3.2). Still, Becky and Jeremy managed to hold a bit of money aside in their checking account, used
five credit cards to buy some time, and occasionally borrowed from
Becky's sister. The result was that their spending and income were
positively but loosely connected from month to month, with a statistical correlation between income and spending of 70 percent (short
of the 100 percent correlation that would indicate literally living
hand to mouth). They were doing even a bit better than that, because the correlation does not account for the fact that their actual
consumption of pork chops, cereal, and canned goods (as opposed
to their spending on them) was even less connected to their income
thanks to Becky's stockpiling. But they were not doing so well that
Becky could be free of anxiety about doing something as simple as
mailing the mortgage check a few weeks early.

To look at consumption smoothing in the Diaries as a whole, we
started by narrowing the focus to all months in which households'
income spiked or dipped. (As in chapter 1, we defined a spike as a
month in which income was 25 percent or more above average and a
dip as a month with income 25 percent or more below average.) We
then looked at spending in those same months. We wanted to know
if the families were so constrained that the dips in income forced
them to make similar-sized cuts in spending. If income dropped by
$200 in the month, did spending drop by $200 too? Or were families
able to keep the income dips from hitting their budget too hard—
and were they able to take advantage of income spikes by saving or
paying down debt?

We found a mixed picture. Few of the households, even among
the poorest, were living hand-to-mouth. When income dropped in a

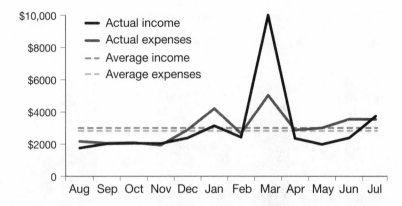

Figure 3.2. The Moores' income and spending. While their spending is clearly influenced by the spikes and dips in their income, it is not fully controlled by it. Even though they spend nearly all of their income during the year they are able to shift their spending from month to month to meet needs or take advantage of spikes in income.

given month, spending dropped too, but not by as much. Still, some saw their spending fall by large amounts in absolute terms, and they sometimes had to take costly measures to try to protect spending. After all, even a 10 percent cut in spending can be a trial in a month when money is already tight.

Figure 3.3 shows how households were able to protect spending. The gray bar on the lower right shows, for example, that when monthly income dipped for moderate-income households (who were the best-off households we tracked), spending fell by 11 percent of the monthly average. The black bar next to it shows that in those same months income had fallen by 44 percent of the monthly average. So households protected much of their ability to spend (spending fell by 11 percent rather than 44 percent), but they still needed to make notable cuts in spending relative to an average month. The story is similar for all income groups—though, as expected, poor households had slightly more difficulty smoothing (for the poor, spending fell by 17 percent when income dipped by 49 percent).[8]

Families' inability to fully protect themselves translates into difficulties during particularly tough times. The Federal Reserve's Survey

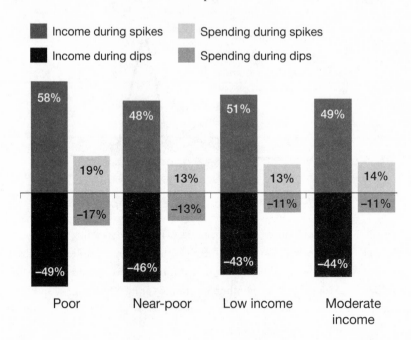

Figure 3.3. Average monthly levels of income and spending in the months when income spikes or dips, by income group. The levels of income and spending are expressed as the percent above or below the household's monthly average. *Note*: Spikes are months in which average income is 25 percent or more above average monthly income. Dips are 25 percent or more below.

of Household Economics and Decisionmaking (SHED) again gives a national picture. The SHED surveyors asked respondents how they would deal with an unexpected car repair or another urgent need requiring $400 quickly.[9] Just about half (47 percent) reported that it wouldn't be a problem: they could handle the emergency with money on hand. Another 38 percent could come up with the money by borrowing or selling something. But 14 percent of the sample said that there was just no way to come up with $400, period.[10]

The SHED shows that, on one hand, most households (85 percent in all) said they could find the money one way or another. On the other hand, a large share of American families—nearly 40 percent— would have to resort to selling assets or taking a short-term loan to obtain $400 quickly, steps that could impose substantial costs. Becky and Jeremy would likely turn to Becky's sister for a loan but many families would put the $400 on a credit card and pay it off over time; roughly, they can expect to pay another 20 percent of the base cost as interest. Among those who would borrow or sell something, 6 percent said they would have to take even more costly actions to come up with $400: procuring a high-cost payday loan or deposit advance, or running a high-fee overdraft on a bank account.[11]

We wanted to go beyond the basic summary numbers, so we obtained the raw data from the Federal Reserve and crunched it ourselves. We split the population into income groups and identified a pattern that aligns with what we found when counting the spikes and dips of families' income and spending: the poorest households have the greatest struggles, but even relatively well-off households are not immune to financial challenges (see Figure 3.4). The SHED data show that about a quarter of poor households (defined here as having household income under $25,000) said that they had no way to come up with $400 in a hurry. They are truly constrained, and that also holds for 11 percent of households earning between $25,000 and $50,000.[12]

It's not so surprising that low-income families face serious financial hurdles. Perhaps more striking in Figure 3.4 is that 21 percent of households earning over $100,000 could not come up with the money easily. Despite what seems like a high income (they are in the richest quarter of American households), the households would still have to resort to selling something or borrowing the $400 and paying it off over time. This is the tip of America's illiquidity iceberg.

The results are starker when turning to bigger crises and bigger needs. The SHED asked the households whether they had set aside rainy-day funds that could cover three months of expenses.[13] This is the sort of buffer needed to cope with a bout of unemployment or a major medical expense. Like Becky and Jeremy, just over half of American families lack that buffer. The SHED again probed further, asking the households whether they could cover the three months of costs by some other means, including borrowing from friends or family.[14] Under a quarter reported being able to get by if those options were added, but 32 percent said that they simply could not last for three months—even when selling assets or tapping friends for

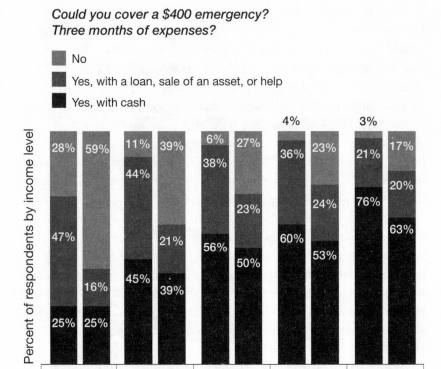

Could you cover a $400 emergency?
Three months of expenses?

No

Yes, with a loan, sale of an asset, or help

Yes, with cash

Figure 3.4. Ability to cope with expense or income shocks in the Federal Reserve's Survey of Household Economics and Decisionmaking (SHED). Respondents at all income levels report coping difficulties. Problems are most pronounced for the poorest.

loans.[15] Most surprising, 17 percent of respondents from households earning over $100,000 a year reported simply having no way to come up with the money.[16]

If families have difficulty dealing with bad shocks, they may have difficulty dealing with good shocks too. Not having a $400 buffer (especially for middle- and higher-income households) could mean that the family failed to save at an earlier time. As Becky and Jeremy knew in principle, months with income spikes present critical opportunities to save and pay down debt, creating buffers to draw on in harder times. By tracking cash flows we can see how, when, and *if* households prepared for bad shocks.

Here, in fact, Diaries families show a clear ability to rein in spending when income spikes. Figure 3.3 shows the same story for spikes as it does for dips: when incomes spike, spending rises too, but not by as much. Moderate-income households saw income spike by 49 percent on average, for example, but their spending jumped by only 14 percent in those same months. Near-poor households saw income spike by 48 percent on average, but their spending jumped by only 13 percent in those same months. Since families were not spending nearly as much as they were earning in those months, the numbers imply that families were actively saving and paying down debt.[17] So why were they so exposed?

Despite their diligence in saving and paying down debt in those months when income spiked, it was hard for Diaries families to end up ahead. Much of the diligence during flush times was compensation for far lower saving and debt repayment in months with less income to spare. So, at every level of income, households were actively smoothing, but the efforts tended to be imperfect across the year, leaving too much debt and too little in the bank.

The Costs of Illiquidity

In sum, Becky and Jeremy, Sarah and Sam, Janice, and the other families take steps to ensure they have money to spend when they need to. Most are able to smooth some of the ups and downs of their finances, but only to a point. Then, illiquidity is felt sharply. The Diaries show that illiquidity can mean that the exact timing of when income is received and money is needed—even varying by a week or a few days—can have big consequences.[18] Dealing with illiquidity took scarce time, created anxiety, added financial costs (through late payments, utility disconnections, and overdraft fees), and could mean delays in making important purchases.

The timing of paychecks and bill due dates was creating headaches for Katherine Lopez, a young professional Mexican American woman from California. She knew that she earned enough to comfortably afford her rent, student loan bills, and car payment, but she constantly felt squeezed. It was not until she made a computer spreadsheet to track her finances that the timing problems became clear. "The due date of the bills . . . were just not adding up with the dates I was getting paid," she explained. Her rent, for example, commanded a large chunk of the spending from her early-in-the-month paycheck. She couldn't afford to pay other important bills that were due at the same time, including her car payment, insurance, credit card, and cell phone bills. Katherine asked her lenders to move the due dates of her credit card bills and her car payment. The scramble to pay bills caused by illiquidity was significantly eased by better aligning when her income hit her bank account and when her bills had to be paid.[19]

Katherine's case is a small example and one that she could address. But her need to shuffle due dates to better line up with her paychecks illustrates how, when households are illiquid, even small misalignments can lead to surprisingly big problems, problems that sometimes spill over with large consequences. Two out of five respondents in the Federal Reserve's SHED survey report that the variability of their income and expenses creates struggles paying bills.[20] As we will explain in chapter 5, bill troubles like Katherine's can eventually lead to overindebtedness or undermine credit scores, which, if severe enough, can then undermine employment, housing, and financial prospects.

In the shorter run, illiquidity leads to temporary shortfalls that create other costs. During the year we spent with the Diaries households, one-third were threatened with (or actually experienced) eviction, the disconnection of utilities or cable, or repossession of an asset—even 31 percent of the best-off, middle-class households. Nearly half of Diaries households with bank accounts (46 percent) had at least one overdraft, a finding that again held for the best-off, middle-class households in the sample. Nationally, 22 percent of Americans reported overdrawing their bank accounts at least once in the previous twelve months, a striking figure given that the national sample has much higher average income than the Diaries sample.[21] Often overdrafts occur by mistake, a consequence of low bank balances. But sometimes overdrafts and late bills are deliberately used as a kind of short-term loan.

To get a better handle on whether households in the study were frequently being pushed to the edge of their ability to cope, we looked at rent payments. Many of the Diaries households told us that their monthly rent payment was their top priority, and we figured that rent was the least likely bill to be missed by accident. When we looked at the timing of rent payments we saw that most were made faithfully. But about three-quarters of the households had at least one time when they paid their rent outside of their usual one-week window for paying. Missing rent was tied closely to a drop in income in that particular week.[22]

In a related way, Clint Key, a researcher at Pew, discovered that the feeling of running out of money at the end of the month is all too literal for a wide swath of families. Pew surveys thousands of Americans on the state of their finances, and Key realized that some people were surveyed during the first week of the month, some the second, some the third, and some in the last week. Following a hunch, Key looked to see if the likelihood that a particular household felt worried about their finances varied based on when in the month they were surveyed. It did. People who were asked about the state of their finances at the end of a month were much more likely to express worry than those asked at the beginning of the month.

Getting Even

There has to be an easier way. That was the conviction that inspired Jon Schlossberg and Quinten Farmer to launch a technology company named Even whose mission is to help families deal with income spikes and dips. Schlossberg and Farmer were struck by the problems created by income volatility that were revealed in *Portfolios of the Poor*, the book on the financial diaries of families in Bangladesh, India, and South Africa that inspired us to bring the research approach to the United States.[23] Farmer had held a string of manual labor jobs in his teens, first washing dishes at a restaurant and then working as a landscaper. He knew from his own experiences that income volatility wasn't "just something that happens with day laborers in Bangladesh."[24] He was in search of a problem to solve with technology, and this seemed like a viable and important one. He and Schlossberg asked themselves questions like the following: What would happen if people no longer had to rely on their own self-discipline to maintain a rainy-day fund? What if they could automatically save their income spikes and automatically get funds back when their income dipped?

Schlossberg and Farmer started thinking about income volatility in the United States at about the same time that we launched the Financial Diaries study, and we regularly compared notes with Jane Leibrock, a member of their Oakland-based team.[25] Their company is young and still a work in progress (with only a few thousand pilot customers by the middle of 2016), and we can't assess its commercial prospects. But their experience so far shows how smoothing can make sense as a concern in itself—rather than, say, just focusing on borrowing, saving, or other specific activities.

Schlossberg and Farmer built their company around a smartphone app that connects to customers' financial accounts. They chose the name Even since the basic idea is to help people maintain a more even financial life, despite the spikes and dips of income. "Technology took us to the moon," their website declares. "Why can't it fix our finances?"

Once a customer signs up, the app is linked to their bank account. The app uses prior data to calculate their average pay (calculated over the previous six months) and then monitors their paychecks. When a customer receives a paycheck that is less than their average amount, the app transfers extra money—a "boost"—into the customer's account, bringing them up to their average. If customers lack sufficient savings, the company advances the money as an interest-free loan. In the customers' best months (periods with above-average pay), the algorithm withdraws funds, either to repay a prior boost or to build a saving cushion. The result is that a customer's once-choppy income stream is automatically made smooth.[26] After a free first month, the service costs $3 a week, though employers usually pay the cost as a benefit, so employees get it free.

The algorithm breaks down the silos between saving and borrowing. Both saving and borrowing are part of the underlying action, but, more immediately, the activity is really about smoothing consumption—that is, moving money through time so that customers have a stable financial life. Because the business model is built on a subscription fee, rather than charging interest on "boosts," the company's success depends on customers valuing increased stability enough to keep paying for the service month after month.

Portfolios of the Poor wasn't the only inspiration for Even. Schlossberg and Farmer also drew from Sendhil Mullainathan's and Eldar Shafir's book *Scarcity*. Mullainathan and Shafir had also read *Portfolios of the Poor*, and they saw the mental tax that income volatility could bring. Mullainathan and Shafir argue that because mental resources are scarce, questions of financial management always require weighing trade-offs. Families need to figure out *what to do* by thinking through everything *not* to do. As humans, though, we can only think about so many things at a time, and the scarcity of money and time makes difficult decisions and problems even harder. Automating some of the near-term decisions can help free up mental bandwidth, and that idea inspired Schlossberg and Farmer.

As a result, a key to their original idea was invisibility. Even's founders envisioned an app that operated in the background of people's lives: users would turn it on, link their bank account, and then never need to think about their finances again. The software would do all the work of analyzing customers' financial data, monitoring spikes and dips in income, and replacing the spikes and dips with a steady income. They imagined that in future versions, perhaps it would even predict spikes and dips in expenses, pay bills, and make it possible to genuinely never think about near-term cash-flow management. Users' mental bandwidth could then be redirected to higher purposes. "We make technology that helps you spend less time worrying about money," their website promises, "and more time achieving the life you want."[27]

Spikier

Smooth consumption usually means smooth spending, but sometimes it requires the exact opposite. To smooth the amount of heat we consume in the winter, we may have to create a spike of spending to repair the furnace. As Sarah and Sam Johnson found, sometimes the need for spending spikes arises because of medical emergencies and unexpected bills. More positively, the holidays or a family vacation often means a big spike in both spending and consumption. As a consequence, families are frequently trying to find ways to simultaneously smooth spending on some things, despite the ups and downs of income, and spike spending on other things, whether income has spiked or not. The language of "consumption smoothing" is thus misleading if taken literally; families want to smooth *and* spike.

Becky and Jeremy couldn't maintain a savings account, but they did have a strategy to save, apart from stocking the cabinets and freezer. Each month, Jeremy paid more taxes than he needed to. In tax jargon, he "overwithheld." When Jeremy handed his W-4 form to his boss at the garage (a document that lets employers know how much they need to hold back from employees' paychecks to cover that year's taxes), he deliberately did not list all four of his children. The fewer dependents employees claim, the fewer deductions they get, and the more tax that is withheld. As a result, Jeremy's employer took more taxes from his paychecks than he would owe. But when Becky and Jeremy filled out their tax forms at the start of the year, they listed all four children and received the appropriate deduction. The strategy produced a big tax refund in March: when combined with the EITC, the overwithholding yielded a $7,300 check (a particularly large sum given that Jeremy's paychecks that year totaled $35,000).

Financial advisors would surely counsel Becky and Jeremy against giving the government an interest-free loan for most of the year. The funds weren't available for an emergency and they couldn't invest the money and gain from any returns. Becky and Jeremy, though, didn't see it that way. Instead, they were taking advantage of a way that the government helps them automatically put aside money every month and keep it locked up, out of reach.[28] Thanks to that "service," Becky and Jeremy got a big, helpful check in March that allowed a big, helpful spending spike. They knew that there were probably better ways to achieve the same goal, but the strategy worked well enough for Becky and Jeremy—especially since their own attempts to save in the bank had repeatedly failed.

Winter was an expensive time for the family, even though Becky and Jeremy did not "go outrageous" at Christmas.[29] The tax refund paid for Christmas and a few family outings, but mostly it was used to repay credit card debt accumulated that winter. Totally smoothing their income was thus not the aim for Becky and Jeremy. They wanted to deal with their ups and downs, but they also wanted times when they could spend in big chunks.

Even, the financial technology company, learned something similar from its early customers. Perhaps not so surprisingly, customers were much more interested in getting help with dips than in having their spikes automatically skimmed off to prepare for the next dip. But it wasn't just that they wanted to have their cake and eat it too. Instead of being grateful for seamless smoothing, many users wanted control over when and how much money was skimmed off their larger paychecks. They looked forward to the spikes and often counted on them as a way to make big purchases, or to get caught up on bills, or as a reward for working particularly hard. Most important, customers did not want any of this to happen invisibly. Instead of wanting the seamless, behind-the-scenes service that Even's founders had imagined, customers wanted transparency, control, and just a little more help than they had otherwise.

"Really, really needs"

The center of Janice Evans's Mississippi town is about fifteen blocks of small stores, banks, and a few large brick churches. Each church is set back from the street with broad stairs that lead up to columned porticos shading heavy front doors. The downtown banks, in contrast, are low-slung and unobtrusive, with large windows that invite views in from the street. The banks share the street with drugstores, boutiques, and discount furniture outlets; like the stores, the banks advertise friendly convenience.

Still, Janice was wary of the local banks. "When you're in a small town like this, it runs on a buddy system. You know, 'good old boys.' It's a 'who you know' thing," Janice said. "Most of the people that run something like the bank, they're from here. You go into a bank, the [white] employees are laughing and talking. They make a loan to Mr. Jim's son [who is white], who they trust and like. But they know that Mr. Jim's son may not ever pay that loan back. In the South you know there's racial attitudes because they don't try to hide it," she said. "You know how to deal with it. You learn to live with it. You don't deal with people who are like that." When a credit union opened right on the main street and specifically sought out the black community, Janice opened an account. She used the credit union for basics like checking and bill paying.

Janice saw convenience as a problem when she got serious about saving, however, so she stowed her savings in a distinctly inconvenient bank. "It's about thirty-five miles away," Janice explained, "and they don't have an ATM and they open at 10:00 A.M. and close at 5:00 P.M." Janice paused to clarify that the bank *does* actually have an ATM, but she cut her ATM card in two the day it arrived in the mail. Like Becky and Jeremy in Ohio, Janice learned from mistakes early in life that temptation could get the best of her if the savings were easy to get to. Without a barrier, she feared spending down her savings until there was nothing left when she really needed it. Her system was a hassle, but that was the logic. "I have to really, *really* need the money before I go get it," she explained matter-of-factly, as if it was perfectly normal that customers would look for banks an hour away and, once there, search for the least convenient option possible. "On Wednesday, they don't open till noon," she said. "But that works for me."[30]

As the summer ended, the local Walmart filled with families buying back-to-school clothes and supplies, and Janice worried about her granddaughter's needs. So in August, Janice made a trip to the faraway bank. "I really, really needed some money because I had to get my grandbaby ready for [kindergarten]," she explained. "*That* was a 'really, really' need."

Janice depended on her system of near and far banks to get through the long winter when the casino slowed down and her paychecks shrank. She thought through the optimal amount of banking hassle (not too much hassle, but not too little), and in the summer months with bigger paychecks, she split what she could save between the local bank and the distant credit union. If Janice could save prudently, her budget would not feel as tight in the winter when her biweekly earnings dipped, or when she had to buy new tires for her car or meet other unexpected costs. So, Janice prepared for her big priorities—the "really, really needs"—like caring for her granddaughter.

Janice worked hard to save, but she was never able to build a large cushion, an amount of savings that could free her from worry and adequately protect her consumption in low months. As a result, when money was short during the winter Janice had to slash her budget. She went without some "needs," or even some *really* needs," in order to protect those most important "really, really needs." Janice viewed her budget as a hierarchy of monthly expenses, and in low weeks there wasn't always enough money for groceries. In those relatively rare times, Janice lived paycheck to paycheck. Despite earning a livable wage—on average—during the year, it was not a huge amount, and in some winter weeks Janice skipped going to the store and the family cut back on what they ate.[31]

For Janice, modest earnings over the year coupled with a lack of wealth made it harder to cope with the ups and downs of income month by month. She faced more complicated financial problems than many others but had weaker tools with which to address them. Her response was to stash surpluses in a faraway bank. Becky and Jeremy were in a similar position; they saw the need to prepare for the future and, to that end, filled up the freezer, stockpiled toothpaste, and overwithheld taxes. They knew these steps were not the "best" or "right" ways to tackle the problems, but they were the ways that were available and workable for them.

The ease of coping is—like income, wealth, and underlying economic steadiness—unequally distributed. Janice could dependably meet her "really, really needs" but not her less important needs. Partly that was because Janice shared her limited income with her son and granddaughter, and there simply wasn't a lot of money to spare. But it was also because of the general challenges in spreading a volatile income across the year.

Tracking cash flows shows that the families that are *most* in need of coping tools are usually those who tend to have the *least* easy access to those tools. The need is not just to have a certain saving balance or a better credit or insurance product. These are all simply ways to move money through time; the bigger goal is to achieve stability. In the next chapters, we'll look more deeply at three critical ways that families try to achieve that goal, by saving, borrowing, and sharing.

How Families Cope

Chapter 4

Saving

Robert

Robert Hill is an expert in making do. He has transformed cost cutting, something most people consider a pain, into a hobby, taking advantage of much of what New York City offers without even opening his wallet. He has seen Stevie Wonder, Jay-Z, No Doubt, and the Roots for free in Central Park. "Most things I do, I do for free. I can get free movie tickets online, so I don't have to pay for the movies." When we met with him, he told us he was planning to attend a screening of a new movie about James Brown the next day. "You just go to certain sites. You can type in your web browser 'free movie screenings,' and sites will pop up. You've just got to catch them when they come to your email, and fill it out, and hopefully you'll get it." At one point, Robert spent his weekends applying to dozens of online sweepstakes. Over the years he has won a free stay at New York's posh Plaza hotel and a trip to the 2010 Stanley Cup playoffs in Chicago.

Robert used to run a summer camp and coach basketball at a community center in another borough, where he put his money-stretching skills to work. His face lit up when he talked about it.

When the center's funds were cut, Robert kept it running: "Basically, I stayed open all the time, so the kids could have somewhere to go instead of being in the street—because we had TV and we had a full kitchen. I would cook if somebody was hungry. . . . I was doing that for a long time without getting paid." Apart from one trip outside the city, everything he did with the kids was in New York, and free. "Zoos, pools, museums," Robert marveled. "Kids can go play golf. You can go anywhere."

Robert learned his frugal ways from his parents. His father was one of fifteen children born into a poor family in Georgia. "The wrong side of the tracks," Robert said. Like six million other African Americans, his father moved north looking for opportunity as part of the Great Migration. He landed in Brooklyn and found a job as a fireman, earning extra money by working as a deliveryman, managing apartments, and running a moving and storage business. Robert's father put him to work early: "I've been doing manual labor since I was five. If I wasn't on a moving and storage truck, if I wasn't cleaning up somebody's building, [I was] delivering telephone books."

The family sent much of their money back to relatives in Georgia, and Robert's mother stretched what was left to care for the children. "I guess [my father] was so busy sending money that he neglected home occasionally," Robert told us. "[But] my mother was always good with money. We always had a roof over our head, we were always fed, we always had clothes, and she took care of other people's kids."

Robert's mother is still caring for people. She shares her two-bedroom apartment, in a public housing complex in Brooklyn, with Robert, three of his adult cousins, and the baby of another relative who is mentally unstable and mostly lives on the streets. On weekends, Robert's grandson—he raised two children of his own, now grown and out of Brooklyn—stays over too. In return for space on the sofa, Robert pays his mother $100 a month for rent and picks up groceries and other necessities at the supermarket and the Family Dollar up the block. With Robert's help, his mother makes a home for them all.

The neighborhood has improved over the years, but it's still far less safe than rapidly gentrifying parts of Brooklyn that are an easier commute to Manhattan. In 1990, the local police precinct was one of the roughest in the city, with forty-nine murders.[1] By 2015, a couple of years after our study, it recorded only five murders. Still, early in the Financial Diaries project, residents warned our researcher who was interviewing Robert to finish up before dark.

Solidly built, Robert doesn't get any trouble from the teenagers idling outside his building. He wears his goatee carefully trimmed and dresses in clean white basketball shoes and black jeans. He is hardworking and ambitious, received a good education (even on their very tight budget, his parents found the money to send him to Catholic school), has a steady job in an in-demand field, and obviously isn't a spendthrift. He could easily be mistaken for a young man on his way up. But Robert isn't a young man anymore. When we met him, Robert was forty-eight, his age betrayed by a few gray strands in his goatee. He was surprised and a bit disappointed to be on his mother's couch.

Robert had moved back in after breaking up with a long-term girlfriend and leaving their shared apartment. As soon as he moved out of the old apartment, Robert put his name on a list for public housing. When we met him, he was waiting to either get to the top of that list or earn enough to afford a market-rate apartment. Either way, Robert knew he needed to save for a first month's rent and a security deposit, which he estimated would cost $1,600.

During the year of the Diaries, Robert worked in tech support for a local nonprofit. The job paid $11.25 per hour, roughly $22,000 per year.[2] It wasn't much—especially for New York City—but it was almost twice the federal poverty line for a single person and 22 percent above the SPM poverty line. Robert had recently received a raise, and he believed this boded well for future increases.[3] Unlike the jobs of many study participants, Robert's job had well-defined and predictable hours and a path to higher pay.

Robert's extreme cost-cutting helped him to save steadily, even on a relatively low income. Robert's behavior was like other savers we met. First, he had a clear, tangible need in mind. Robert was not saving for savings' sake, and he didn't aim to build a large balance that would go untouched for a long time. Instead, he aimed to set aside a seemingly small, but nonetheless consequential, amount of money. Second, Robert's need would not arise in the distant future. The need was going to arise, he hoped, very soon.

Financial "Illiteracy"

Financial literacy is often touted as the answer to consumer financial troubles. It is tempting to imagine that if only people knew better and understood more, they would save more. We asked Robert and other Diaries participants three questions that have become part of standard tests for financial literacy:

1. Suppose you had $100 in a savings account and the interest rate was two percent per year. After five years, how much do you think you would have in the account if you left the money to grow? (i) More than $102; (ii) Exactly $102; (iii) Less than $102.
2. Suppose you had $100 in a savings account and the interest rate is twenty percent per year and you never withdraw money or interest payments. After five years, how much would you have on this account in total? (i) More than $200; (ii) Exactly $200; (iii) Less than $200.
3. Assume a friend inherits $10,000 today and his sibling inherits $10,000 three years from now. Who is richer because of the inheritance? (i) My friend; (ii) His sibling; (iii) They are equally rich.[4]

The first answer is correct in each case, and Robert missed all three. The first and second questions concern basic numeracy and the power of compound interest. The third question focuses on the "time value of money"—the idea that getting hold of money sooner is more valuable since the friend can invest the $10,000 and end up with more than that after three years. In financial literacy research, these questions are often asked along with two others, and less than half of Americans can answer all five correctly.[5] Among Diaries participants, 70 percent correctly answered numeracy questions, but less than half answer correctly about compound interest and only a third about the time value of money.

But when you look at Robert's goals, his financial literacy as measured by these standard questions is almost irrelevant. The financial literacy questions capture the sort of knowledge useful for households deciding how much to save for long-term needs like retirement. But Robert's time frame, and that of most of the families in the Financial Diaries study, was much shorter. Even the five-year time frame specified in these questions was longer than the families' time horizons. For Robert to achieve his goal of accumulating $1,600 toward a new apartment, he needed focus and the ability to keep his costs down, not generic financial knowledge.

The idea of compound interest, a core of financial literacy curricula and tests, provides a good example. Compound interest, which combines principal interest with interest accumulated from an earlier loan or deposit, is an idea that gets financial planners excited. Financial planners can describe the magic of compounding in their sleep. Vanguard, the world's biggest provider of mutual funds, makes the case for retirement saving this way on its website:

> The key is the power of compounding, the snowball effect that happens when your earnings generate even more earnings. You receive interest not only on your original investments, but also on any interest, dividends, and capital gains that accumulate— so your money can grow faster and faster as the years roll on.[6]

Dave Ramsey, the popular money management guru, trumpets this financial wisdom more colorfully:

> One awesome thing that you can take advantage of is compound interest. It may sound like an intimidating term, but it really isn't once you know what it means. Here's a little secret: compound interest is a millionaire's best friend. *It's really free money* [emphasis in original].[7]

Ramsey gives an example that makes the case for starting to save for retirement as soon as possible, allowing young people to transform a flow of steady deposits into an exponentially growing balance. In Ramsey's example, compounding allows a teen named Ben to turn $16,000 into more than $2 million.

Surely if more Americans knew about the power of compound interest they would stop overspending and start saving—at least that's the logic of financial literacy programs, advertising campaigns by financial firms, and financial advisors. It's true that compound interest can be a powerful tool for building up balances. But miraculous examples like Ramsey's depend on very high and steady returns on savings and long time horizons. To get his result, Ramsey assumes that Ben starts saving for retirement at age nineteen, puts aside $2,000 a year for eight years, then doesn't touch the money for forty-seven years, all the while earning a consistent return of 12 percent per year. But most experts project stock market returns closer to 6 percent over the long term, not 12. If you assume that Ben's money grows at 6 percent a year, he ends up with only about $200,000 at retirement.[8] Not bad, but well shy of $2 million.

The fact is that Robert does not have $16,000 to tuck away for decades. He knows he needs to think about retirement and contributes $25 each month to an employer-sponsored retirement plan. He also knows it's a token effort and won't get him very far. When we met with him, however, he was focused on saving up to rent an apartment, and the miracle of compound interest wouldn't help him. He counted his time horizon in months, not decades.

Not only are retirement savings goals too ambitious for many families, so too are shorter-term savings goals for emergencies. Among Financial Diaries households, most had an emergency savings goal of three months of income or less. But most financial literacy programs say that three months is the bare minimum. That time frame is not as daunting as the eight months that finance guru Suze Orman recommends, but it's still ambitious.[9] And while households in the Diaries with relatively high financial literacy scores often had loftier goals for their emergency savings, they were only slightly more likely to have met those goals than other households were. Financial knowledge appeared to increase families' ambitions to save, but not necessarily their success.

Vanguard and Dave Ramsey can't be faulted for encouraging Americans to save more or for teaching financial concepts like compound interest. They are right: we don't save enough for the long term. Over the last several decades, experts have been trying to move beyond financial education and heartfelt appeals to save more. Whatever we're doing to mobilize more Americans to save for the long term, however, isn't yet working.

The Poor Can Save

In the mid-1980s, Michael Sherraden, then a young professor at Washington University in St. Louis, attended an information session on campus about retirement savings plans and the tax benefits that accompanied them.[10] The room was filled with professors like him. Other kinds of workers, Sherraden noted, were absent. Where were the janitors, he wondered? The grounds crew? Cafeteria staff? Weren't they going to retire one day? Programs to help people build long-term savings with public subsidies via tax benefits, it seemed, were reserved for those with white-collar jobs.[11]

At around the same time, Sherraden had been interviewing mothers on public assistance. The women complained that their government benefits were at risk the moment they started to accumulate savings. The government cut off benefits if families had saved $1,000 or more, and the women felt trapped.[12] The women understood that government programs were meant for the truly needy, but how could they ever get off of welfare, they asked, if they were not allowed to build a cushion first?

The two observations coalesced for Sherraden. As he further investigated savings programs, he found that the bias toward subsidies for better-off Americans to build savings extended well beyond Washington University. Most government savings policies—especially tax deductions for retirement saving and housing—were directed toward high-wage employees, not janitors and cafeteria workers. In 2013, the United States spent almost $400 billion in federal tax subsidies for homeownership and retirement savings. That was 30 percent of all federal tax expenditures. About 70 percent of the savings from the mortgage interest and property tax deductions went to the top 20 percent of earners. Almost none went to the bottom 40 percent. The proportions were similar for retirement-related tax deductions.[13] On the bottom end of the income spectrum, if government policy served any function, it was to create hurdles for families trying to save.

Sherraden was convinced that the poor could save, especially if given the sorts of structures and supports offered to middle-class households. He laid out a plan to help low-income families build up their savings. It wasn't complicated: the basic idea was to provide them access to the same carrots and sticks that wealthier families had. But given that these low-income families had to make greater sacrifices in order to save and that they didn't have as much to put aside, he argued for giving them a boost. In the language of economics, he wanted to provide them with positive financial incentives to build up savings. Put more simply, he suggested subsidizing them by matching their savings (in much the same way higher-income households are subsidized to use 401(k)s or IRAs with reduced taxes).

Sherraden proposed a new kind of savings account that would be universal, progressive, and lifelong, called Individual Development Accounts, or IDAs. However, as a demonstration program, IDAs were implemented as a short-term program targeted to the poor. Like other savings incentives, the benefits of IDAs were restricted for particular long-term goals deemed worthy: buying a home, paying for education, and investing in a business. For every dollar that households saved in an IDA, Sherraden proposed that the government chip in a dollar (and sometimes more).

In 1998, Congress authorized IDAs and allocated matching funds. Less than a decade later, 400 programs had opened across the country. Thirteen of those were part of the American Dream Demonstration, a project sponsored in part by the Ford Foundation and others to evaluate the effectiveness of IDAs for helping lower-income households build up savings and turn them into long-term assets.[14] Demonstration sites were selected through a competitive process and chosen to reflect the breadth of the country, from Ithaca, New York, to Oakland, California.[15] By the end of 2000, some 2,350 people had signed up for IDAs in the thirteen sites.[16] In 2002, survey teams fanned out to see what progress the IDA participants had made.

The results were mixed. The good news was that many people were interested in the program, and some saved a considerable amount given their low incomes. Those who managed to save for retirement had accumulated $702 on average. Those who saved toward the purchase of a home had accumulated $559 on average, and those who had saved for home repairs had $491. The bad news was that by the end of the study, only half had accumulated more than $100—despite being given $2, on average, for every $1 they saved.[17]

Across the thirteen sites in the Demonstration, a third of participants successfully used their savings for one of the future-oriented purposes at the heart of the IDA idea: home buying, education, or investing in a business. The total sum they accumulated for the long term (pre-match) was $672,577. This result helps make the case that even families with low incomes can set aside substantial resources for the future.

But 64 percent of families took an unmatched withdrawal, totaling $763,903. The amount of subsidy forfeited by these withdrawals averaged $1.77 for every dollar saved. After doing the hard work to save, participants willingly left $1.4 million on the table. Each of these participants—drawn from a population that was poor or near-poor—walked away from an average amount of $892 in lost matches.[18]

The size of these unmatched withdrawals was a "surprise and a concern" for Sherraden and his colleague Mark Schreiner.[19] The reasons for the withdrawals were not recorded, but Schreiner and Sherraden speculated that the primary cause was the volatility and uncertainty in people's lives, something we also saw in the U.S. Financial Diaries data. "Some participants may not only be very close to subsistence," Schreiner and Sherraden wrote, "but also subject to sharp variations in their streams of income and expenses. If income dips (for example, due to job loss) or if expenses spike (for example, due to illness), then the short-term need for cash may outweigh the long-term costs of unmatched withdrawals."[20]

This pattern—of people trying to save for the long term but often dipping into funds sooner—also happens with long-term savings vehicles like the IRAs and 401(k)s that IDAs were modeled on. More than a quarter of American households have withdrawn money from retirement accounts for reasons other than retirement, including Jeremy, the truck mechanic we met in the introduction, and Sarah and Sam Johnson, whose expenses we explored in chapter 2. These withdrawals are often large and frequent. In 2010, for example, some

$60 billion was pulled out, about 20 percent of the worker contributions and employer matches held in the accounts. Overall, approximately 25 percent of Americans have withdrawn money from employer-sponsored plans at some point.[21] A retirement expert at Vanguard concluded that, "in effect, [IRAs and 401ks] have become dual-purpose systems for retirement and short-term consumption needs."[22]

A natural response to this data might be to double down and add even higher hurdles to prevent people from withdrawing savings for all but long-term goals. But that gets it backward. The American Dream Demonstration showed that households work hard to put aside money they will need and use. Although the program was designed to study how to help poor families accumulate wealth, it unintentionally demonstrated that low-income households were willing to pay a high cost—by sacrificing the match—to meet other savings goals. The data on early withdrawals from retirement accounts tell the same story on a larger scale.

Part of what keeps households from the goal of long-term savings isn't a lack of awareness or a lack of discipline. Rather, it's that the day they're saving for isn't very far away. IDAs, like the retirement and homeownership policies that preceded them, offered just one solution: long-term savings. For many families, that focus missed the mark. Take Robert. When he moved into his mother's apartment, he wanted, and was able, to save. But an IDA wouldn't have done him any good. He was trying to put money aside for the short-term goal of renting his own apartment, not a long-term goal like a home purchase or retirement.

Now, Soon, and Later

The usual narrative about Americans is that we are terrible savers. In January 2015, for example, Americans saved just 5.6 percent of their disposable income. That's an improvement over the dismal 2.2 percent recorded in April 2005 but still low.[23] The numbers are worrying. Nearly half of families have no retirement savings, for instance. And among lower-income families, minorities, and women, that figure is even lower.[24] Households generally do not have much money put aside for emergencies either. As we discussed earlier, just over half do not have enough savings for three months—even just to live at the poverty level—if they were to experience a major income loss.[25]

A fair assumption, judging by these numbers, is that Americans are recklessly overspending. And it's true that few of us spend as carefully as Robert or search out as many bargains. Americans appear to be living for today, rather than thinking about the long term. We seem too focused on now, rather than later. This belief helps explain why the United States has introduced many policies to help people better orient their finances to the long term. The mortgage interest deduction aids people in buying houses, for example, while individual retirement and 529 accounts help people save for retirement and education. These programs contain tax incentives that encourage people to prioritize goals that will happen "later" and penalties to discourage succumbing to the temptation of withdrawing money to pay for things "now." They're designed to help people accumulate large sums, over a long period of time. And in order to be successful, they require people to save consistently over the course of a lifetime.

But our existing narrative about saving—based on the assumption that people are overspending today instead of saving for later—is incomplete. Data on low balances support that narrative, but the data miss much of the action. The data distort the view of what American families need, and what they can achieve.

Robert is one of the many people who do not fit that narrative. He is up at 5:00 every morning, in time to take the subway to the bus to arrive at his office by 7:15 A.M. He eats breakfast and starts work by 7:30. He works a full day and comes home to a full house where he helps support an extended family of seven. He also minimizes spending today in favor of the future. A lack of knowledge, or an inability to resist temptation, is hardly Robert's problem. If you think of saving as an activity rather than as something measured by the size of a bank balance, Robert is an impressive saver.

Despite Robert's drive to save $1,600 for his rent deposit, financial experts might not even think of his accumulation of cash as "saving."

That term is typically used to describe money set aside for loftier goals, in larger quantities, and over a longer time frame. Robert's accumulation was indeed impressive; within a few months, he had put aside $1,600 on an annual take-home income of $15,360. But no long-term balance would result from that dedication.[26] Were he to move out of his mother's apartment, the deposit would be handed over to the landlord, and he would again have little or no assets.

And he was far from the only person we met through the Diaries who could be called a "saver with no savings." In the Financial Diaries, we see flows into savings vehicles dwarfing balances. The median household deposited three times more money into their savings accounts during the year than their balance at the end of the year. These households are saving, but their bank balances don't reflect it.

We asked households how quickly the money in their bank accounts would be spent. Figure 4.1 shows that, on average, 72 percent of the money in their bank accounts was intended for needs within the next six months. Eighty-three percent would be spent within a year. Only 10 percent was being saved for needs three or more years away.[27] When we only looked at balances in non-transactional accounts (e.g., not checking accounts or prepaid cards), the kind of accounts explicitly designed to be savings accounts, households still expected to spend 65 percent of those balances within the year. In other words, the households are saving, but not for the long term. Money comes in, but it goes out "soon" for the necessities of life.

The Diaries didn't show households spending every dollar as they earn it. As we described in chapter 2, few households were technically living paycheck to paycheck. Instead, the cash-flow data we collected show what Nobel Prize–winning economist Angus Deaton calls "high frequency saving."[28] In contrast to "low frequency" saving— the slow-and-steady, long-term saving over the life cycle—high frequency saving requires people to make many smaller decisions to save, over and over. They are constantly saving and spending, then saving again and spending. High frequency saving is a crucial strategy for weathering volatile incomes and expenses, especially for those with limited access to financial tools that might otherwise smooth the ups and downs.

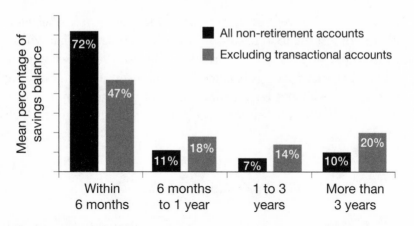

Figure 4.1. Expected time to spend savings balances in the U.S. Financial Diaries. Households report that nearly 50 percent of their balances in savings accounts will be spent within six months and 65 percent within one year. Only 20 percent of balances are expected to be spent in more than three years.

The funds saved for near-term needs, like Robert's goal of $1,600, often reflect hard work and good choices. High frequency savings provide a crucial cushion for financial ups and downs. They can also enable small gains to add up and become larger gains. For example, saving enough to purchase a slightly more reliable car might mean getting to work more reliably, which in turn justifies a raise. Small amounts of savings, held for short amounts of time, can be a foundation for larger changes.

As much as Dave Ramsey is a proselytizer for the power of compound interest, his approach to financial planning is also anchored in an awareness of this idea. His core advice is to set aside $1,000 in savings before attacking other goals. This is his "Baby Step 1," and he advises people to focus on it before paying down debt, setting aside a three- to six-month fund, and saving for other goals like college or retirement. One of the reasons to start here, he says, is that even a relatively small cushion of $1,000 can build confidence to tackle those other goals. Without this cushion, the pressures of "soon" will exert the strongest pull, edging out longer-term goals.

Once we recognize this, we can start to focus on people's behavior rather than just the total balances they've accumulated. That will allow us to redefine Robert and others as successful savers—not as individuals who lack savings balances. We can invest more in building on their successes and establishing the right tools to help. Tracking cash flows allows us to see the wealth of saving activity from which to build.

Revolving Savings

One of the challenges of IDAs was that the functionality and user experience of the American Dream Demonstration were clunky at best. The nonprofits administering the program generally held the funds in a custodial account on behalf of the saver so they could monitor saving and approve withdrawals. This created complications for banks, several of which nonetheless went to great lengths to support IDAs by building new, expensive account infrastructure. As a result of this complex relationship, resolving errors in account statements was tedious and customer service was inconsistent. This account structure was held together by the ingenuity and force of will of the organizations involved, but it was challenging and few (if anyone) believed it could be scaled to meet the needs of millions of Americans, at least not without modification.

Commonwealth, formerly Doorways to Dreams Fund (D2D), was founded in part to solve this problem. The organization's goal was to find new ways to help low-income families save, at scale. From the beginning, Commonwealth was interested in how to use new technology to deliver incentives and structures to savers. The group's ambition was to make saving easy—or better yet, fun. Among other efforts, Commonwealth has created savings games, sponsored pilots that offer sweepstakes to savers, and sold savings bonds at free tax preparation sites.[29]

But despite Commonwealth's best efforts, it was a constant challenge to persuade people to set money aside for the future. By listening to the target audience for their tax-time work, the Commonwealth staff began to understand one reason why. Many tax filers already knew how they were going to spend their tax refunds—and long-term savings wasn't on the list. Instead, they focused on paying for urgent needs they'd long put off—a car or home repair or a medical procedure. Commonwealth decided to try a new tack: help these households accumulate an emergency reserve so their tax refund wasn't essentially spent before the families had even received it. The organization teamed up with Banking Up, a prepaid card company, to offer the Rainy Day Reserve.[30]

The Rainy Day Reserve is a higher-tech version of the age-old envelope budgeting system. Users could, with a few taps on a mobile app, segregate their money into "spend" and "save" accounts. Once dollars were designated "save," the cardholder could not spend them without first moving the funds back to "spend."

Commonwealth and Banking Up marketed the savings opportunity as a way to prepare for emergencies, for a rainy day. They set no minimum balance or deposit requirements, making the account easy to begin using. But they added one small twist: a minor roadblock at the point of withdrawal. When customers indicated that they wanted to move funds from the "save" to the "spend" account, they were shown a pop-up box asking them to confirm that they *really* wanted to spend their savings.

The Rainy Day Reserve turned out to be popular. In its first fifteen months, 17 percent of Banking Up's active customers used it, a much higher percentage than Commonwealth expected based on its experience selling saving bonds. But the results in terms of savings were mixed. When they launched the pilot, the team hoped to see steadily rising balances. They wanted clients to build a $2,000 emergency fund. In the fifteen-month pilot phase, 7,000 savers, two-thirds of whom had annual household incomes below $40,000,[31] deposited more than $14 million, for an average of $1,980 flowing through each account. But savers rarely accumulated balances close to $2,000. "In hindsight," said Tim Flacke, Commonwealth's executive director, it was "naive" to imagine most families could put aside $2,000 and leave it untouched.[32]

Instead, savings were built up and then depleted, then built back up and depleted again. But that was exactly what many families needed in order to manage their financial ups and downs. The Rainy Day

Reserve pilot was not set up as a scientific experiment with a control group, but Commonwealth surveyed Banking Up customers who used it as well as ones who did not. Rainy Day savers reported that they withdrew their money to pay for financial emergencies (46 percent), to help a friend or family member with a financial emergency (17 percent), or to pay monthly bills like rent (52 percent) or weekly expenses like groceries and gas (44 percent).

The data suggest that the reserve fund helped people cope more effectively with financial emergencies. Among those who encountered a budgetary crisis during the study, people with access to the fund were half as likely to report that the emergency caused hardship, compared to customers without access. Four in five savers reported feeling more confident about their ability to handle future expense spikes. And the product carried no stigma around drawing down savings and no barrier to starting to save anew. When cardholders withdrew money, they often began saving again almost immediately.

Weak Commitment Savings

Research conducted outside of the United States provides another example of how to help people save for "soon." In the Philippines, Kenya, Rwanda, Malawi, and elsewhere, economists have been testing what they call commitment savings. The basic concept shares elements with IDAs. People choose a savings goal and put money toward it into an account (with a formal bank, a nonprofit agency, or even a simple lockbox). They forgo access to the account until they reach their goal. In some cases the goal is an amount of money, in others, it's a future date. The savings are intended for near-term needs: paying school fees or buying fertilizer for the next planting season.

In each pilot, commitment savings accounts worked: those with access to the accounts saved much more than comparable groups without them. But the most surprising thing to consistently emerge from these studies is not that the commitments help—it's that so-called weaker commitments help more than stronger ones.

In Rwanda, for example, one group of account holders received their savings in vouchers they could use only for school supplies and fees. A second group received their savings in cash, which they could spend however they wanted. Both groups managed to save more than a control group without access to the accounts. But those who got their savings back in cash not only saved more than those who received vouchers, they also spent more on school items.[33] In Malawi, farmers who had access to a commitment savings account that would have locked up their savings until planting time saved more and spent more on fertilizer and seeds than farmers who didn't have the accounts. But remarkably, the farmers didn't save *in* the commitment accounts. They kept their savings at home.[34] In Kenya, women were given a simple metal lockbox for their savings. For one group, the program's village leader held the key. To get their money, savers needed to ask the leader to open their lockbox. Another group was given the key to the lockbox, and participants could open the box themselves. The women who had the key to the lockbox saved more.[35] These studies suggested that people were more willing to use accounts that gave them the freedom to withdraw for urgent needs if they arose. If savings were truly untouchable, people were inclined to put aside less.

Robert and several other households in the Diaries devised their own version of commitment savings, which we thought of as the Bank of Mom or, sometimes, the Bank of Far Away. In a previous job, Robert had a credit union membership. But he stopped using it when he left that job. When we met him, he was using a prepaid card. He could store savings on it, but that wasn't how he saved for his apartment. Instead he gave the money to his mother. Robert turned to the Bank of Mom because he needed to organize his savings in a way that wasn't possible with a typical bank. Saving with his mother didn't require him to go to a bank during bank hours or set up a direct deposit with his employer. All he had to do was give her cash when he had extra.

Instead of bank fees or penalties, Robert relied on his mother to strengthen his resolve to leave his savings untouched. He knew she would hand over his money if he really needed it; otherwise, she said no. "She's like Fort Knox," Robert told us. "I won't get to the money.... She's impossible to break into."[36]

Janice's reliance on a bank an hour's drive away, with inconvenient hours, is a variant of this strategy. As described in chapter 3, she uses the Bank of Far Away for what she calls "really, really needs."

Because a trip to the bank requires planning, it serves as a weak commitment for Janice to stick to her goals.

It's a Sprint, Not a Marathon

We're all familiar with the idea that saving large amounts is easier if done slowly in small increments. It's common financial advice: start by putting aside a very small amount and steadily ramp up the percentage of each paycheck that goes to savings. That certainly works for some. Save More Tomorrow, a program developed by Richard Thaler, one of the creators of behavioral economics, and his colleague Shlomo Benartzi, allows workers to automatically increase their retirement savings contributions whenever they get a raise. It has been successful in increasing the amount people save in retirement accounts.[37]

But one of the world's most successful savings programs takes a very different approach. Savings groups—also known as Roscas (rotating savings and credit associations), *tandas*, lending circles, and many other names—have been around for centuries. They arose independently in many cultures around the globe. While there are important variations, the basics are the same: people who trust each other agree to save together for a limited amount of time. Each week or month, they get together and contribute a set amount—say $100. For a group of ten, that means $1,000 is "deposited" each meeting. Each member gets the pot once during the cycle. This structure helps people collaborate to turn small cash flows into large, useful chunks of money.[38]

Mateo Valencia and Lucia Benitez are Ecuadorian immigrants living in Queens, New York, with their young child. They both work multiple jobs and serve as de facto landlords by subletting rooms in the house they rent. Altogether they earn about $40,000 a year. It's not a big budget, at least for New York, and every dollar counts. In other words, you wouldn't expect them to be able to put much money aside. But they go on savings sprints by participating in a large savings group in their community.

In Mateo and Lucia's group, thirty to fifty savers contribute $300 each week for a set period. With thirty savers, the weekly pot totals

$9,000. When the group expands to fifty, it hits $15,000.[39] Mateo and Lucia have used this savings group on several occasions in recent years to help them afford a significant investment. A few years ago, they went on a savings sprint to buy music equipment. Mateo's primary job is at an auto shop, but his passion is his side business: hosting an online radio show and deejaying events. The equipment allowed him to expand that business.

Savings groups are effective for several reasons. They create a sense of commitment, as in the case of the commitment savings accounts described above. With savings groups, though, the commitment is to others in the group, not to a monetary goal. Mateo, for instance, described making his weekly contribution to the savings group as "sacred." But savings groups are also effective because they require strict discipline for only a relatively short time. In that sense, they're like crash diets. They don't permanently alter participants' daily routines or necessarily establish a lifelong savings habit. Nutritionists—or in this case, personal finance experts—might not approve. But savings groups enable people to accumulate substantial, sometimes life-changing amounts of capital. Saving in short, concentrated bursts is particularly effective for people experiencing financial volatility. In a burst of concentrated effort over eight months, Mateo and Lucia put aside over $10,000.

Grabbing Spikes

Conventional wisdom urges people to make savings automatic. In summer of 2016, we checked the first twenty Google results for the phrase "savings advice"—every single one included some version of "make it automatic," and more than half used that exact phrase. The idea is that to save successfully, you should have a certain percentage of your paycheck automatically deposited into your savings account. That way, you don't have to routinely summon the willpower to put the money aside, and you'll be less tempted to spend it.[40]

However, it is a risk to sign up for regular, consistent payments when income or expenses are unsteady. Sarah Johnson, who manages school budgets for a living but strains to juggle her own finances, signed up for only two automatic bill payments, opting for control over which bills to pay when. Many Diaries families made this same choice to tightly control which bills were paid when, avoiding most automated payments, including automatic savings.

Instead, some families save sporadically, but systematically, by grabbing income spikes when they happen. These families follow a clear saving rule: "when I have extra, I put it aside." Instead of fighting volatility and trying to smooth out their financial lives, or creating rigid structures to save, they cope with ups and downs by taking advantage of the spikes.

For many families, the annual tax refund fueled by the EITC is the biggest such spike. In 2010, the average refund for tax filers earning less than $50,000 per year was $2,300. Almost 70 percent of Diaries participants received a tax refund, with a median value of $3,800. Families count on this annual spike in income to pay down prior bills, get a little ahead, or make a big purchase. Commonwealth saw a significant spike in savings in the Rainy Day Reserve at tax time, as did the programs in the American Dream Demonstration.[41]

The tax system also provides a way for families to create a spike. As we described in chapter 3, Becky and Jeremy Moore could reduce the estimated tax they pay during the year, but instead, like many others, they maximized tax withholdings during the year to get a higher amount back as a tax refund. For Becky and Jeremy, the refund during the Diaries year was over $7,000. This is a form of saving, though the monthly accumulations don't show up in personal bank accounts. Financial planners may argue that there are more flexible ways to save and more stable ways to spend, but saving through the tax system and leveraging an annual income spike works for many of the Diaries households.

Balancing Structure and Flexibility

Families rarely have much control over their financial spikes and dips. Getting laid off or having the roof spring a leak isn't a moral failing. But the primary mechanisms for coping with financial volatility—

saving and borrowing—are freighted with moral judgment. In Ae-
sop's fable of the Ant and the Grasshopper, the hardworking ants
store food for the winter while the Grasshopper lives for the moment. The Ant is the clear hero of the story. As a society, we tend to
view the accumulation of savings as a sign of industriousness and
prudence. Those without financial reserves are seen as shortsighted
and prone to temptation.

But our data, along with other research, point to new ways of understanding saving among low- and moderate-income Americans.
Many of these families are committed, effective savers; they're just
not saving in the ways financial advisors might imagine. They put
aside money for expenses they anticipate in the next few months,
not the distant future. Their bank accounts are flat not because of
overspending but to balance the needs of now, soon, and later.

To paint a more accurate picture of saving in America, we need to
reframe the discussion and pay attention to additional data. Too often we examine saving only through the lens of rich people in rich
countries—those who are saving up for the big "life-cycle" events and,
eventually, retirement. Or we draw on analyses of poor people in
poor countries—individuals who are putting away money primarily to cope with near-term economic shocks such as illness and job
loss. Most Americans, though, are neither so rich that they're insulated from short-term ups and downs nor so poor that the future
feels out of reach. Programs, policies, and products that focus on just
one part of the savings picture are prone to failure because they're a
poor match for families' actual financial needs.

The families we followed as part of the Financial Diaries were remarkably inventive savers. When existing financial products were too
rigid, were too costly, or did not properly suit their needs, they came
up with their own solutions. They made adjustments and used products in ways that financial institutions didn't anticipate (with varying
degrees of success).

Their adjustments were often driven by the need to find a balance
between structure and flexibility. Standard savings accounts have
structure, for example, but it's not always the right kind. A bank has
structured fees, locations, and hours—but those hours might not be

convenient for someone who works long days. At the same time, the structures banks offer to limit withdrawals can be too strong, or nonexistent. People face significant financial penalties if they withdraw their retirement funds early, for example, but aren't limited in any way from withdrawing from a basic savings account. Financial providers have developed a multitude of products and a multitude of ways to make those products available through retail branches and online. Nonetheless, finding a balance between the structure necessary to maintain financial discipline and the flexibility to deal with the unexpected remains a challenge for both consumers and providers.

Saving also illustrates a related financial tension, between stability and mobility. People save money in order to secure a better life, but that means different things for different people. For the affluent, a better life might mean building wealth over decades; for others, small amounts of saving, built up and drawn down, and then built up and drawn down again, can improve one's circumstances—even if large, long-term balances never accumulate. Ideally, pursuing the two strategies—stability and mobility—would be complementary. With basic financial tools in place to address issues in the near term, building for the future could become possible.

We met Robert for lunch one day in Manhattan in the spring of 2015, two years after the U.S. Financial Diaries study had concluded. We chose an upscale sandwich shop in the lobby of the building where he works, but Robert had never tried it. He saves money by eating at his desk. Robert is still cutting costs and was pleased to inform us that he had received a long-awaited raise. He had become a manager, and his annual salary had risen to $30,323. He proudly enunciated the numbers, "thirty thousand, three-two-three."

We asked: What's happened with his savings? Where is he living now? His $1,600 goal must be long past. Robert paused, and smiled a little. He was still living with his mother. He was still saving with the Bank of Mom. He didn't know exactly how much she was holding for him. "I can't tell you right now," he said. "I don't ask. It's about four or five thousand."

The right apartment hasn't come along yet—so he keeps on saving. He has an impressively large savings balance, at least compared to most Americans. In the meantime, he's continuing to help his extended family while his mother continues to help him. Robert did tell us that he had booked a short vacation in Cancún for his birthday. After a long winter in New York he was ready for some sunshine, and apparently the Bank of Mom agreed.

Chapter 5

Borrowing

In many ways, Katherine Lopez's story is the kind we in the United States love to tell. She grew up in farm country, California's fertile central valley. Her father emigrated from Mexico as part of the Mexican Farm Labor Program, or Bracero Program, which brought hundreds of thousands of guest workers to the United States to fill labor needs during and after World War II. With Katherine's mother, also a seasonal field worker, he spent decades driving tractors and tending tomatoes, almonds, cotton, wheat, and chilies.

Katherine worked hard in high school and paid her way through college with a combination of jobs and student loans. When we met her, she was working as the coordinator of a federally funded literacy program she affectionately called Reading 101. Her small office, tucked in a Northern California library, was packed with paper and reports, stacked on a table and shelves and on the extra chairs. She spoke candidly, in detail, about family, relationships, work, her goals, and her financial life.

"We're trying to work with kids of immigrants, encouraging them to read," she said. She had been one of those immigrant kids and loved the idea of helping children aspire to college, as she did. She joked about how, today, she lacked motivation, how she preferred to sit on the couch and watch TV. Then, in the next breath, she marveled at how far she had come—and how much more she wanted to achieve.

Katherine's big goal was a master's degree in psychology, and, dressed in jeans and a sweatshirt, she still had the casual look of a student. She thought about putting aside the extra money she was earning thanks to a recent raise toward tuition, aiming to become the first in her family to receive an advanced degree. She was working on an application to the local university, and during the Diaries year she spent early evenings on her application essay before her boyfriend arrived home from work.

Katherine worried that her college grades weren't good enough for admission, so she took a few classes in the graduate school department in hopes that she would do well enough that her professors would pull for her. But it wasn't just the application that stood in her way. The other part of Katherine's story involved debt. She had funded her college degree with student loans and supported her middle-class lifestyle with credit cards. Taking on debt allowed her to manage when her car broke down, for example, but it also saddled her with yet another obligation. Debt had been a critical tool in her upward climb, but it also threatened to derail her hard-won progress.

An Old Problem

Katherine's story captures the complicated and often contradictory way American society views borrowing. According to Pew Research, seven in ten Americans say debt is necessary in their lives but they prefer not to have it. And while seven in ten also say that "loans and credit cards have expanded their opportunities by allowing them to make purchases or investments that their income and savings alone could not support," they nonetheless often see it "as a negative force in the lives of others." Most believe that other people use debt irresponsibly, propping up spending they cannot afford.[1] Among Diaries families, more than half felt that making purchases on credit was "good in some ways" but "bad in others." Katherine had to agree.

Even more than savings, debt is freighted with moral baggage. We even use two different words for the same thing: credit and debt. When you apply for a loan, you fill out a credit application, while lenders make a decision to give you money based largely on your credit score. The most common borrowing vehicle for Americans is a credit card. If instead the process involved filling out a debt application, checking our debt score, and using a debt card, many of us might consider our actions differently.

Ambivalence about debt is an old problem, transcending time and culture. In his book *Debt: The First 5,000 Years*, anthropologist David Graeber writes that "the most obvious manifestation [of the profound moral confusion about debt/credit] is that most everywhere, one finds that the majority of human beings hold simultaneously that 1) paying back money one has borrowed is a simple matter of morality, and 2) anyone in the habit of lending money is evil."[2]

Moral judgments surrounding debt and indebtedness underlie policy debates about how lenders operate. They inform public discussions about the interest rates that can be charged, the types of loans that should be allowed, the collection practices that are acceptable, who can file for bankruptcy, and the consequences of doing so. In the aftermath of the 2007–8 housing crisis, these judgments reverberated through national discussions of who was to blame—overly optimistic home purchasers or overly greedy mortgage lenders—and who deserved help recovering. These judgments and the related policy decisions determine which credit products make it to market—and into the financial lives of American households.

Yet the debate is often oversimplified, framed within a binary argument that borrowing or lending is either bad or good. Depending on one's point of view, lenders or borrowers might be heroes enabling investment and growth or villains causing ever-downward spirals. But when we take a closer look, we find that it is far more complicated than that—and requires a different kind of frame.

From a Good Score to "Doomed"

Most of what Katherine knows about finances, she taught herself. When she was growing up, money was always cash and always tight.

Katherine's father opened his first bank account just a few years before we met her. "My mom still won't put money in a bank," she told us. In high school, Katherine took a mandatory financial literacy class, but much of it was useless. She was taught to track stock prices in the newspaper and to balance a checkbook. But by the time she needed to manage her own money, debit cards and ATMs had replaced checks for routine payments. She wondered at first if she was supposed to be using checks instead of a debit card, but she adapted. When she began receiving credit card offers in the mail, she opened some credit accounts. But she always paid the full balance each month.

In college, Katherine applied to rent an apartment and the landlord checked her credit history. When the landlord asked to see her, Katherine was afraid something was wrong. Instead, the landlord said she was impressed with Katherine's credit score, especially given her young age. These scores, which assess borrowers' credit worthiness, often based on a 300 to 850 range, are used by employers, insurers, landlords, and lenders to make decisions.[3] Feeling very grown up, Katherine began tracking her credit score "obsessively," she said. She read blogs about how scores are calculated, and how to protect and raise them. She learned, for example, to leave her old, unused credit cards open, because a long credit history is good for her score. Her solid credit score, like her college degree, became a matter of personal pride.

Student loans were Katherine's first real experience with longer-term debt. She was working full-time, but she still took out $42,000 in student loans to fund her degree. Despite her best efforts, Katherine wasn't able to maintain her credit score. What first got her in trouble wasn't the student loans per se but the rocky road of her insecure financial life. After college, she lived with a boyfriend who had health problems. He was unable to contribute equally to their finances, and his medical expenses became a financial drain on Katherine. Soon she was overextended. She fell behind and started cycling bills—one month she would pay one bill, the next month another. Her good credit rating melted away. "Next thing I know, my credit [score] is like a 500," Katherine remembered.[4] "I started crying."

Her boyfriend at the time didn't understand why she cared so much about the score. Eventually she left him and moved into her own apartment. Over time, she earned more, and she dedicated herself to fixing her finances. Over the next several years, Katherine clawed her way back up to a credit score over 700, just one tier below the best rating. Early in our year with her, she had even saved a $2,000 emergency fund—placing her in the top half of American households in terms of emergency savings. She hoped she was, perhaps, six months away from being free of all of her credit card debt. But then her financial situation turned again.

When asked a few years after the Diaries had concluded how she felt about her credit cards, Katherine responded, "How should I say this? ... Doomed? ... Doomed might be too strong. But in that direction.... A few levels down from doom."

How did Katherine go from a solid credit score and a clear upward trajectory to feelings of doom? It happened in steps. First, she needed to replace her increasingly unreliable, ten-year-old Toyota. On top of other mechanical problems, the car door locks were temperamental. Sometimes, they wouldn't unlock and Katherine would climb into the car through its hatchback trunk, reassuring passersby that the vehicle was hers. Other times, the doors wouldn't lock at all. Katherine worried she might come out to her car one morning and find a homeless person living inside it—not an unreasonable concern in her neighborhood. Still, she held onto the car because her bank advised her against taking on more debt. One Saturday morning though, her car wouldn't start. The battery had been lifted overnight. For Katherine, that was too much. She searched online and quickly found a lender that would help. That same day, she purchased a Mazda that was fuel efficient and only a few years old.

Katherine had owned her old car free and clear, so the payments put new pressure on her monthly budget. But she felt the new car was a necessity. And after looking closely at her budget, Katherine decided she was "doing pretty ok" and could afford the car payments.

Not long after, she moved in with a new boyfriend. Excited about their future together, she bought a new desk and a few other items for their apartment, using her credit cards. Then one morning as she hurried to work, she found herself stuck behind a slow-moving truck and "misjudged the space." Her recently purchased Mazda, she said, was "scrunched." Luckily she was uninjured, and her insurance covered the outstanding principal on her car loan. Still, she was out the money she had put down on that vehicle—and now she needed a new car for the second time in a year. Her boyfriend took the $2,000 she'd saved for an emergency to a friend who worked at an auto dealership and returned with a leased Acura. Katherine was glad to have the matter resolved quickly but upset that her savings were gone. With the benefit of hindsight, she described that moment as the "nail in the coffin of credit card paydowns."

Going Cold Turkey

Knowing debt's dangers, some simply opt out. About 20 percent of Americans choose to avoid credit altogether.[5] Sandra Young is one of those people. At age twenty-three, Sandra enlisted in the military. Her mother didn't think the army was right for her, but as a young African American, Sandra saw it as a path to the independent life she wanted. Her army aptitude tests suggested she was well suited for a career as a bookkeeper, and she embraced the training and the work. Her first posting was in Belgium. She used the opportunity to travel throughout Europe, to France, the Netherlands, England, and more. After her tour ended, she chose to be discharged, and she married another soldier. After a few years in Florida, he was posted to Italy, so she had a second stint abroad, this time as a military spouse with young children.

While overseas, though, her marriage broke up. She decided to move back to the States, this time to New York. It was "where I could get to when I was coming from Italy, and I knew a couple of people here," she said. "I came here with nothing, like five suitcases, the kids, and that was it."

Twenty years later, she is still there. When we met her, she was living in a bright apartment in Brooklyn with sliding glass doors that opened onto a small garden on her terrace, several floors above the bustling street life below. Every summer, she takes on a home improvement project. The year of the Financial Diaries, she had decided to paint, and her new pale green walls gave the apartment a fresh, clean feel. She also takes a short vacation each summer. In the Diaries year, she went upstate for the woods and open skies. At least in the summer months, Sandra, now in her fifties, is relaxed and easygoing. But her calm belies the discipline and drive it has taken her to get to where she is—and the intense budgeting she has embraced to stay there. As she said, "It's more expensive [to live in New York], and you have to be creative and you have to really, really, really budget."

New York *is* expensive, but the main reason Sandra needs to "really, really, really" budget is her work situation. Building on the skills she gained in the army, she works as a tax preparer and bookkeeper. Sandra typically spends the first part of the year, during tax season, working more than sixty hours a week. The rest of the year she works part-time in bookkeeping. As a result, she earns more than half of her annual income in just three months, nearly a third in February alone. This arrangement is intentional. She likes the rhythm of her year: work hard in winter, relax in summer. She also doesn't think she could tolerate a corporate job where you couldn't wear jeans "and you have to do corporate politics and you're in a cube . . . and all the other stuff."

In order to make her earnings stretch, Sandra said she has to be "extremely fanatical about budgeting." Opening her laptop to show off her spreadsheet, she said: "I just do it by years. So, I figure out what my income is going to be, how much is in my bank account. And then I want to get back into saving, so I figure out how I'm going to save and what I want to do. Anything I want to do, like how I wanted to paint and do stuff for the house." She looks at her budget spreadsheet every day and tries to track her money to the dollar, making constant adjustments. "I adjust it if something comes up. I budget car fare, I budget food, I budget entertainment, I budget every single thing. I budget if I have to do stuff for the kids or if they're gonna give me money. I budget if I'm going to have clients. I budget everything." Sandra checks her bank balances regularly, too. If she spends more or less than planned, she adjusts her future spending accordingly.

Sandra's discipline is hard-earned, the result of her upbringing and army training, but it also stems from some bitter personal experience. In her thirties, Sandra got into trouble with credit cards. "The doctor is the worst patient," she said. "Just 'cause you know, don't mean you will." She recalls, "The person I was dating was spending.

We were just spending." She also found it difficult to limit how much she spent on her kids. "Sometimes you get caught up," she said. "You don't pay attention, you just buy, buy, buy, and you just do stuff." At the time, she had a steady, year-round job. At first, Sandra ignored the credit card offers that came in the mail. But those borrowing limits—"Up to $5,000!" "Up to $10,000!"—were just too tempting. "Once you start using them," she said, "and you realize you got a big limit and then you only have to make a little payment, and nobody's really bothering you as long as you make that little payment, then I wasn't really thinking about it until I saw that it was getting bigger and bigger. Then I worried, but not enough that I stopped."

Eventually Sandra realized that she was in over her head. She wasn't earning enough to make the minimum monthly payments on her debt, much less pay it down. After falling behind, she started getting credit collection phone calls day and night. "They start calling you . . . and calling and calling," she said. It was a lonely, painful time. She knew she'd made a big mistake. Finally she decided declaring bankruptcy was her best option, so she hired a lawyer with her tax refund that year and went to court.

Almost two decades later, Sandra is still focused on not making that same mistake again. Unlike Katherine, who reacted to her first lapse with credit by working to rebuild her credit score, Sandra avoids all borrowing. She is aware she could take nicer vacations, and do more for her home, if she used credit cards. But, she said, "I don't want to mess about with that [again]." A few years earlier she had a large, unforeseen, urgent expense. Rather than borrow, Sandra withdrew the money from her IRA. The penalty felt less painful to her than the prospect of going back into debt.

Perhaps the biggest illustration of her aversion to debt is her children. Sandra's two daughters, toddlers when she came to New York, are now in their twenties, working full-time, but dead-end, jobs. After graduating from high school, they both considered college. But Sandra would not let them take out student loans. If they couldn't get grants or scholarships, she advised them, then they should not go to college.

Given the growing numbers of people like Katherine starting off their lives with thousands of dollars of student loan debt, Sandra's advice is understandable. But it's also flawed. While it's true that the cost of going to college has increased dramatically in recent decades, the gap between lifetime earnings for those with college degrees and those without has grown faster.[6] There are cases in which college loans don't pay off: when they're from poor-performing for-profit colleges, for example, or for those who never finish their degrees. But for the majority of people, the return on a college education is well worth the attendant debt. Sandra didn't have to take out college loans to get an education. But she took on a different form of debt: for nearly a decade, she ceded control to the army of what job she would do, where she would do it, and how much she would be paid. That debt has yielded a substantial return. She was trained in a marketable skill, and her veteran status gave her access to subsidized middle-class housing and health care benefits. Her children won't have those advantages.

Why Borrow Then?

The experiences of Diaries families show that too much debt can be a problem and so can too little. That explains why, regardless of our conflicted feelings and judgments about it, credit (along with the risk of overindebtedness) is part of life. Debt predates even money. As David Graeber tells it, at the dawn of civilization, harvest cycles determined when most people had goods to trade. Anyone wanting to sell something to a farmer before harvest had to accept an IOU; in other words, they had to offer the farmer credit. "We did not begin with barter, discover money and then eventually develop credit systems. It happened precisely the other way around," Graeber writes.[7] Many of the oldest examples of writing, dating from ancient Mesopotamia circa 2500 BCE, are records of IOUs. Americans today owe $3.5 trillion in outstanding debt, not including mortgages. That's $10,000 per man, woman, and child if distributed evenly across the population (which, of course, it is not).[8] In late 2015, outstanding credit card debt in the United States rose to more than $900 billion, or about $4,000 per person over eighteen.[9] Among Diaries families, 42 percent carried credit card debt.

Borrowing enables us to make major investments in the future: relocating for a better job, getting a college education, buying a home. If we had to save up for these things, modern society would look very different. Lack of access to credit is a major source of the racial wealth gap in the United States. For decades, communities of color have been denied the credit necessary to invest in homes, businesses, higher education, and other assets that build generational wealth.[10] Microcredit—arguably the most significant global financial services innovation of the last forty years—is built on the idea that a lack of access to credit keeps the poor in poverty.[11]

In the United States, there is another consideration. Taking on debt is the only way to build a credit score. Those scores are used not only by credit card companies but also by landlords, employers, and insurers.[12] And a significant share of Americans—one in five, many of them African Americans and Hispanics in poorer neighborhoods—have logged insufficient information with the three nationwide credit agencies to be scored. The Consumer Financial Protection Bureau (CFPB) dubs these individuals "credit invisible."[13] Being credit invisible or having poor credit because of limited information has major repercussions. More than 10 percent of Diaries participants reported that they had been denied an apartment, or avoided applying to rent an apartment in the first place, because of their credit score. About 6 percent reported that they had either been refused, or avoided applying for, certain jobs because of their credit history.

Borrowing is also the easiest way to manage illiquidity challenges, at least in the short term. Credit cards help people cope when expenses temporarily exceed the money they have on hand. At least half of credit card holders rarely carry a balance, paying their bill in full each month instead.[14] Almost a third of the credit cards tracked within the Diaries were paid off in full each month. Cardholders who regularly pay their bill in full are effectively managing their liquidity by consolidating many of their expenses into a single credit card bill and paying it off at a moment when cash flow is high. Katherine uses credit cards this way too; they allow her to make smaller purchases easily without worrying about her day-to-day cash flow.

However, 20 percent of Americans pay only the minimum on one or more of their credit cards, and that share is higher among lower-income borrowers.[15] Among the Diaries families, 19 percent reported paying only the minimum required by one or more credit cards. When we looked at repayment by card, versus by cardholder, though, the number grew: families were making only the minimum payments on about half of the credit cards we tracked. For these cardholders, credit cards were no longer a useful tool to manage illiquidity; instead, they'd become an ongoing burden. While credit can help many people cope with ups and downs in their income and spending, it also makes it easy for people to act against their financial best interests.

Better Underwriting

Thinking back to ancient Mesopotamia, all those IOUs that farmers issued and merchants accepted were based on a prediction of the harvest. As you can imagine, an economy built on IOUs from farmers was subject to collapse any time harvests disappointed. When a harvest was bad, farmers who had issued IOUs during the growing season were unable to honor their debts, creating what today we call a debt crisis. As a consequence, there were regular decrees from kings forgiving all debts and wiping everyone's slate clean. (This still occurs today in some countries; farmers are shielded from the volatility of harvests through various mechanisms including regular rounds of debt forgiveness.)[16] The origin of debt in agricultural societies illustrates a central feature of borrowing and lending that causes trouble: it requires both borrowers and lenders to predict the future. And like Mesopotamian farmers, and other prognosticators, borrowers and lenders are frequently wrong.

The process by which lenders evaluate borrowers, their ability to repay, and the risk they pose is known as underwriting. Lenders try to distinguish illiquid potential borrowers from insolvent ones, and to do so quickly, cheaply, and before lending too much money. The word "underwrite" first came into use in the insurance industry in the 1700s, when the insured person or company representative would literally write his name under the description of the item being insured.

If a lender underwrites loosely, making credit easily available, then the lender will likely face higher losses. The lender will have to charge higher fees to make up for the higher losses, and there will be more debt in the system. This is what payday lenders do. Their underwriting approach has not changed much since the 1700s: borrowers write their name on a check underneath the amount they promise to repay. The payday lender accepts that postdated check as collateral and hands over the borrowed money. This process is quick and convenient for both lender and borrower. Unsurprisingly, payday lenders experience some of the highest loss rates in the U.S. lending industry. A 2007 study finds that the loan loss rate (the ratio of average of annual loan losses to average outstanding loans) for older payday businesses is about 60 percent.[17] For a while, as the housing bubble grew in the 1990s and 2000s, some home mortgage lenders loosened their underwriting standards as well, offering what were called "no documentation" mortgages.[18]

Generally, however (and certainly after the mortgage crisis), mortgage lenders are more cautious. The underwriting processes for larger loans usually require collecting verifiable information about the borrower's income, expenses, and credit history and about the value of the home. This slows down the process and adds cost to the transaction. That is fine for a big event like buying a home, but both borrowers and lenders would be reluctant to undergo an onerous underwriting process to enable someone to get $300 to bridge from now to the next payday, or even $3,000 for a medical expense or for a new car. That is one of the reasons that credit cards are such powerful financial tools. Credit card companies underwrite their borrowers for the maximum loan they think the cardholders can repay and then rely on them to pay off what they can, when they can. The companies don't underwrite the borrower for each new purchase.

Different types of lenders operate on different parts of this spectrum, some charging higher fees and engaging in less underwriting, others relying on lower fees and more underwriting. However, over the last several decades, as lenders compete on the ease and availability of their services, the trend has been toward faster and faster decision-making processes. Lending decisions can be made while a busy parent waits at the register to pay for Christmas presents or while a tired worker sits across the desk from a car salesperson, imagining his new SUV. This pushes underwriting practices away from customized assessments of individual applications toward "automated" decisions, in which the credit "yes" or "no" answer is the result of computer-calculated algorithms using electronic data that can be evaluated within minutes or even seconds.

The problem is that lenders' assessments are based mostly on credit scores, with little consideration of the rest of the potential borrower's financial life. For example, a borrower's payment history on prior loans—whether he or she paid consistently and on time—accounts for 35 percent of the credit score, the single biggest factor.[19] This information tells the lender that the potential borrower has a pattern of repayment, that he or she tracks the bills that need to be paid and considers it a responsibility to pay them regularly. The second-largest variable, accounting for 30 percent of the credit score, is the amount of debt the borrower owes as a percentage of the total amount available to borrow. That is called the credit utilization rate. Having a low credit utilization rate tells the lender that the potential borrower could use some of that available credit in a pinch, to pay for an emergency expense or to cover the loss of income if the borrower loses his or her job. It indicates a source of future economic options.[20]

Payment history and credit utilization offer potential lenders useful ways to determine whether borrowers are likely to repay. However, the variables say far, far less about how much credit a person can truly afford. Think about Katherine. She always pays her credit card bills on time, generally pays more than the minimum payment (though not the full amount), and has never declared bankruptcy. Her credit utilization rate is also fine, in part because her credit card providers keep raising her credit limit. As a result, her credit rating is strong, above 700.

But if lenders looked instead at how much free cash flow she has after paying her bills, or her ratio of debt to income, or whether or not she is paying down her balances over time, they would see a different picture. At the beginning of the Diaries year, Katherine was solvent: her total earnings covered her living expenses and discretionary spending. She even had some slack, a small difference between her annual income and annual expenses. She borrowed during the year, especially when she needed a lump sum that was larger than she could afford with one month's worth of extra money. She needed braces, for example, and opened a new credit card account to pay the dentist a large advance.

But when she took on a car payment midway through the year, she became illiquid. Because her spending was pushing the bounds of what she could afford, Katherine often did not have cash on hand at bill payment time. It makes sense that she would use credit cards to bridge those gaps; that's what they are best designed to accomplish. But, over time, she was unable to pay her principal down, and as Figure 5.1 shows, more of her income went toward paying interest. Her increasing debt load and the costs to service that debt nudged her closer to insolvency.

In our conversation after the Diaries had ended, Katherine estimated that a quarter of her income was going to her monthly car payment. She prioritized paying her student loans next, then rent, and then the minimum payment on her credit cards. After living expenses, she said there was nothing left—no room to make significant progress on paying down her debts. That's why Katherine felt doomed: even with no new spending on her credit cards, it would take her eight years to pay off the balances.[21] When you consider her income relative to her expenses and debt-servicing costs, Katherine's debt may indeed have become inescapable, except through the extreme step of declaring bankruptcy.

Despite Katherine's self-assessment of her own debt level, she was not even close to maxing out the credit available to her. She had only borrowed about 30 percent of her credit card limits, and she was still receiving offers for even more credit. According to FICO, the most widely used credit score, she was still a "good" credit risk because she paid her bills on time and wasn't using all the credit she had available.

The point is similar to the one we made about savings. Analyses of savings focus mostly on collecting snapshots of savings balances rather than tracking saving behavior or cash flows in and out of savings accounts. With credit, the analysis includes measuring cash flows over time alongside outstanding credit balances, but it is limited to

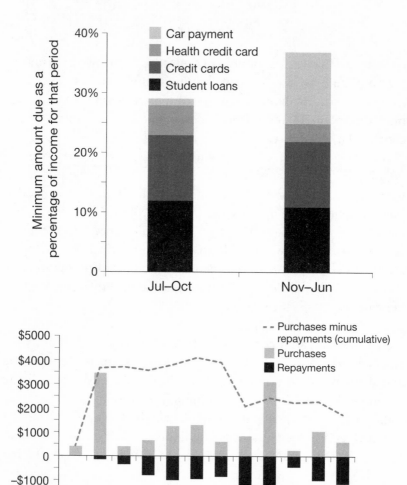

Figure 5.1. Katherine's debt during the year. Above are her minimum required debt payments as a percentage of her income, which increased markedly over the year. Below we show her monthly credit card spending and repayments (including her health credit card), as well as the change in her credit card balance from the beginning of the study year. Her balance spiked in August when she paid for her braces and dipped in February when she used her tax refund to pay down debt. She transferred some of her balance to a zero interest card in March, which partially explains the large increase in both "purchases" and "repayment" and enabled her to put more money toward balance repayment instead of interest charges. This helped her end the year with her balance trending downward. After the study ended, however, her credit card borrowing continued to increase to the point where she feels "doomed."

the cash flows most directly related to the borrowing itself. Payments toward rent, utilities, and other bills—or ongoing saving behavior— are infrequently included in the assessments of whether someone is creditworthy or has exceeded his or her capacity to borrow safely.[22] The Diaries help us see why a wider analysis is helpful. Yet lenders typically lack incentives to take on that analysis.

Blunt Tools

Establishing policies that give lenders incentives to conduct a more comprehensive assessment of borrowers' creditworthiness isn't easy. Meanwhile, the availability of credit not only has implications for individuals, it also affects society. Too little credit results in lower investments in homes, businesses, and education, while too much can lead to a debt bubble and excessive risk-taking.

When it comes to underwriting and the resulting availability of credit, the interests of individual borrowers and lenders are inherently at odds. In order to earn profit and manage their risk, it's not necessary that lenders get their underwriting exactly right in the case of every single borrower. Lenders are able to spread the risk of making a bad prediction across many borrowers. Their objective is to sustain a certain level of profit across their entire portfolio. If they have high losses, they can counterbalance those with high fees or vice versa, while still maintaining profitability.

For borrowers, spreading risk isn't an option. They each bear the full risk if they are wrong about their future ability to repay. Katherine is liable for her full loan, regardless of whether her creditors estimate that 4 percent or 8 percent or even 16 percent of their loan portfolio will default. And for individuals, failing to repay has dramatic consequences. Late fees and interest charges build up, increasing the amount that has to be repaid. Illiquidity problems are amplified. And once someone declares bankruptcy, that black mark stays on his or her credit report for up to ten years and makes it difficult to obtain credit at affordable rates in the future.

There are other misalignments between borrowers and lenders, too. For a borrower, paying only the interest on a loan, and not the principal, spells trouble. But lenders can profit greatly from that kind of behavior. In other words, there is an incentive in some kinds of loans for lenders to seek out not borrowers who will succeed but borrowers who will just get by.[23] And for other types of loans, it's even worse. Payday lenders are the most prominent example, infamous for generating their profit from borrowers who continually take on new loans to repay the prior ones. Some mortgage lenders during the housing bubble had a similar strategy. They depended on origination fees and interest-only mortgages to generate quick profits, while assuming that ever-rising home prices would enable borrowers to ultimately refinance loans that were not likely to be paid otherwise.

What can be done? Efforts to better align borrowing and lending behavior date back to ancient Hindu, Chinese, and Roman civilizations. In Hindu law, a rule known as Damdupat caps the total amount that a lender can recover from a borrower at twice the amount borrowed—no matter how large the loan, how long the term, or the specific interest rate. Chinese law had similar provisions: for over a thousand years, from the Tang dynasty (618–907 AD) to the Qing dynasty (1644–1911 AD), this rule applied to long-term debts. Roman law included an equivalent mandate, documented in the Institutes of Justinian, published in 513 AD. The Roman rule was known as *alterum tantum*, which means "as much more."[24]

Usury laws, which limit the interest rate that can be charged, work in a similar way, as do rules about credit collection practices and bankruptcy.[25] Laws limiting how much lenders can recover (whether by regulating interest rates or by giving borrowers the ability not to repay) serve two purposes. The most immediate is that they recognize that borrowers shouldn't be permanently punished for bad luck, errors in judgment, or even foolish mistakes. They protect borrowers by limiting the consequences of overestimating their ability to repay in the future. The second, and less heralded, purpose is that by pushing more of the consequences of underwriting decisions onto lenders—in the form of losing their money—they make lenders more cautious and selective in how much, and to whom, they lend. The regulations introduce stronger incentives to carefully evaluate the level of losses that they can sustain profitably, nudging lenders toward gathering more data and making better assessments about the effect of their loans on their customers. By doing so, they acknowledge that neither borrowers nor lenders have perfect information about the future, and they take some risk off of borrowers' shoulders. However, these are blunt tools with which to solve complicated challenges. We can, and should, go further in developing sharper ones.

See More of the Picture

Tinkering with the individual elements of loans by changing how loan terms are disclosed to borrowers, or the specific length of the loan, or the maximum interest rate won't be enough. Instead, we need to begin engaging lenders in protecting the rights of borrowers. Global standards are beginning to emerge. The G20's High-Level Principles on Financial Consumer Protection provide a voluntary standard of conduct for regulators and providers. They state that financial services providers "should have as an objective, to work in the best interest of their customers."[26] In the United States, the CFPB's rules for mortgage lenders and their recently proposed payday loan regulations move in this direction by imposing requirements for lenders to assess borrowers' "ability to repay."[27] The U.S. rules prescribe specific underwriting criteria and business practices giving financial institutions stronger incentives to offer loans that make people's lives better, not worse.

This is a big shift. Even if a loan is well designed and responsibly offered, whether it will turn out to help or harm depends on the specific situation. If we assume that Sandra and Katherine know more about their own financial situations and their ability to repay than lenders do, then it might seem fair for them to shoulder a disproportionate amount of the risk that comes with borrowing. But this assumption is often false.

Borrowing decisions are often made in complicated circumstances and based on incomplete information. For example, payday loans have plenty of obvious downsides and often result in a cycle of dangerous, expensive, and painful indebtedness. But for someone who will lose a job if he or she can't come up with the money to replace a tire on the car needed to get to work on time, a payday loan can be a lifeline. One study participant told us she prefers using payday loans to deal with illiquidity rather than a credit card because, for her, payday doesn't carry the same temptation to overspend.[28] Choosing to borrow can require making trade-offs about earning more, spending less, and imposing on friends and family, not just among different types of credit.

While weighing these trade-offs, people can be too optimistic about their own likelihood of repaying. Katherine, for example, only considered her monthly cash payment toward her car loan. She did not factor in the other ways a new vehicle would stretch her budget and neglected to account for the higher insurance payments and inevitable repairs. She was influenced by her boyfriend and did not sufficiently investigate the difference between a lease and a loan. She got some very good advice when her bank advised against taking an auto loan until she paid down other debt. However, it was far too tempting to ignore their advice, so when other lenders presented other options, she took one.

In part, that was because Katherine focused on her long-term financial goals and her most immediate needs, instead of taking into account a fuller picture of her near-term financial life. Her behavior was, in this sense, the opposite of Robert's (in chapter 4). She knew her goals for "later": graduate from school, earn a higher salary, and pay down debt. She also knew her goals for "now": spend less on regular monthly expenses and make sure she could cover her bills each month. But she wasn't considering as carefully how her decisions for "soon"—taking out a car loan or lease, for example—would affect the present and the long term.

Perfectly predicting the future is difficult in the best of cases, and lenders and borrowers will continue to make mistakes. Volatility in income and spending makes predictions all the more difficult. The challenge is to set up rules that take into careful consideration who is most able to assess financial risk and who is most able to bear it. In doing so, poor credit options can be limited, and more space can be created for good advice and good financial decisions. Any such rules will require both borrowers and lenders to take into account a more complete financial picture.

This will require us to collect and use different information than we do today, paying closer attention to the ongoing ebb and flow of money within a household rather than relying too much on one-time snapshots or slices of information. The sheer amount of transactional data and increasing analytical power will make this possible in new ways, allowing us to move toward a much deeper understanding of our financial lives—and, in principle, toward much better credit assessments and financial advice.

Katherine tracked her credit score closely. But at best, her credit score offered an incomplete view of her financial status; at worst, it was distracting and discouraging. Monitoring her credit score motivated Katherine to make regular debt payments, but it was almost like a game: take this specific action, pay this much, keep your score within this range. The guidance she received from consumer finance sites about managing her credit score could have done more than simply help her to keep her credit score within a certain range; it could have helped her better manage her financial goals for "now," "soon," and "later." Instead, she was too often steered to do the opposite. Musing about the possibilities, Katherine told us she wished her lender would give her reward points for paying down her credit—not for spending more.

Chapter 6

Sharing

Tahmid and Abida

Ten to twelve hours a day, at least six days a week, Tahmid Khan stands on a crowded sidewalk in midtown Manhattan, selling fruit. He is one of New York City's roughly ten thousand street vendors. In the morning, coffee and donut sellers crowd the sidewalks, giving way by midday to those hawking hot dogs, pretzels, falafel, and other lunch food. Many food carts have loyal followers, who count on the sellers' presence on the same corner every day and, for a few, track their whereabouts on Twitter. Yet the details of these vendors' lives generally escape the focus of busy pedestrians.

Tahmid sets up his fruit stand before the morning rush hour, piling up apples, bananas, and other merchandise. He closes down in the evening, when the crowds have thinned. The fruit stand's owner pays Tahmid $50 to $100 a day, depending on business. He earns the most in summer, when fresh fruit is a big draw. Winters are slow. In a good month, he can make almost $3,000. In a bad month he might not even crack $1,000. Including his tax refund, in the year of our study, he earned just under $30,000.

Tahmid's wife, Abida, worries about his health. He is outside, all day, on his feet and works even when he feels ill. A doctor's visit is out of the question; he never wants to miss work. Abida worries, too, that he doesn't have enough time for friends, activities at the local Muslim Center, and, most important, their son, Faiz.

Tahmid and Abida Khan graduated from college and held white-collar jobs in Bangladesh. But when they arrived in the United States a few years before our study, this was the job Tahmid was able to find. Abida stays home to raise their child. "How long are you going to do this work?" Abida asks him. She wishes he would find a different job.

New York City's street vendors account for nearly $200 million in annual wages and contribute almost $300 million annually to the local economy.[1] Meanwhile, they're subject to a thicket of city regulations that dictate how and where they can work. Tahmid's table, for example, can be no larger than ten feet by five feet. He cannot keep items under the table or next to it. The table must be at least twenty feet away from the nearest building entrance, be eighteen inches from the curb, and provide twelve feet in clearance for pedestrians. Vending is only allowed on certain streets. Vendors must display their license and permit at all times.[2] While it's relatively easy to get a street vendor license to sell food in the city, food vendors also need permits from the Department of Health. And those are limited to about five thousand citywide, including just one thousand for fruit and vegetable vendors like Tahmid.[3] Therefore, many vendors either work without permits, risking penalties, or, like Tahmid, work for someone who already has one.

Breaking any of the rules can lead to steep fines, up to $1,000 per violation. The Street Vendors Project, an advocacy group, reports that 50,000 tickets are given out each year.[4] A few months before we met him, Tahmid was cited for a series of infractions, incurring fines that totaled $5,500. He expected that the owner of his stand would pay the city, since the owner was the one who made the decisions that led to the fines. But the owner told him to pay them, assuring Tahmid that he'd be reimbursed. Taking him at his word, Tahmid borrowed the $5,500 from his friend Nayeem. The owner then sold the vending license and the business, and the new owner refused to repay

Tahmid. Around the same time, Nayeem needed his money back for a long-planned trip to visit family in Bangladesh. Tahmid and Abida had to come up with $5,500, about 20 percent of their annual earnings, in a hurry.

Families' coping mechanisms often extend beyond nuclear family units. In chapter 4, we described savings groups, which are one prominent example, but there are many other ways that people's finances are interconnected with their neighbors, family, and friends. This financial interconnectedness can bring advantages to a community, bolstering the resilience and mobility of families within it. But it also has clear limitations and can introduce new problems even as it solves others. In this chapter, we broaden our focus from individuals and households to explore how communities cope with volatility. Tahmid and Abida, for example, are not only borrowers, they're savers, lenders, and givers too—in spite of their low income and their location in one of the most expensive cities in the world.

Sharing

Our field researcher usually met with Abida, whose schedule was less busy than Tahmid's, though it was important to her that Tahmid agreed to the meetings. She was reserved yet upfront about her family's finances and the adjustment to life in New York. The family left Bangladesh because of the worsening political situation; Tahmid had been involved with politics and feared retribution from the opposition party. They were also thinking about their son's future. They applied to emigrate to European countries as well as America and, eventually, won a visa to enter the United States. When the U.S. Embassy first notified them in a letter, they were afraid it wasn't real; reports of fraud and blackmail in the visa process in Dhaka were common. But once they were assured the letter was genuine, they moved quickly. Within six weeks, they bought plane tickets, gave notice at their jobs, and said their good-byes.

Now they live in a three-bedroom apartment in Queens with two other families. The Khans inhabit one room and share the bathroom and kitchen with the others. Their neighborhood is less busy than midtown Manhattan, but it is still a stark contrast from the quiet towns where Becky and Jeremy, Janice, and Sarah and Sam have spent their lives. Yet Tahmid and Abida seem to have found a sense of community. They now have friends and family in New York. The community members rely on each other to manage the volatility of their financial lives. And while Tahmid and Abida miss celebrating birthdays and weddings back home, they are still connected to their family in Bangladesh, too.

Tahmid and Abida brought $8,000 with them when they emigrated, but they view that money as untouchable, reserved for Faiz's education. Aware of the seasonal ups and downs of Tahmid's income, they always put money aside during the summer. The year we spent with them, Tahmid had been working extra hours all summer, so they had put away several thousand dollars, more than usual. They used much of that year's savings to repay Nayeem. In a way, it is surprising that they borrowed from Nayeem at all, given that they had this money set aside. But, like their savings for Faiz's education, the funds had been earmarked for a purpose. They preferred to borrow rather than disrupt their savings for the winter.

Then in late October, Hurricane Sandy, a deadly and destructive storm, hit the eastern United States. Tahmid, Abida, and Faiz lived far from the devastating flooding, but the storm surge swamped subway tunnels. People couldn't get to the shops, offices, and schools near Tahmid's fruit stand. He couldn't get there either. Tahmid stayed home for a week. He earned barely $1,000 that October, a month when his earnings might normally exceed $3,000, as they had in September. It was a difficult start to the worst season for a fruit vendor. From November to February, he averaged less than $1,500 a month. And this winter was harder than usual because they couldn't rely on their summer's savings, having used that money to repay Nayeem. Relief finally came in February, in the form of their $4,350 federal income tax refund, aided by the EITC. By March, fruit sales began to pick up again, and Tahmid earned $2,300.

But despite their tight finances during the Diaries year, Tahmid and Abida loaned money to friends on three separate occasions, for a total of $3,900. They gave $1,500 to Tahmid's cousin and her husband, who had lost two months of income after Hurricane Sandy damaged their shop in Manhattan. Tahmid and Abida made this loan in November, at a time when they were also short on cash. The second loan, for $400, was to a friend of Abida's, who repaid it so quickly that Abida did not even discuss the loan with Tahmid. The third loan was $2,000, which was for a friend who urgently needed to visit his ailing mother in Bangladesh. Tahmid and Abida were also traveling to Bangladesh around the same time, and they figured they wouldn't need the money until they were back in the States. The friend agreed to repay them when they returned, and he did.

On top of the loans, Tahmid and Abida sent an average of $270 a month to relatives back home, most of it to Tahmid's mother. All told, that money was about 12 percent of their annual earnings. In addition, Abida sometimes gave other assistance as part of a community of local mothers. For instance, she often took a neighbor's child to school, and sometimes she bought food and prepared meals for neighbors returning from Bangladesh. She figured they would be jetlagged and too tired to cook.

Though their income was low, just 113 percent of the local poverty line in New York, Tahmid and Abida devoted much of it to helping others. That was only possible because they received from others roughly what they gave. Their community is an oasis of interconnectedness within the vast, often impersonal metropolis of New York.

These kinds of informal financial interactions were common among Diaries families. Across the 235 households we tracked, 95 percent said they had some sort of informal financial arrangements during the study year. About 40 percent borrowed from friends and family, 40 percent loaned money informally to family and friends, and more than 20 percent were like Tahmid and Abida, both borrowing and lending.

In some cases, these informal financial transactions are a last resort for those who lack access to the traditional banking system or who have exhausted other forms of credit. In others, informal financial transactions complemented formal ones. Among Diaries families who borrowed from friends and family, 90 percent had a bank account and 57 percent had credit cards. While some families had maxed out their credit cards, those who borrowed from relatives and friends weren't any more likely to have maxed out their cards than those who didn't.

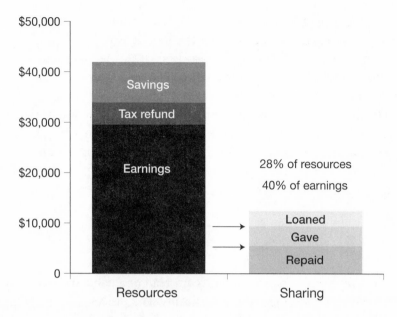

Figure 6.1. Tahmid and Abida's income, resources, and sharing. Tahmid and Abida share a remarkable amount of their resources with their family and network by borrowing, lending, and sending remittances home. *Note*: Their savings is the amount the Khans brought with them from Bangladesh.

Tahmid and Abida, for example, used a credit card for purchases they knew they could repay immediately, in order to build a credit history. They also had a bank account, but they did not use it for daily spending or even for all of their savings. Instead, Abida kept cash at home and used it for most transactions. Only when she had accumulated a significant amount did she take it to the bank, usually about once a month. Many Diaries families actively save at home: 63 percent had at least $250 in cash at home at some point during the study, 41 percent had at least $500, and 16 percent had $1,000 or more.[5] Of these families, more than 90 percent had bank accounts. Overall in the Diaries study, informal loans—those with no institutional involvement— were more common than payday, pawn, and auto title loans.[6]

The U.S. Financial Diaries is a small sample, not a nationally representative one. But results from the Federal Reserve's 2014 SHED

survey were broadly consistent with ours. Among those in the Fed
survey who had experienced a financial hardship in the previous year,
30 percent had provided financial assistance to a family member or
friend. Approximately 28 percent had received financial assistance
from a family member or friend, and 10 percent did both.[7]

For many families, informal interactions like these are both frequent and represent a meaningful amount of their financial activity.
For the Khans, about a third of their income (or 40 percent of their
earnings) and one and a half times their total savings balance flow
through their community during the year.

The Benefits of Sharing

Borrowing from a friend or relative, instead of a bank, has many advantages. Chief among them is flexibility. The process of borrowing
can be fast and convenient; there is no loan application, no need
to produce supporting documentation. It is also generally low cost:
only rarely in the Diaries sample, about 2 percent of the time, did
friends and family charge each other interest. Loan terms themselves
are highly flexible. Among those who borrow from family or friends
in the Diaries study, a full 15 percent said the lender of their most
important loan had no clear expectation for when the money would
be repaid. Over half, 65 percent, reported that the lender expected
the loan to be repaid when possible but not by any specific date.
Among the other 20 percent—those who did have a clear understanding of when to repay—half said they expected the lender to be
very flexible if they didn't meet that date.[8]

Another advantage is that friends and family can assess creditworthiness in ways automated algorithms cannot. Tahmid lends money
to a cousin he knows is good for it. But because the cousin is new
to the country and lacks a credit history, most formal lenders would
likely consider him credit invisible.

Another Diaries participant, Lauren Walker, borrows from her
mother for similar reasons. Lauren lives in eastern Mississippi with
her young son. As long as she lives frugally, her job as an administrative assistant (along with her tax refund) provides just enough

income to cover her expenses. For the most part, she was able to time her bill payments to her paychecks, paying her rent and gas at the beginning of the month and her electric bill at the end. When she needed to make a bigger investment, she saved for it gradually or negotiated payment terms. Lauren's landlord let her pay her security deposit over several months. And she started setting aside party supplies and presents for her son's birthday four months in advance.

But her EITC is a crucial piece of income. Without that February check, Lauren wouldn't have enough to support herself and her son. She needs a way to cover her expenses during the year before she receives her refund check, and formal credit is out of the question. She declared bankruptcy a few years before we met her, after a divorce left her with credit card debt she couldn't repay. Instead her mother loans her money each month, which Lauren uses to pay for her son's daycare and make ends meet. Lauren pays her back when she gets her refund. In theory, Lauren could put aside her refund for the upcoming year instead of relying on her mother. But it is difficult to get ahead of this cycle once she is already behind.

Credit cards can accomplish this same objective, enabling borrowers to spend when they need to and pay when they have the money. Lauren is actually a good credit risk for a loan structured like her mom's loan, as a yearlong advance repaid when Lauren experiences a predictable tax-time spike in her income. But it would be hard to know this unless you were her mom. Because of her prior bankruptcy and overindebtedness, Lauren does not look like a great risk on paper. She has been refused a job in the past as a result of her poor credit history and has avoided applying for others. The instability of her financial life makes it difficult for a formal lender to figure out if she is insolvent or merely illiquid. But her mother knows her backstory, and also knows that Lauren takes her responsibility to repay seriously. The loan she offers is flexible in ways that formal loans are not; it offers flexible loan timing, terms, and availability. But it is also structured tightly to Lauren's ability to repay and with a high expectation of repayment.

Savings groups provide another example of how informal financial services can be structured effectively to help people meet near-term financial needs. In chapter 4, we described Mateo and Lucia, an immigrant couple, living in Queens with their young son. Mateo works as a mechanic and deejays on the side. Their income is $40,000 annually, yet they set aside an astonishing $10,200 as part of a savings group.[9] Savings groups have been used around the world for centuries, and they have been studied extensively. About 9 percent of Diaries families participated in one during the year (most of whom were immigrants, but not all).

Savings groups depend on trust. Participants must trust that everyone will reliably pay in to the group and that they will be paid out when it's their turn. Generally savings groups are not composed entirely of close family or friends. They tend to be more successful when members have more distant relationships: coworkers or friends of friends, people who will see each other again but who don't feel so comfortable with each other that they can let each other down easily.

This was one reason that Mateo described his contribution to the group as "sacred." Under few circumstances would he consider missing a payment. Melinda Perez, another Diaries participant in a different New York savings group, would even borrow if she did not have the money to meet her weekly obligation otherwise. The peer network creates a strong, structured requirement to save that is largely absent from formal savings accounts. Abida talks in similar terms about repaying the loans she and Tahmid received. When we asked Abida what they would have done if they had not had the money to repay Nayeem, she was perplexed. The question as we had phrased it was impossible to answer. They would have worked more. They would have found the money somehow.

Perhaps most significant, informal financial relationships are fluid. Their terms can easily shift between structured to flexible and back as needed, and this is key to why these informal networks are so important to families and communities experiencing financial volatility. Tahmid and Abida have accounts with formal financial institutions for their long-term goals, like saving for Faiz's education or building a credit score in order to invest in a home or a business, yet for their near-term financial needs, such as budgeting for daily purchases or borrowing for a few months, traditional financial accounts are too inflexible. Their financial life is inherently unpredictable, and planning for it requires flexibility. Informal financial transactions have another important quality: they are personalized, and their balance of structure and flexibility can be adjusted to the needs of the specific moment.

The Limits of Sharing

Sharing resources across a community has many benefits. It can allow for personalized financial interactions, and it can move money around a community to those most in need. However, sharing also puts pressure on the community's financial resources, introducing new costs and new risks. And ultimately, the benefits of sharing are bound by the total amount of money available within the community.

Informal borrowing and lending can sometimes complicate relationships. While most of the Diaries families were grateful for the ability to borrow and loan informally, feeling indebted and obligated to others wasn't always easy. One of the Diaries borrowers described this downside well: "I was given no choice. . . . He offered to help out. There's no interest. Even though you get the leeway and they understand your situation, I know I owe him. He knows I owe him. The bank doesn't know when you take a vacation or go out of town. He does know. He wouldn't mention it, but he knows." Some community members stretch their own financial limits in order to avoid these complications.

Lending also increases the financial insecurity of the lender. Knowing this, many people appreciate financial structures that enable them to avoid sharing, or to at least be more judicious about when to lend or give. In the American Dream Demonstration, for example, savers said a benefit of locking up their money in a matched savings account was that those funds were protected from the needs of friends and family.[10] Savings groups and the weak commitments described earlier are often described as having this same benefit: because the money is so firmly committed to another socially acceptable purpose, it makes it socially acceptable to say no to requests for help.

Other people go ahead and lend or share resources, even if that decision makes their own financial life more insecure. They are faced with the trade-off between helping the community and building their own, individual financial security. Carol Stack, in *All Our Kin*, her ethnography of two extended families in the Midwest, describes sharing as a way that community members protect their well-being in the face of harsh financial conditions. Communities move resources around based on need, with each family knowing that if they give today, it will come back to them later. Stack quotes a research subject as saying, "You have to have help from everybody and anybody, so don't turn no one down when they come round for help."[11]

But while sharing resources can be a critical coping mechanism for many individuals within a community, for others, it can be costly and raise the risk of future financial upsets. Moreover, the capacity of any community to keep everyone afloat is limited by its collective financial resources. Tahmid and Abida had to pay Nayeem back much sooner than they would have liked because Nayeem needed the money himself. Similarly, when they loaned money to their friend who needed to visit his ill mother, they wanted to be repaid within a few months. Like others in their circle, they did not have enough extra money to make a long-term loan.

The Khans' Bangladeshi network had relatively high savings balances, given the low incomes in their community.[12] Their friends and family were generally recent immigrants. Our field researcher, who was also a recent Bangladeshi immigrant, said that most families had set aside several thousand dollars before making the leap to move to the United States. This meant that their community had a cushion they could share around. Still, it was unlikely that many in their circle could give a large loan, the kind big enough to invest in a home or business.

The Diaries family in Tahmid and Abida's community that took the most informal loans received only $12,800 during the year we followed them, and the median family borrowed only $2,300. Given our sample it is impossible to generalize, but other communities in our study had even lower lending capacities. The median household in our other sites borrowed less than $1,500 a year from family and friends.

Another Financial Diaries story shows both the potential and the limits of sharing within a community. Peter Garcia came to the United States with his parents from Mexico as a small boy. Eventually his parents decided to return home. But Peter felt like an American by then.

He didn't want to leave California. So he found himself completely on his own by the time he hit his mid-teens. Since then, he has worked a series of customer service jobs, first in a restaurant and then at a department store. His friendly manner and responsible work habits led to his promotion to shift manager, with store manager in sight. Then he had a life-threatening accident. While at a concert with friends, he slipped and fell down several flights of stairs. He was in the hospital's intensive care unit for a couple of weeks to treat his serious back injury. It would be months before he would be ready to go back to work.

This was before the passage of the Affordable Care Act, but California's state health insurance covered his medical costs. However, Peter lived alone. It was unclear how he would pay for rent and food during the long months while he recuperated. Luckily, Peter's social network came through. His closest friends put together an online campaign to share his story with a wider group of his friends, and their friends and their friends. They raised over $7,000. His friends are like him, young people with low-wage jobs. They gave, but their capacity to give was small: of more than one hundred donations, only nineteen were over $100. The coworker of a friend—someone who was a few steps removed from Peter and earned more than he did—donated more than $1,000. Peter's friends were able to come up with the money he needed only because they reached out to an extended network of those who might help.

Bringing More Money In

The challenge, then, is to bring more money into struggling communities. Banks and other financial institutions have the potential to excel where informal financial networks stumble: they can bring resources from outside. Yet it appears difficult for large organizations to replicate many of the benefits of social networks. Big companies have trouble engaging with a network; instead they structure their relationships with individuals, and consider the services they provide as contracts between the company and one person, or a couple. The Internal Revenue Service follows the same protocol, identifying a "primary taxpayer" on any jointly filed return. Financial researchers do the same, seeking to ask questions of the "financial decision maker" of the household. Yet, sitting with Abida, it was clear that neither she nor her husband could accurately be described as "the primary financial decision maker." They together decided to emigrate. Tahmid was responsible for earning, but Abida was responsible for saving and budgeting. Separating their financial capacity from that of their community also ignored meaningful complexities.

Decisions that communities make about saving, lending, borrowing, and sharing money across the community are "high touch" in the sense that they come with extensive personalization and don't require major investment in information gathering, financial product design, or customization. Individuals are able to respond to the context surrounding the numbers because they understand how the whole network functions. Informal financial transactions succeed because they enable personalized decision making around when to be flexible and let a payment come in late, and when to have structure and demand immediate payment. Smaller, community-based financial institutions, especially those with a strong, mission-driven commitment to their customers' well-being (such as community development credit unions), are sometimes able to replicate this sort of nuanced, personalized, high-touch treatment. However, even they have trouble taking into account not only individual situations, but also the interactions across the network.

For large, national financial institutions, however, providing personalized, high-touch service at a large scale is challenging. The financial services industry over the last few decades has moved in the opposite direction, toward increased automation and standardization in order to boost efficiency and lower costs. Technology, data, and analytics are paramount in this model, and they have diminished the human touch. To make decisions, they rely on different data and criteria than friends and neighbors. However, this same technology, the same data and analytics, are gradually beginning to enable new experiments in financial services that seek to combine the best aspects of both informal and formal financing.

The start-up lender Vouch was one such experiment.[13] Vouch closed in June 2016 when it was not able to raise sufficient equity capital, a sign of how difficult it is for these kinds of businesses to work, but its model offers some ideas for how to think about lending to, say, a determined divorcée like Lauren in the same way her mother would. Vouch asked members to take a survey about each other, answering: How long have you known each other? Do you trust each other? Do you trust each other with money? And then, would you sponsor each other? Sponsorship essentially meant cosigning part of a loan. Vouch loaned amounts between $500 and $15,000. The loans had interest rates of between 7.35 percent and 29.99 percent and terms of one to three years. Having a bigger or stronger network, or greater sponsorship, would lower the interest rate charged and/or increase the amount that could be borrowed.[14] Meanwhile, sponsors were on the hook only for the amount that they sponsored. If Nayeem were to sponsor Tahmid for $250 out of $5,000 borrowed, and Tahmid were to default (and Vouch couldn't collect in any other way), then Nayeem would have to pay $250, not $5,000. Vouch not only brought in new resources to the community, it factored in personal trust and reduced risk to the community.

Among the first thousand Vouch borrowers, many were like Tahmid and Abida, people whose creditworthiness is easily undervalued by traditional scoring algorithms. Whereas traditional underwriting models are based on individual assessments, creditworthiness is networked. Tahmid and Abida's ability to repay depends on whether or not they are reimbursed the money they have loaned. It depends on whether or not Tahmid's employer—likely someone with a similar financial life to his—continues to be able to pay him for the work he does. Taking these relationships into account has the potential to improve the accuracy of underwriting for people with a limited or mixed credit history. It would enable lenders and payment companies to experience fewer losses and therefore offer their services for lower fees. Vouch's loss rates on loans to borrowers with poor credit scores were a third to a half lower than losses typical for lenders using traditional methods.[15]

There were other benefits to Vouch's approach. Sponsors on Vouch had the ability to limit their exposure to risk. Instead of saying yes or no to her friend's request for a loan, Abida could say, "I'll help you get a lower rate" or "I'll sponsor part of your loan." This provided the community with a better way of managing its total risk. It also provided a path for borrowers to pool the power of their sponsors and get access to larger amounts of credit than they would otherwise have been able to find. Vouch, as a business, did not grow fast enough to survive, but, as a demonstration of concept, it showed the ideas could work.

Companies like Vouch need to be very cautious about not repeating the mistakes of the past. The roots of lending lie in relationship- and character-based decision making, with lenders taking into account a range of factors other than the straight math of incomes and asset values. In other words, before computers made decisions about loans, people did. In the United States, that led to redlining, in which whole communities had no access to fair credit because banks literally drew a red line around areas on the map where they would not lend. In response, fair lending laws were passed to limit which variables lenders are allowed to take into account when they make decisions: race, especially, is off-limits.[16] Data from social networks, however, are not. These data are already being used to augment traditional credit scores to lower rates or increase borrowing limits. But using social media data to inform lending decisions carries a serious risk of a new kind of redlining, in which entire communities' access to capital could again be unfairly restricted.

Kiva US, a nonprofit lender that provides individuals in the United States with zero interest loans of up to $5,000, is another example of a company that uses social networks within its underwriting process, in part to increase the likelihood of repayment.[17] Kiva requires anybody seeking a loan to do two things: first, to support another entrepreneur with a $25 loan themselves, and second, to recruit fifteen to twenty-five people to lend to them. These provisions build the social cohesion of the Kiva community by giving participants reasons to work for each other's success. As a not-for-profit, Kiva assesses its success primarily by its impact on participants, by its ability to fundamentally democratize access. Kiva believes that the strategy enables them to maintain reasonable loss rates while lending to people who would otherwise be overlooked by traditional lenders.

The Social Meaning of Money

To economists, financial matters shape our relationships. But often it is the other way around: relationships influence what we can achieve with our finances. Recognizing this helps us better understand how, and why, people make the financial choices they do. Often, decisions that might seem confusing when viewed from a purely economic perspective make more sense when we take into account the influence of relationships. While this may seem obvious, financial policies, products, and advice are rarely designed with these insights in mind.

Katherine Lopez, for example, whom we met in chapter 5, knew that her spending habits had been affected by her boyfriend's approach to money. She never bought soda before moving in with him, for example, and she ate most meals at home. During our year with her, she started eating out more often, and her spending on restaurants jumped from about $9 per week to $46. Her boyfriend urged her to fret less about money, and she worried he would grow tired of her frugal lifestyle. While her financial future and indebtedness were concerns, she also remembered how lonely she felt before meeting her boyfriend and worried about losing him. It is a reasonable fear; relationships can suffer when people refuse to match their friends' and family's financial habits. The Vargases, another Diaries family from California, were frugal, focused savers and were criticized for it. They put any extra money they earned toward saving for their retirement and their children's education. Their extended family felt insulted when the Vargases limited how many people they invited to their children's birthday parties to save money. Shrugging it off, Rose Vargas said, "They think I'm weird."

Almost every story we've shared about a Diaries family's finances could be recast as a story about relationships. Relationships have a deep impact on how we deal with money—and sometimes make it impossible to follow, or even understand, the textbook pieces of money management advice proposed by economists and personal finance experts.

Viviana Zelizer, a pioneer in the field of economic sociology, describes "the social meaning of money," arguing that, contrary to economists' assumptions, money is not entirely fungible. Rather, people often earmark funds and think about money in different ways depending on how it is earned or what it will be used for. For example, we establish "moral boundaries among categories of money" based on how that money was acquired. We differentiate among "dirty" money, "easy" money, and "blood" money.[18] Similarly, we differentiate between money paid to workers as entitlements or gifts, by calling the payments wages, honoraria, bonuses, or tips.[19] In Zelizer's thinking, money itself can be categorized based on what it will be used for, who can use it, how it is allocated and controlled, and its source.[20]

As people in the Diaries talked about money and relationships, they repeatedly revealed how social meanings matter to households' long-term financial decisions and even their day-to-day cash flows. Money is more than a symbol of financial worth, and people rarely make financial decisions based purely on math. Instead, money can be a way that people structure their choices and express their values.

We don't save simply to save; we might do it, for example, to afford Christmas presents later. Sarah Johnson's parents cosigned an auto loan for her son, Mathew, so he could drive to college and work. He received much better terms that way and a more reliable car. But for them, the loan wasn't simply a financial transaction, it was an opportunity to support and connect with family. On the other hand, paying down debt can be particularly unsatisfying, because the thing it paid for has already been used. Katherine Lopez felt that way about her credit card debt. Sarah Johnson stopped making payments on her car loan for a while after the vehicle broke down.

During the Diaries year, the Khans were careful to avoid most formal borrowing. They used credit cards but only for small payments they could repay quickly. When we checked in with them a few years later, after the conclusion of the study, their computer had broken and Faiz needed one for school. To buy a new one, they had immediately taken on store credit of $1,975. Abida had gone to work part-time, with the goal of repaying the loan before the end of the eighteen-month interest-free period. Abida's commitment to her son's education made both the loan and the job palatable. As we think about the trade-offs that people make among sharing, saving, and borrowing, it's critical to remember that these choices are made in the context of relationships.

Together on the Rocky Road

Over and over in our study, we see gestures of generosity, even among families with very little. Think of Janice in Mississippi stretching to tithe to her church. Or Sandra, the tax preparer, who avoids all credit and earns just enough to get by. After a close friend died, for instance, Sandra didn't think twice about taking in the woman's daughter and toddler. It was fall, the time when her money was tightest. Her apartment felt cramped, and food costs soared. But Sandra's decision-making process was governed by her values, not her budget. Recognizing that values often inform financial decisions helps us understand why people take the actions they do.

Sharing is sometimes a reflection of mutual responsibility and deep, ongoing caretaking. Take Janice, who buys diapers for her granddaughter, or Robert in Brooklyn, who pitches in for groceries. But even people without direct family obligations are intertwined with others financially.

Informal financial arrangements aren't perfect, but they are remarkably effective at meeting the needs of participants by offering both structure and flexibility. Formal financial institutions may never be able to replicate all of these strengths and, most likely, their services will continue to serve as complements, not substitutes. However, lending institutions can draw on the core insights of informal financial relationships in order to better serve financially struggling families. They can expand the data they use to underwrite borrowers, capturing a fuller picture of people's financial lives. They can experiment with more flexible loan repayment terms. Savings groups can be formalized and the payments documented so that the contributions can help inform participants' credit scores.[21] They can do more to help people protect savings for the near-future, the way weak commitments and revolving savings accounts sometimes do. Most important, they can be more creative and ambitious in their efforts to bring resources into struggling communities. And as they do so, they can learn from members of these communities, who understand that helping each other is part of ensuring financial security.

New Ways of Seeing

Chapter 7

Sometimes Poor

Becky and Jeremy

The small town where Becky and Jeremy Moore live is not the most obvious place to go to understand poverty in Ohio: suburban, largely white, and mainly middle class. Statistics would instead point you to the high-poverty Appalachian counties to the south, or to cities like Dayton, Youngstown, and Toledo, which have recorded worrying increases in concentrated poverty in recent decades.[1]

We were in Becky and Jeremy's town because we were interested in more than poverty, and, in line with that, most of the families we got to know there were not poor. Becky and Jeremy's annual resources, just below $38,000 after taxes, put them safely above the government's regional poverty line. That line, known as the Supplemental Poverty Measure (SPM) to differentiate it from the government's "official" poverty measure, has the important advantage of taking regional price differences into account, and we have used it throughout the book. Becky and Jeremy and their four children were in fact living on an income 43 percent higher than the SPM poverty line for a family of six in their part of Ohio.[2]

Like many families, however, their income was unsteady. When we looked closer, we realized that the ups and downs in Becky and Jeremy's income meant that during the year of our study, they spent six months living below the poverty line. Becky would never describe their family as poor, yet, by the numbers, they sometimes were.[3] When their income dipped so low that they had trouble putting food on the table, Becky reluctantly signed up for food stamps—$295 received on the first of the month—and secured help from the state for health expenses for the children.

Becky was conflicted and somewhat embarrassed. "I didn't want the state to have to be the primary insurer for the [kids]," she told us. "I didn't want the taxpayers to have to pay." She paused for a moment, looking for the right words. "I feel there are folks who are worse off." She wasn't the only person we met who spoke this way, reluctant to accept public benefits. Nor was she the only person we met who wrestled with the unfamiliar situation of being both poor and not poor. Becky's experience of poverty is common. In fact, temporary poverty like Becky experienced is far more common than the chronic, grinding deprivation that easily comes to mind when thinking of poverty. The idea that most people who require help are born poor and will always be poor, subsisting only thanks to state benefits, is increasingly out of whack with the facts.

This chapter describes two ways to see poverty in a broader frame. First, to the lists of challenges faced by the persistently poor we need to add the problem of volatility described in chapters 1, 2, and 3. Those chapters show that the instability of income and spending revealed in the Diaries is most pronounced and most challenging for the poorest. This is a core part of America's hidden inequality. Second, episodic poverty like Becky's accounts for a large share of poverty and requires new and fundamentally different policy solutions.

Other Americas

The Other America, Michael Harrington's influential book on poverty, deserves a spot on the shelf of books that have transformed the way Americans view our society. Published in 1962, Harrington's book helped build the momentum that culminated in passage of Lyndon Johnson's War on Poverty legislation. It exposed growing, and often shocking, economic and social divisions in postwar America.[4] At a time when the middle class was expanding and many (white) families found themselves on a firmly upward path, Harrington denied readers the comfort of assuming that life's blessings were equally shared.

Harrington described the poor as segregated, trapped, and caught in "cultures of poverty," unable to capitalize on America's postwar boom.[5] The poor people that Harrington described were marginalized, yet hardly marginal in number. He cited U.S. Census data, available in government reports that were not yet widely reported, which showed that the poor comprised one in four Americans. An estimated 40 million people, he wrote, were getting by on less than $3,000 per year. Translated into today's dollars, that's roughly $24,000, close to the 2015 federal poverty line of $24,250 for a family of four.[6]

Harrington's book sparked outrage. Americans of all stripes were shocked by the concentrated poverty in inner-city neighborhoods and the economic decay of rural communities. More than anything else, Harrington argued that poverty was often invisible:

> That the poor are invisible is one of the most important things about them. . . . Poverty is often off the beaten track. It always has been. The ordinary tourist never left the main highway, and today he rides interstate turnpikes. He does not go into the valleys of Pennsylvania where the towns look like movie sets of Wales in the thirties. He does not see the company houses in rows, the rutted roads (the poor always have bad roads whether they live in the city, in towns, or on farms), and everything is black and dirty.[7]

At the same time that *The Other America* made the invisible visible, it also codified the ways people imagined poverty. Harrington focused on poor communities concentrated in large cities and isolated hamlets, their disadvantage reinforced by the overlapping curses of geography, racial injustice, weak education, poor jobs, inadequate housing, and, more than anything else, pervasive hopelessness.

Fifty years later, the veil Harrington pierced has been lifted.[8] Today, it's not hard to see the kinds of poverty that Harrington dragged into the open—poverty-related news stories, documentaries, movies, books, and even popular music are available at a click.[9] Yet people like Becky and Jeremy do not fit into Harrington's picture, and they still are out of the frame of most conversations about poverty. Harrington's gaze landed far from communities like theirs where, most of the time at least, people are not poor. When people think of poverty in America the dominant images are the ones that Harrington focused on—inner cities, Appalachian hollows, and the rural South and West—where deep poverty persists.

Despite the increased attention to poverty it continues to be difficult to understand *how* poor families spend their lives—what combination of factors holds them back; how some escape; how some trespass poverty lines, moving in and out of poverty; and how they seek to cope. We have an even tougher time comprehending why Becky and Jeremy—and other families that are not poor by standard measures—still feel the tug of poverty.

As we've noted, the Diaries households are not a statistically representative sample. We purposefully selected households so that a quarter of the households in our sample are poor, but the data do not capture important parts of the American experience with poverty. Because we were interested in American workers, we excluded households that didn't have at least one employed member. We recruited people who were not the most disadvantaged households in their communities. As a result, we didn't encounter people living in entrenched poverty.[10] The Diaries, however, allowed us to see other aspects of poverty often missed by broad-brush approaches.

Taisha

Taisha Blake, almost thirty, lives near downtown Cincinnati, not far from her sister and parents, whom she calls an "awesome family and support system." Taisha is raising her seven-year-old son, Rashid, alone. In her early twenties, before Rashid was born, Taisha hopped from job to job. "If something would upset me, I would leave and find another job," she told us. But those days are past. "Now when I have problems at work," Taisha said, "I suck it up and keep moving."

"Plus," she added, "the economy is different." A few years before the study, Taisha trained for sixteen weeks to be a nurse's aide; she learned interviewing skills and how to write a résumé, and received eighty hours of supervised training. A manager she'd worked with during training was impressed. "She said to call her when I completed the program," Taisha recalled, "and I would have a job." She did. Taisha was hired as a nurse's aide, working part-time for $13.75 an hour, three nights a week, for a total of twenty-four hours. Her mother and sister took turns watching Rashid in the evening so Taisha could work her shifts. Then she shifted to PRN basis—Latin for *pro re nata*, which translates to "as needed." For Taisha, that meant she wouldn't be sure how many hours she might work in a week, but she assumed she would get more hours and earn more. In fact, she earned much less. "With the job change [from part-time to as-needed status], I had expected to get a lot more than eight hours every two weeks," Taisha said.

Taisha managed to pick up extra shifts when Rashid started first grade and needed new clothes. The extra shifts not only offered more hours, they also paid a higher hourly wage via an incentive plan. Taisha, short on money, took special care to make sure her boss logged her hours correctly. The hospital, however, soon faced a budget crisis. The incentive plan that had provided a higher hourly rate for overtime was cut, first from 60 percent over $13.75 to 45 percent over. For Taisha, that amounted to a $2 an hour wage cut. Then the 45 percent bonus was cut to zero.

Taisha's income fell below $15,000 that year, which put her 21 percent below the SPM poverty line.[11] That total included the value of food stamps and housing assistance she received, and a $3,700 tax refund aided by the EITC. On top of her low yearly total, Taisha had to deal with unsteadiness from month to month. In September she earned $500. In October, she received close to $1,000. But in November, December, and January, her income hovered back around $600. By spring, the hospital was busier, and for a couple months she brought in more than $1,000. And then it dropped again.

Back in January, when Taisha's income had dropped so precipitously that she couldn't pay the month's gas and electric bills, she was forced to use her rent money toward the utilities, even though it meant paying a $25 late fee to the landlord. When Taisha's tax refund arrived in the third week of February, she paid the March rent, gas, and electric early, able for once to keep a step ahead of her bills.

Taisha would like to work more, and, at the end of the Diaries year, she was discussing a full-time position with her supervisors at the hospital. "Gradually, I would like to go to school, graduate, and get a better-paying job so that I can move away from subsidies and be more financially independent," she said. But for most of the year she was caught in a double bind shared by many of the families in our study. "I don't have any money," she said. "You can't save something you don't have." Along with insufficient resources, though, her ability to save was undermined by instability, making it more important, but even more difficult, to plan and build.[12]

Poverty and Instability

Taisha's experience living on a very low and volatile income echoes the results we found in chapter 1. From the Diaries, we learned that households like Taisha's, with incomes below the poverty line, had income in nearly six of twelve months that was far from average (above or below by at least 25 percent). Not only were these spikes and dips frequent, they were large. Figure 1.2 shows that income spikes for the poorest households averaged 58 percent of monthly income, and their dips were 49 percent below average.[13] The finding that poor households experience more volatility than better-off families was echoed in a variety of studies described in chapter 1, including analyses of bank transaction data, national economic surveys, and self-reported qualitative assessments.

The data show that living in poverty is not usually about struggling to make ends meet each month on a small, but predictable, budget. Rather, insufficiency of resources is accompanied by instability. Poor families thus do far better during some months and far worse in others. The income spikes present chances to catch up on overdue bills and make postponed purchases. The income dips, on the other hand, can present severe financial challenges that are not always evident in yearly data. Figure 3.4 showed in nationally representative data that the poorest families are also the most vulnerable to major crises: 60 percent report having no way to get through three months with the resources they could muster, even if borrowing from family and friends. Poverty is accompanied by volatility and illiquidity. Studying poverty only through the lens of yearly income misses much of this—and overlooks possible solutions.[14]

While we were gathering our data, other researchers were investigating income volatility for poor households in other ways. Bradley Hardy and James Ziliak, researchers at American University and the University of Kentucky, respectively, used data from the Current Population Survey to examine the year-to-year volatility experienced by families between 1980 and 2009. They found that the richest 1 percent of the population saw the sharpest increase over the period.[15] But in any given year (rather than over the entire nineteen years), income volatility for the poorest 10 percent was far greater for the poor than for the richest. And because the poor had fewer tools to cope, it likely also had much bigger ramifications for their lives. At the same time, once-reliable strategies for coping were disappearing. Before 1990, the earnings of spouses tended to be negatively correlated, meaning that one partner typically experienced earnings spikes and dips at different times than the other partner, cushioning the family's total volatility. But Hardy and Ziliak showed that changed after 1990. Spouses' incomes became more likely to move up and down at the same time, amplifying rather than buffering volatility. Moreover, while government support helped reduce volatility for lower-income households, as it did for Taisha, its role became less significant than in the past.

As noted in the introduction, there are some limited month-to-month data on the finances of households from the Survey of Income and Program Participation (SIPP). A team of researchers studying family welfare assembled data across a twenty-five-year span of the SIPP (which covers families qualifying beginning in 1984).[16] Overall, month-to-month income volatility for families with children was relatively stable in that time. But two groups saw substantial changes. Volatility increased for the poorest 10 percent of households, and it fell for the richest 10 percent. Thus, over the past generation, the gap in income volatility between the poorest and richest grew by more than 400 percent, reinforcing divides based on income and wealth.[17]

Sometimes Poor

Most poor households in our data were not, in fact, poor during the entire study year. As Figure 7.1 shows, only 8 percent of poor households were always below the poverty line. The other 92 percent saw their incomes rise above the line an average of three months during the year.[18] At first, the magnitudes surprised us. We thought, perhaps, that part of the reason was related to months in which tax refunds arrived, usually February or March. So we removed tax refunds from

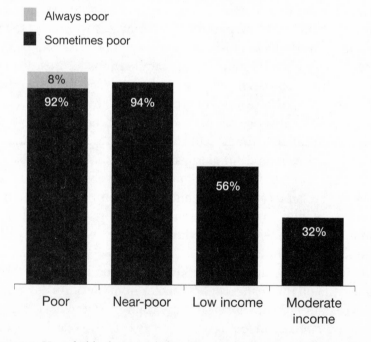

Figure 7.1. Households that were below the poverty line for at least one month during the year in the U.S. Financial Diaries. Only 8 percent of families whose annual income was below the poverty line spent all year below the line. In contrast, 32 percent of households with annual incomes above 200 percent of the poverty line spent at least one month below it.

the data. Even then, 81 percent of those judged poor by annual incomes had months when they weren't poor.

More striking, though, was the experience of Becky and Jeremy and other households that we initially thought would be insulated from poverty. Nearly all of these households in our sample were sometimes poor as well. Looking across the study year, 94 percent of those living on annual resources near the poverty line (between the poverty line and 1.5 times the line) spent at least one month in poverty. And that was also true for 32 percent of those with yearly resources greater than twice the poverty line, people whose yearly incomes located them squarely in the middle class. As the first row of Table 7.1 shows, the near-poor families who spent any time below the poverty line spent an average of 4.8 months in poverty during the year, while those with incomes above twice the poverty line nevertheless spent 1.6 months in poverty.[19]

Outside the community of social service providers, policy wonks, and poverty researchers, episodic poverty is not well appreciated. Four decades after Harrington's book, a group of prominent poverty scholars noted that the perceptions of poverty that *The Other America* helped create remained: "Popular perceptions of the permanence of poverty and welfare receipt are widespread. We speak easily of 'the poor' as if they were an ever-present and unchanging group. Indeed, the way we conceptualize the 'poverty problem,' the 'underclass problem' or 'the welfare problem' seems to presume the permanent existence of well-defined groups within American society."[20]

But Becky and Jeremy's experience moving in and out of poverty is common. The most recent data available from the U.S. Census's SIPP show that 90 million people, *nearly one-third of all Americans*, experienced poverty for two months or more between 2009 and 2011. In contrast, just 10 million people, less than 4 percent of the population, were poor for the entire three years. As with Becky and Jeremy, most spells of poverty did not last long: about two-thirds lasted less than eight months, and 44 percent lasted four months or less. If we look only at one year (2011), 8.3 percent of Americans were poor every month of the year, but about one-quarter of Americans spent two or more months below the poverty line. While these data are from 2009 to 2011, years in which America was pulling itself out of the

Table 7.1. Months in Poverty Defined by Income and by Spending

	Income group based on yearly income			
	Poor	Near-poor	Low income	Moderate income
Months in income poverty	9.1	4.8	2.1	1.6
Months in income poverty that are also months in spending poverty	8.1	3.7	0.6	0.6
Percentage of months in income poverty that are also months in spending poverty	89%	77%	29%	38%
Number of households	53	68	27	20

Source: U.S. Financial Diaries.

Note: The columns show poverty status based on yearly income, while the rows give a monthly view. This analysis is limited to households that had at least one month of income below the poverty line during the study period.

Great Recession, the picture of episodic poverty then is in fact not dramatically different from the experience in 2005 to 2007, the years before the recession.[21]

The data tell a clear story: families leave poverty in great numbers, and they enter poverty in great numbers. Only a small share lives in poverty for long periods. Most Americans who experience poverty are far from Harrington's depictions. They are not trapped in poverty, even if they are never so distant from it; neither do they permanently escape it even when their income rises significantly.[22]

The results make sense given the large number of people living near poverty. In 2015, 58 million people, 18 percent of the U.S. population, had household income that placed them above the federal poverty line but below twice the line.[23] The group includes Becky and Jeremy Moore, Janice Evans, Sandra Young, and Abida and Tahmid Khan. Couple the large population living near poverty lines with the volatility problem, and the broad extent of episodic poverty in America is inevitable, a mathematical certainty.

Over the years, others have attempted to draw attention to episodic poverty. Mary Jo Bane and David Ellwood, both Harvard professors, wrote in the 1980s about the prevalence of poverty "spells," experienced by people who temporarily enter and exit poverty. They later took those ideas to Bill Clinton's administration, where their studies provided a basis for rethinking poverty reduction policy. Bane and Ellwood based their understanding of episodic poverty on an analysis of the University of Michigan PSID survey described in the introduction. In data from the 1980s, they found that nearly 45 percent of spells below the federal poverty line lasted no more than a year; 70 percent lasted no more than three years; and just 12 percent stretched beyond a decade.[24] The prevalence of relatively short spells led them to propose time limits on the receipt of public support, coupled with job training, an expansion of the EITC, and, if needed, wage subsidies. (Bane famously resigned to protest Clinton's signing of the Republican-led welfare reform bill in 1996 that featured time limits but stripped out much of the support they had recommended.)

Still, perceptions of short-term poverty episodes—and what they mean for the fight against poverty—tend to rely on the same sort of incomplete picture that informs the life-cycle arc. The shocks commonly blamed for knocking families into a poverty spell are the same major life changes that are assumed to be responsible for pushing families off the life-cycle tightrope.[25] In a 2010 essay in the *Stanford Social Innovation Review*, for example, Rourke O'Brien and David Pedulla wrote: "Episodic poverty is often precipitated by the loss of a job, a sudden illness, or another unexpected crisis."[26] This is true in part. The Financial Diaries reveal, however, that poverty spells also occur as the result of less significant events, such as a series of smaller-than-normal paychecks or the end of a side job. Indeed, among our households, it was these supposedly minor changes that accounted for much volatility. Sometimes these problems build on each other, sending even higher-earning households into a poverty spell, although none on its own would ordinarily pose an insurmountable challenge.

Becky and Jeremy's spells of poverty were driven by the ups and downs of paychecks, not by major shocks. There is no reason to think this would have changed had Jeremy not switched jobs. Episodes of poverty would remain part of their life as long as they remained near-poor, with regular income spikes and dips.

Statistical Slices

We are not suggesting that concern for the temporarily poor displace concern for the persistently poor. Rather, both types of poverty must be considered to see the full picture. It is a counterintuitive fact of statistics that *at any given time*, a large share of the poor may include those who experience long-term, persistent poverty, even if at the same time the large majority of people who have *ever* been poor are in fact poor for short periods.

To see the math, consider a year in an imaginary society occupied by just one hundred people. Further imagine that five people out of the hundred are persistently poor—they are below the poverty line every month for a year. Another fifteen people are poor temporarily for four months each, with their poverty episodes spread evenly through the year; thus, five people are in the midst of temporary poverty episodes each month. In any given month, then, ten people are poor: five persistently and the other five temporarily. The average poverty rate is thus ten out of one hundred, or 10 percent. The percentage of poverty attributable to persistent poverty is then 50 percent in each and every month, a relatively high figure. Yet among the twenty people who experience poverty at some point during the year, the fraction that is persistently poor is five of twenty, or just a quarter of the whole. In other words, most people who are ever poor—75 percent—are temporarily poor.

We give this example to show how perspectives can vary depending on the way you measure poverty, and even the statistical slice you analyze. But the example is not far from the actual facts in the United States today. In national monthly data from the SIPP, the persistently poor comprise 35 percent of those ever poor in 2011; the episodically poor comprise the other 65 percent (not radically different from the 25/75 split in the hypothetical example).[27]

As with the example, the persistently poor are a relatively large share of people who are poor at any given moment, but they are a much smaller share of all those who are ever poor during the year. If your interest is in aiding those who are poor right now, the persistently poor should command much of your attention. But if your interest is also in aiding all who will be poor this year, or reducing the national poverty rate, focus must expand to include the tens of millions of households that are sometimes poor.

How We Measure (and Think About) Poverty

When Harrington published *The Other America*, the United States did not yet have a standard way of defining poverty. It wasn't until seven years later, in 1969, that the government started using the "official" federal poverty measures. Based on research conducted by Mollie Orshansky, an economist at the Social Security Administration, the measures used the cheapest of several food plans developed by the Department of Agriculture to reflect a nutritionally adequate diet for a year. Since food costs generally accounted for a third of household spending, Orshansky then tripled the food budgets to arrive at a minimum cost-of-living estimate for a single person. That figure was then adjusted for household size and has been updated for inflation ever since. While the line remains the primary way that the government assesses poverty, economists have for decades debated its relationship to a family's actual needs or whether it estimates an adequate standard of living. A few years ago, the Census Bureau worked with experts to define the Supplemental Poverty Measure, which narrows the focus to money available to spend on basic necessities, such as food, clothes, and shelter (and which most of our analysis refers to).[28]

While both the federal poverty line and the Supplemental Poverty Measure are rendered in terms of income, they are rooted in ideas about spending. So why don't policymakers assess poverty by directly monitoring spending instead? The main reason is practical: it is usually much easier to collect data on income than on spending.[29]

For families, though, what matters is whether they can actually spend as needed. If Becky can keep food on the table and fill the van with gas, she has a sense of security even if her income is unsteady. So even if, for practical reasons, we continue to track, measure, and monitor poverty in terms of income (which captures the general availability of resources), we need a policy frame that is also rooted in protecting and supporting families' ability to spend when needed.[30] In short, we need a framework that incorporates both insolvency (which is essentially the traditional view of poverty) and illiquidity (which emerges from a cash-flow view). As chapter 3 showed, even poor households can partially stabilize their consumption in the face of income spikes and dips. They do so by drawing on their own resources and those of their family and neighbors. At the same time, the fact that households can only partially and incompletely protect their consumption means that even temporarily low incomes often mean sharp cuts in consumption.

As Bruce Meyer and James Sullivan document in national data, measuring poverty in terms of spending shows very different trends over time than poverty measured by income. While income-based poverty has shown relatively little progress over time, poverty measured by consumption has clearly fallen. Meyer and Sullivan attribute the divergence partly to measurement error in the income of the poorest households and partly to households' ability to smooth consumption. Their work illustrates the value of bringing consumption more fully into poverty analysis.[31] Evidence from the Financial Diaries reinforces this distinction between "income poverty" and "spending poverty." The first and second rows of Table 7.1 illustrate how the incidence of poverty depends on whether you measure poverty by levels of income or spending. The first row shows the number of months people spent in poverty, on average, based on monthly income (as measured according to SPM guidelines and conditional on spending at least one month in poverty). As noted above, those whose annual income is below the poverty line spent nine months of the year in poverty. Those who are near-poor, like Becky and Jeremy, spent nearly five months below the poverty line. In contrast, for those counted as "moderate income" (with yearly income more than twice the regional poverty line), 1.6 months were spent in poverty. These better-off households see their incomes dip into poverty less often, both because they experience somewhat less income volatility and because they start at a greater distance from the poverty line.

We see a different picture, though, when we ask how many of those months would still be counted as months in poverty if measured directly by their spending levels. Did people manage to maintain their spending through borrowing, relying on savings, and perhaps getting help from others? The analysis here is restricted to households with at least one month when income fell below the poverty line. The second row of Table 7.1 shows that households spent fewer months in "spending poverty." The average "near-poor" household experienced only 3.7 (about three-quarters) of their income-poor months below poverty thresholds. For the average "moderate-income" household, just 38 percent of their months in income poverty were also months in spending poverty. Again the best-off households fare better: the percentage of income-poor months that are also spending-poor months falls as households become richer.[32] So, in line with what we found in chapter 3, some households can maintain spending above the poverty line even if their income drops below. To do so, they depend on the coping tools described in previous chapters—saving, borrowing, and sharing. But when coping tools are weak, spending falls with income and avoiding the experience of poverty is impossible without public support.

New Ways of Seeing

As we came to know Becky, Jeremy, and others in the study, we saw that conventional wisdom about fundamental economic and social relationships—particularly around earning, spending, saving, and borrowing—was outdated. Just as our year with the households led us to reevaluate common ideas about income and wealth, we saw the need to reassess ideas about poverty, too.

America desperately needs solutions that will lift more families from poverty. The entrenched poverty described by Harrington persists as an American dilemma, and the geographic segregation of the poor has only widened in the past half century.[33] Families who spend long periods in poverty are the most disadvantaged, and the safety net meant to bolster their livelihoods has withered and must be rebuilt.[34] Most of the ideas that are offered to solve poverty focus either on bolstering income itself (the EITC, TANF) or on ensuring a minimum level of specific types of consumption (for example, the SNAP "food stamp" program or the health care supports in the Affordable Care Act).

But seeing that many families are not consistently poor and are instead regularly in and out of poverty, and seeing that this is occurring as a feature of their economic lives—and not as an exception—suggests that a broader framework is needed. For these families, the mechanisms to cope with the ups and downs that we've described in this book—saving, borrowing, and sharing—have particular urgency. Policymakers and advocates who seek to reduce poverty are usually distinct from those who seek to help people better manage their financial lives. But, in fact, the lives of the Diaries families show that their agendas need to intertwine.

When poverty is the result of volatility and illiquidity, public assistance should be provided with a less onerous application process that relies on broader, yet more easily gathered, data. Applying for public benefits today is often clunky and slow. It can require standing in lines, filling out extensive forms, parsing complicated eligibility criteria that vary for each type of public benefit, and answering burdensome follow-up questions. This is expensive not only for applicants but also for taxpayers. Moreover, the data gathered do not necessarily capture cash-flow information or generate sufficient insight about instability. As a result, they do not inform the best possible decisions about how to spend our assistance dollars. Government's assessment of benefits eligibility—in both form and substance—should carefully take new data into account, with a premium put on becoming quicker and more nimble in the process.[35]

When considering income and spending volatility, one aim should be to help households help themselves. Yet policy too often undermines that goal. In more states than not, families must deplete most available resources before they are eligible for public assistance. This makes it difficult for families to build up a buffer stock that will help them smooth their consumption on their own. So far, only eight states have eliminated asset restrictions before families can receive funds from the TANF program. The numbers are more encouraging for food stamps and emergency energy assistance, with 34 and 39 states, respectively (plus Washington, D.C.), having eliminated asset restrictions.[36] Research by the Urban Institute shows that when asset limits have been relaxed for food stamps (SNAP), low-income households are more likely to save and have bank accounts, and, most important, once they leave the SNAP program, they are less likely to keep returning for additional periods.[37]

TANF also has work requirements: individuals are eligible for help only if they are working a certain amount. For low-wage workers with volatility in the number of hours or amount of earnings they receive week by week, this is a complicated provision to comply with. Too many hours, and they lose eligibility as a result of too much income, but too few hours, and they lose eligibility for failure to work. Work requirements need to build from the realities of today's labor market described in chapter 1.[38]

Finally, most of the public support to help the poor is designed to pay for specific, approved expenses, such as food or medical care. However, given the nature of the spikes and dips that cause families to dip below the poverty line, this distinction becomes difficult to implement. Often, what people need is a flexible bridge to a few months from now.

The cash-flow perspective pushes toward an expanded poverty-reduction tool kit, one that accommodates the vulnerability of the near-poor while recognizing the pervasive instability in the lives of the persistently poor. As was the case in the previous chapters, conversations need to embrace both illiquidity and insolvency as distinct but often overlapping problems. The families' stories reveal that, alongside efforts to help those whose poverty drives instability, we also need new ideas to keep instability from driving people into poverty.

Chapter 8

Secure and in Control

Financial Diaries

Conversations with the families in our study often returned to one topic: financial instability. We've shown that it is tempting, but dangerous, to assume that Americans' financial trajectories trace steady climbs, their upward momentum stymied only by big events like lost jobs or medical emergencies. Instead, the households we got to know—even those whose annual incomes put them in the middle class—experienced financial uncertainties that consumed their attention and led them down costly paths. Many saw their earnings fluctuate, often dramatically, not just from year to year but month to month, and even week to week. Pay was unpredictable and hours irregular, and, on top of that, spending needs fluctuated too. Even some of the middle-class families experienced months in which their incomes dropped to the poverty line.

The Diaries families were preoccupied with frequent (and often difficult) decisions about when to save, spend, and borrow. They were trying to stretch their incomes, predict their spending needs, and balance competing financial priorities. Think of Sarah Johnson, who was forced to pay the utility bills one month and the mortgage the next while trying to minimize the impact on her family. Or Jeremy Moore, who traded a higher-paying job for one with steadier hours and a more predictable paycheck. Or Katherine Lopez, whose dreams of graduate school were dampened by the debt she accumulated while trying to acquire a reliable car to get to work. They struggled to plan for their futures and remain financially secure in the present, but achieving both mobility and stability was too often impossible.

This type of financial instability emerges in other national surveys too, and it has ripple effects—preventing people from taking important steps to adequately care for their health, prioritize their education, move to better jobs, spend time with their family, or contribute to their communities. It is intertwined with income and wealth inequality, but distinct from it. We came to see this instability as a third, less visible inequality, growing amid the widening gaps of income and wealth inequality in the United States.

Volatility doesn't have to be a problem. People with high incomes and ample wealth often have the liquidity to weather the ups and downs. But the national surveys described in chapter 3 show that most Americans lack easy options. Rising costs and stagnant incomes—along with changes in the labor market, public policy, and the financial services industry—have disproportionately affected poor and middle-class families. They have made it harder for families to help themselves, and they have eroded protections, like safety net benefits, that once supported families in the most difficult moments. This has left families increasingly vulnerable.

How people are able to cope influences whether they can achieve the lives they seek. The families we met had developed a range of strategies for managing their cash-flow challenges, as well as for balancing their longer-term goals with their immediate and near-term financial needs. They borrowed money from informal networks, built small but critical pots of savings, and took simple but meaningful steps such as asking creditors to move the due dates for bills. The strategies were often thoughtful and creative, helping families preserve their resources for their highest priorities. Ultimately, however, their strategies were often insufficient, highlighting the gaps in aid available to families.

We need new approaches, both to reduce the instability that families face and to help them cope with its costs. This will require shifting risk from low- and middle-income Americans onto those more able to bear it, through better employer practices, stronger government policies, and fairer and more beneficial financial services. It will also require finding new ways to help workers and families manage the cash-flow challenges they experience as a result of income and spending volatility. No single policy or market-based innovation will remove all the risks or solve all the challenges, but we hope the examples that follow will provide inspiration for the change that is needed.

Putting Risk on the Right Shoulders

In today's America, families bear a larger share of economic risk than ever before. Employers have pushed the costs of business ups and downs onto their workers, banks and other financial institutions have left families unprotected, and the government safety net has failed to meet the challenges of people experiencing ups and downs. This is neither fair nor wise. Companies, financial institutions, and governments are much better equipped than individuals to cope with volatility by sharing the risks across a larger pool of people. Transferring greater risk onto those institutions will require a mix of legislation, regulation, collective action, and recognition by businesses that worker and consumer protections are in their corporate self-interest.

Better Jobs

The most fundamental way to reduce the volatility that Americans face is through improvements in job quality. As we saw in chapter 1, the Great Job Shift has resulted not only in lower wages but also unpredictable scheduling, inadequate hours, and less job security. Alongside those challenges are diminishing opportunities for training and advancement, and an erosion of benefits such as paid leave and employer-provided health care and retirement coverage.

We need the sort of changes that decades ago helped transform manufacturing jobs—once dangerous and financially tenuous positions—into careers that provided economic security and mobility for millions of American families. Manufacturing jobs were never inherently good jobs, but government regulation and collective action (and to a lesser extent business self-interest) helped workers secure a louder voice, stronger rights, and a larger share of the wealth they helped create. Similar shifts are needed in our current service economy, though they will be difficult to achieve. To secure wide-scale change, we'll need new ways of organizing workers across industries and bolstered support for collective action. In the last few years, we've seen a few promising developments—worker campaigns such as the fight to increase minimum wages, for example.

As we explore how to make the jobs that our economy offers today into better jobs, we will also need to develop new models of workplace benefits. A group of labor experts and business leaders assembled by the Aspen Institute has proposed "principles for delivering a stable and flexible safety net for all types of work." They argue that work-related benefits (such as health care insurance and paid leave) should be independent of specific employers, flexible and prorated so that part-time workers can accrue benefits, portable across different work scenarios, and universally available to all workers regardless of employment status.[1]

Meanwhile, some states and municipalities are starting to mandate measures aimed at giving workers more stability. San Francisco's Retail Workers Bill of Rights is an early model.[2] A federal bill, the Schedules That Work Act, was proposed in 2015. It would require employers with fifteen or more workers to establish a "right to request a flexible, predictable or stable schedule." Employers could still deny these requests, but workers would be given protection against retaliation for asking. Employees in three specific industries—retail, food preparation and services, and building cleaning—would receive additional protections, as would those with caregiving responsibilities, a second job, or a health condition, or those who are enrolled in an educational or job training program. Legislation to raise the tipped wage would help workers too, particularly those in the service industry, who experience volatile incomes even when their hours are steady.

These protections are far too limited to guarantee job quality, but they point a way forward. The measures would create costs for employers, and Susan Lambert, a University of Chicago expert on job quality, argues that "even a seemingly formidable business case is unlikely to persuade many employers to voluntarily improve jobs lodged at the bottom of today's labor market."[3] More optimistically, though, Zeynep Ton, in her book *The Good Jobs Strategy*, argues that investing in employees and operations can be good for business over the long term. Ton suggests that companies should view their labor force as an asset, hiring workers who are paid and managed well, in jobs that allow them time for family and civic life and opportunities to contribute and grow within their work. She points to examples such as Costco, arguing that the retail company's investment in improving labor conditions has led to greater customer satisfaction and higher labor productivity.[4] While some businesses may voluntarily adopt these sorts of principles, wide-scale implementation will require legislation.

Fairer Finance

The financial tools available to help low- and middle-income families save, lend, and borrow are insufficient and in some cases harmful. This is especially true in the case of lending, as we described in chapter 5. Bolstering consumer protections to ensure that financial services are safe is critical. The establishment of the Consumer Financial Protection Bureau was an important step forward, and it has made smart investments in researching consumer experiences and complaints, enhancing financial education, and investigating and prosecuting unfair, deceptive, or abusive practices.

However, we need to think more deeply about the framework for consumer protection. Existing U.S. consumer protection laws and regulations primarily emphasize disclosure requirements—which obligate financial providers to share extensive information about their products—and enforcement actions to punish companies in extreme cases of harm to customers.

This leaves important gaps. Often loans and other products cause financial harm not because they are poorly designed but because they're ill-suited to consumers' needs. In other cases, products can lead to financial distress even when offered in accordance with the described terms and conditions. Sometimes a product doesn't cause outright harm, but it does nothing to benefit the consumer. We need to extend the conversation around consumer protection to include a discussion of providers' responsibility in circumstances like these— when a loan is not predatory per se, but it is not in the best interest of consumers. (Katherine Lopez's auto financing described in chapter 5 is one such example.) Financial outcomes result from people's personal choices and the quality of the services available to them; regulators need to continue working toward rules that reflect that.

Stronger Safety Net

Even if families work hard and play by the rules, they sometimes need assistance beyond what they can secure on their own or through their family and community. Becky and Jeremy Moore, for example, found that Jeremy's earnings from a full-time job did not always provide enough support for their family, so they reluctantly turned to the government for food and health insurance. The availability of benefits varies greatly by state; the families we met in Mississippi had far weaker protections than did Becky and Jeremy in Ohio or the families in California and New York. We need to do more as a country to equalize the basic protections of food, shelter, and health available in different states, so that the growing inequalities between rich and poor are not echoed by inequalities between low-income families living in more generous states versus those living in less generous states.

Meanwhile, as described in chapter 7, over the past two decades the safety net has become less responsive to the fluctuating needs of families. At the same time, a large share of American households experiences movements in and out of poverty. New approaches should consider episodic poverty as an integral part of anti-poverty frameworks, with an eye toward cash-flow issues faced by low-income families.

A strong safety net will include better ways to help households help themselves. One step is by continuing to remove or greatly reduce limits on the assets that recipients of public support are able to accumulate. Evidence cited in chapter 7 suggests that allowing households to build assets keeps people from returning to public support. Another meaningful step is to shift tax benefits for saving toward lower-income, lower-wealth, and less financially stable families. In the current system, the bulk of the benefits go toward wealthier families for long-term goals. Today's system is upside down, with public money largely subsidizing the richest in society.[5] Several proposals aim to help people save more via adjustments to the tax code. Incentives could be provided as a new refundable savings credit, for example, or as part of the EITC.[6]

The Right Money at the Right Time

The Diaries families coped with erratic incomes, checks that arrived too late to make payments, and variable and sometimes unpredictable spending needs. As they juggled medical bills with retirement savings, and utility bills with tuition payments, they were often trying to balance immediate, near-term, and long-term financial goals (what we came to refer to as "now, soon, and later"). None of the Diaries households was recklessly spending in the present rather than saving for later, but they were often prioritizing what they needed "soon" over ambitious and long-term financial priorities.

In deciding what to prioritize, they rarely had adequate financial tools and resources to make the wisest trade-offs. While the U.S. financial services marketplace is large, its products and services are typically tailored to wealthier Americans and often geared toward helping families make big decisions about financial planning and investing. The marketplace for services to help struggling families balance their needs for now, soon, and later—with better ways to save, spend, borrow, and plan—is growing and improving, but still insufficient. We need new products and policies designed to benefit lower- and middle-class families.

Smooth and Spike

To manage financial instability, families borrow, save, and plan so they have money to spend when they need it most. Sometimes this means evening out their incomes so that spending can be smoother over time. Other times families need a spending spike—to buy airplane tickets or put down a security deposit on an apartment. As families try to both smooth and spike their spending, they often face dilemmas: If their earnings one month are unusually high, should they immediately put their extra money aside for a later dip? Or should they seize the chance to finally repair the car or purchase the airline tickets?

The policy discussion about tax refunds shows the dilemma well. Many of the Diaries households experienced their highest-income month during tax time, when they received a refund. Families anticipated the refund and often knew exactly how they would spend the money. Seeing the spike in earnings that this creates for families, some have proposed enabling tax filers to divide their refund check into smaller checks, perhaps received quarterly, rather than annually. When this idea was tried as a pilot, however, less than 3 percent of tax filers took advantage of the opportunity. That may be because filers were counting on the future spike, in the same way that Becky and Jeremy Moore did in chapter 3. As newer experiments to split tax refunds are developed, they will be most effective if they provide ways for families to both smooth and spike their incomes and spending.[7]

Given the complexities of aligning income spikes with spending needs, families can benefit from expert guidance. We highlighted the early efforts of the financial technology start-up Even in chapter 3 and the Rainy Day Reserve in chapter 4, and there are others. The company Digit,[8] for example, tracks customers' earning and spending patterns and transfers money (usually between $5 and $50) from their checking to their savings account when its algorithm assesses that the customer won't need the cash. Approaches like Digit's help people with at least some of the complexity of knowing when and how much to save.

Align Cash Inflows and Outflows

Families that smooth spending and create income spikes are trying to align cash flows with spending needs. Challenges arise when their paychecks arrive at the wrong time or in the wrong size relative to their needs, even if their annual income is sufficient to cover their expenses overall. Similarly, their options for paying bills flexibly and quickly when they do have cash on hand can be expensive. But the digital age has afforded easier ways to help people match their earning and spending.

Since most employers pay their workers electronically, instead of by paper check, companies could, in principle, give workers access to their earnings on a more flexible basis. Ridesharing companies, such as Lyft and Uber, enable drivers to receive their earnings instantly, and third-party companies such as PayActive, Active Hours, and FlexWage have emerged to enable other kinds of workers to receive their pay outside of their usual pay cycle.[9]

Families who experience roller-coaster finances often turn to the services of check cashers, paying a fee in order to get immediate access to cash rather than wait three to five days for a check to clear. They pay fees to rush bill payments in order to pay on the exact date the bill is due or because they don't have the cash far enough in advance to risk mailing a check. They sometimes avoid bank accounts when they have volatile earnings and spending, likely in order to prevent overdrafts.

These families would benefit greatly if the financial services industry enabled real-time payments, but until recently, it has had little incentive to develop a faster system. The U.S. payments system moves a jaw-dropping $175 trillion through the economy on an annual basis in over 120 billion transactions with inspiring accuracy, so delays of a few days to move money have not been perceived as justifying the extraordinary investment and coordination required to develop the infrastructure for faster payments.[10]

By establishing the Faster Payments Task Force, made up of leading payments infrastructure companies, financial providers, and consumer advocates, the Federal Reserve recently took an initial step to change that. The task force has been asked to develop a basic framework for a faster payments system and solicit proposals for achieving it. There are teeth behind this process: if it does not result in an improved payments system, the Federal Reserve has said it will declare a "market failure" and act unilaterally to build a better system. This is a powerful threat, crucial to pushing the private sector to make the necessary infrastructure investment.

Balance Structure and Flexibility

When families sought to devise their own financial workarounds, they were often trying to balance structure with flexibility. Existing products sometimes provide the wrong mix. Lenders, for example, offer little structure around borrowing limits but a lot of structure (and little flexibility) around the consequences for borrowers who cannot repay. Katherine Lopez, the Californian who struggled with car payments, wished her credit card company had been less flexible in increasing her credit line.

This is the case for savings products, too. Behavioral economists identify lack of discipline, rather than simple impatience, as a main reason people don't save more. As we discussed in chapter 4, this has led to the creation of a variety of savings products that provide discipline (by requiring deposits or restricting access until a goal is met). That discipline can be useful, but it can also be counterproductive. Workers experiencing a high degree of volatility often need cash in emergencies. Chapter 4 described savings products, like the Rainy Day Reserve, that provide simple cues to help savers maintain discipline while allowing them the flexibility to make their own financial decisions.

A related idea is the "sidecar" proposal for retirement plans. According to this model, highly disciplined retirement accounts are paired with flexible emergency funds. A share of workers' wages would be automatically deposited into both accounts. The hope is that households with access to a flexible pot of money could more easily maintain the discipline to lock up money for retirement, ultimately decreasing leakage from long-term savings.[11]

Another promising example is the U.S. Treasury's myRA account,[12] which is designed to provide an easy and low-cost savings plan for workers who do not have access to one through their jobs. Because the myRA is a type of Roth IRA account, funds contributed to it can be withdrawn anytime without penalty, giving users the ability to save both for short term ("soon") and long term ("later").

Enhance Control

Volatile earnings and expenses make it difficult for people to set or keep budgets, put aside savings, or determine how much they can safely borrow. This uncertainty keeps families from feeling financially secure. Poor service, hidden fees, and overly complex products and advice aggravate this sense of instability, leaving families distrustful of financial institutions. We need to restore a sense of trust by developing financial advice and tools that are straightforward, transparent, and effective—and give people a sense of control.[13]

Research by the Urban Institute suggests that common sense rules of thumb about "*what* consumers should do"—as opposed to complicated explanations of *why* they should take certain actions—could better guide people in financial decision making. The researchers offered credit union customers two rules for how to use credit cards: "Don't swipe the small stuff. Use cash when it's under $20" and "Credit keeps charging. It adds approximately 20% to the total." In a randomized trial with nearly 14,000 customers, they found that this straightforward guidance increased net saving and reduced debt, especially for younger customers. Moreover, the rules of thumb could be learned and remembered easily (and conveyed extremely cheaply), in contrast to detailed financial education curricula or intensive financial coaching programs.[14]

The Safe-to-Spend feature offered by online bank Simple (owned by BBVA) provides another example. Safe-to-Spend shows customers their balance, minus the amount they've said they want to put aside for goals and any scheduled payments that will be withdrawn from

their account in the next thirty days.[15] The Safe-to-Spend feature provides an example of how banks can use straightforward and clear
cash-flow-based advice to benefit consumers. This model could, in
theory, be developed further by factoring in additional consumer information such as recurring charges, historical earnings, and spending patterns. Over time, people may come to expect that the financial
advice they receive be informed by a more comprehensive view of
their financial lives.

Coping in a World of Uncertainty

The Diaries show the power of a cash-flow view into families' finances.
They reveal instability that is hard to see when measuring income or
spending on an annual basis or comparing point-in-time snapshots
of savings accumulated and debts owed. They document month-
by-month ups and downs of income and spending that complicate
families' already complicated choices. They reveal gaps in employer
practices, government programs, and financial products, which do far
too little to help families negotiate these realities.

One benefit of the Diaries project is that we see across silos. We see
how work and health and education intermingle with finance. We see
how families and friends both complicate and help. We see how even
small interventions can sometimes have big results because of how
things are connected. Scheduling improvements that are intended to
give workers more power and improve family life, for example, also
help them budget and think long term. What seem like small steps can
meaningfully enhance greater stability—and ultimately mobility—for
struggling families. On the flip side, the Diaries show how big, long-
term interventions, like some designed to help build retirement savings, fail for lack of attention to households' short-term constraints.

We have entered a new economic reality, in which even a middle-
class annual income is no longer a guarantee of financial stability. Government, employers, and financial institutions must work together in
new and different ways. The Diaries reveal *why* people are struggling.
Our challenge now is to help people feel more secure and in control,
week by week, month by month.

Notes

Introduction: A Hidden Inequality

1. In 2010–14, 34.5 percent of Ohio adults had attained a high school degree only; 11.2 percent had completed less school than that, and 54.3 percent had an associate degree or higher. "Educational Attainment for Adults Age 25 and Older for the U.S., States, and Counties, 1970–2014," U.S. Department of Agriculture Economic Research Service, http://www.ers.usda.gov/dataFiles/CountyLevelDatasets/Education.xls.

2. Data on manufacturing are from the U.S. Bureau of Labor Statistics, "All Employees: Manufacturing 2016–01: 12,356 Thousands of Persons (+ see more) Monthly, Seasonally Adjusted, MANEMP, Updated: 2016–02–05 7:51 AM CST," https://research.stlouisfed.org/fred2/series/MANEMP. Data on union membership are from the U.S. Bureau of Labor Statistics, "Union Members Survey," January 28, 2016, http://www.bls.gov/news.release/union2.nr0.htm.

3. The life-cycle story is formalized in Brumberg and Modigliani, "Utility Analysis and the Consumption Function."

4. Mullainathan and Shafir, *Scarcity*.

5. Pew Charitable Trusts, "Americans' Financial Security Perception and Reality," 7 (figure 5). The Pew Survey of American Family Finances is a nationally representative survey of 7,845 households conducted in November and December 2014. The survey question was "Which of the following is more important to you (financial stability/moving up the income ladder)?" The Pew brief notes that this is "an increase of 7 percentage points since 2011. This probably reflects families' desire for greater control over their financial situations—something focus group participants mentioned frequently—but it may also indicate a growing recognition that moving up the income ladder can be challenging. In 2009, nearly 4 in 10 Americans (39 percent) felt that it was common for someone to start poor, work hard, and become rich. Five years later, just 23 percent of Americans believe that." The portion of U.S. Financial Diaries (USFD) households that chose financial stability over moving up the income ladder was 78 percent. In the USFD sample, poorer households were more likely to choose mobility, with financial stability becoming more important as households gain income.

6. The research in India was led by Orlanda Ruthven, in Bangladesh by Stuart Rutherford, and in South Africa by Daryl Collins. Rutherford created the original financial diary study, and the three further developed the methodology. Collins led efforts to systematize the method and was an integral member of our team as we brought the financial diaries to the United States. We are greatly indebted to Daryl as a cocreator of the U.S. Financial Diaries project. She and Stuart Rutherford have continued to refine and extend the method in applications around

the world, as have others, including the organization Microfinance Opportunities. For more, see Collins et al., *Portfolios of the Poor*.

7. Data analyses using the Panel Study of Income Dynamics (PSID) are from the PSID website, accessed August 6, 2015, https://psidonline.isr.umich.edu/Publications/Bibliography /search.aspx. Other data sets have also been used to shed light on economic insecurity in America. These include the Survey of Income and Program Participation (SIPP) (see, for example, Wolf et al., "Patterns of Income Instability among Low-Income Families with Children") and the Current Population Survey (see, for example, Hardy and Ziliak, "Decomposing Trends in Income Volatility"). Other specialized surveys, like the Fragile Families Survey run by researchers at Princeton and Columbia, also illuminate the changing situations of American families (see Garfinkel, McLanahan, and Wimer, *Children of the Great Recession*).

8. The data are from a cross-sectional snapshot of earnings of full-time male workers in 2013, taken from the U.S. Census, "Annual Earnings of Men, by Age and Highest Level of Education Completed," table P-32, "Educational Attainment—Full-Time, Year-Round Workers 18 Years Old and Over by Mean Earnings, Age, and Sex: 1991 to 2013," http://www2.census.gov /programs-surveys/cps/tables/time-series/historical-income-people/p32.xls.

9. This depiction comes from Duncan, "The PSID and Me." This story is told in several places. We also draw on Duncan, Hofferth, and Stafford, "Evolution and Change in Family Income, Wealth, and Health."

10. Duncan, Hofferth, and Stafford, "Evolution and Change in Family Income, Wealth, and Health," 164.

11. Ibid., 165.

12. Gottschalk and Moffit, "The Rising Instability of U.S. Earnings."

13. Hacker, "The New Economic Insecurity," 113. The ideas there draw on Hacker, *The Great Risk Shift*.

14. Gosselin, *High Wire*.

15. Among the earliest social scientists to write on precarity is the French social theorist Pierre Bourdieu, who links precarity to the deterioration of social relationships and the rise of social isolation. In an essay translated as "Insecure Jobs Are Everywhere Now," Bourdieu writes: "It has emerged clearly that job insecurity is now everywhere: in the private sector, but also in the public sector, which has greatly increased the number of temporary, part-time or casual positions; in industry, but also in the institutions of cultural production and diffusion—education, journalism, the media, etc." (*Acts of Resistance*, 82).

16. In summarizing the literature, Jonathan Latner shows that all of the major studies find increasing year-to-year volatility in national surveys. Latner, "Income Volatility and Social Stratification." A notable exception to these findings is Dahl, DeLeire, and Schwabish, "Estimates of Year-to-Year Volatility in Earnings and in Household Incomes from Administrative, Survey, and Matched Data," who find that income volatility is flat between 1984 and 2004 in national administrative data on labor earnings.

17. Dynan, Elmendorf, and Sichel, "The Evolution of Household Income Volatility." They measure volatility by the standard deviation of percent changes in annual income across two-year spans.

18. By 2011, the latest year captured in the 2015 Pew study, families on average had a roughly equal chance of experiencing a large gain or a large loss. Previously, gains had outweighed losses as families advanced, but the chance of losses has increased over time. The new data show about one in five households benefiting substantially from one year to the next, with a gain in income larger than 25 percent. But about one in five experiences a loss of the same size. Pew Charitable Trusts, "The Precarious State of Family Balance Sheets," figure 2. The data are from 1979 to 2011.

19. The PSID has been analyzed over and over by different researchers. They agree that income volatility is pronounced but disagree about how quickly it has grown or when. Some recent work suggests that there is considerable heterogeneity, such that evidence for average

volatility may be driven by a small, highly volatile subset of the sample. See Jensen and Shore, "Semiparametric Bayesian Modeling of Income Volatility Heterogeneity." The other PSID analyses cited here suggest more widely felt experiences of volatility.

20. Pew Charitable Trusts, "The Precarious State of Family Balance Sheets," 3.

21. The ability to view distant events through the PSID is captured by the depiction of the PSID as a "telescope on society" in House et al., *A Telescope on Society*.

22. We knew we were undertaking a much more ambitious and complicated way of collecting data than that of a typical survey. The extent that was true soon became clear. The project was designed to take two years, but getting the details right meant spending four years on basic research and most of an additional year verifying numbers.

23. In addition to adjusting for regional differences in cost of living, the SPM framework modifies income to yield a measure of resources available to spend on food, clothing, shelter, and utilities (often abbreviated as FCSU). See Short, "The Supplemental Poverty Measure: 2014."

24. Under those region-specific (SPM) lines, a family in rural Mississippi made up of two adults and two children was considered poor if their yearly income in 2012 was no more than $20,744. In the Cincinnati metro area, the costs of city living push the poverty line up to $23,415 for that family. In New York City, the line was much higher at $29,849. It was higher still in San Jose at $34,296. The lines here are from 2012, the year that is most relevant for the Financial Diaries sample. Separate lines are specified for renters and homeowners. The lines illustrated in the text apply to renters.

25. The real median household income in the United States was $56,516 in 2015 (in 2015 dollars). See Proctor, Semega, and Kollar, *Income and Poverty in the United States: 2015*.

26. To acknowledge the major time commitment and sharing of personal data that went along with participation in the study, families were given up to $600–700 worth of gifts, as well as nonmonetary gifts (e.g., coffee mugs, notepads, and pens), over the course of the study. Money was distributed in the form of gift cards that could be used at a wide variety of retailers. Households were generally not notified about these gifts in advance, nor were gifts provided on a predictable schedule.

27. Attrition slightly changed the composition of the sample, though given the goal of the study (a deep dive, rather than a statistically representative view), not in a material way for our findings. See the U.S. Financial Diaries issue briefs that describe the sample and how we identified and recruited households (www.usfinancialdiaries.org).

Chapter 1: Earning

1. Throughout the book we report net incomes (after all payroll deductions), rather than gross income. There are a variety of reasons for this including the fact that households usually don't think of their income in gross terms. In places where we refer to income in terms of the SPM, we make adjustments to net income according to the SPM guidelines so that our reported figures are consistent with measures of poverty and access to benefits that use SPM thresholds. The SPM framework modifies income to yield a measure of resources available to spend on food, clothing, shelter, and utilities. See Short, "The Supplemental Poverty Measure: 2014."

2. Mullainathan and Shafir, *Scarcity*, 107.

3. Central Mississippi Yellow Pages (2012 Aspenwood Directories, Pittsburg, Kansas).

4. Neshoba County African-American Heritage Driving Tour (pamphlet), http://www.neshobajustice.com/documents/RootsofStruggle.pdf.

5. While the U.S. Supreme Court ruled in the landmark 1954 case, *Brown v. Board of Education of Topeka*, that maintaining segregated schools was unconstitutional, school districts in

the South delayed implementing integration. The delays continued for fifteen years until the Court's 1969 decision in *Alexander v. Holmes County Board of Education*. Immediate integration was ordered. *Alexander v. Holmes* applied to nineteen school districts in Mississippi, including several near Janice's district, but the reach of the ruling stretched across the South.

6.   Because eleven months of the year have a few days more than four weeks, people who are paid biweekly receive three paychecks in a month twice a year, and people who are paid weekly receive five paychecks in a month twice a year. This is a source of income volatility and in theory is predictable. We discuss this in more detail later in the chapter, but our measures of income volatility are not primarily driven by these calendar issues.

7.   Swings, spikes, dips, and the coefficient of variation (CV) were calculated from net income, while excluding tax refunds, in order to focus on earnings, and money given from friends or family, to avoid including informal credit. Details on the methodology and evidence can be found in Morduch and Schneider, "Spikes and Dips" and Hannagan and Morduch, "Income Gains and Month-to-Month Income Volatility." Income from tax refunds acted as another significant income spike for most households in the study and figured prominently in household financial management.

8.   These results, and other sample-wide results unless otherwise noted, include 235 households. For income volatility analyses we exclude household-month observations where spending or income was below $100 and months when households received any tax income. In Figure 1.2 we also exclude four months spread across four households that were in the top 1 percent of spikes, which skew the result for the top income group. These four months have income spikes ranging from 448 to 569 percent of their households' average income. The number of spikes and dips is annualized.

"Poor" households have income below the local threshold established by the U.S. Census Supplemental Poverty Measure; "near-poor" households have incomes 100 percent to 150 percent of the threshold; "low-income" households have incomes 150 percent to 200 percent of the threshold; and "moderate-income" households have incomes 200 percent or more of the threshold.

9.   Short, "The Supplemental Poverty Measure: 2014." This measure takes into account that the cost of living in Mississippi or rural Ohio is much lower than in New York City or San Jose. In 2013, the benchmark poverty threshold for the nation was $21,397 for a family with two adults, two children, and no mortgage.

10.   The bank data included over two years' worth of data on all Chase consumer products, including checking accounts, savings accounts, credit cards, mortgage and home equity loans, and auto loans. The Chase research was led by Diana Farrell and Fiona Grieg. See Farrell and Grieg, "Weathering Volatility" and "Paychecks, Paydays, and the Online Platform Economy."

11.   The Chase report notes: "We acknowledge that our estimates of volatility may be underestimated across the income spectrum but particularly in the lowest quintile because our sampling approach requires that individuals have a minimum of $500 in deposits each month." Farrell and Grieg, "Weathering Volatility," 10.

12.   Farrell and Grieg, "Weathering Volatility," 3; Farrell and Grieg, "Paychecks, Paydays and the Online Platform Economy," 10.

13.   The Federal Reserve's Survey of Household Economics and Decisionmaking (SHED) was first run in September 2013. The survey has been repeated subsequently with different samples and questions. The SHED focuses on adults over age eighteen. An online panel of 50,000 individuals was sampled randomly, and 8,681 were asked to take the survey in 2015. About 65 percent (5,695) agreed. Weights were used to recover nationally representative answers. The survey was administered online, and if households didn't have a computer, they were provided a laptop. The question (I9) is: "In the past year, which of the following best describes how your (and your spouse/partner's) income changes from month to month?" There were 5,642 respondents. Board of Governors of the Federal Reserve System, "Report on the Economic Well-Being of U.S. Households in 2015," 151.

14.   The data here are from 2015, based on publicly available data, weighted to be representative of the broader population using sample weights. Our analysis was aided by a set of extra calculations performed at our request by researchers at the Federal Reserve. We are grateful to David Buchholz, Arturo Gonzalez, and Jeffrey Larrimore of the Federal Reserve's Division of Consumer and Community Affairs for sharing that unpublished information.

15.   In turning to year-to-year volatility, there is also evidence that the poorest households fare the worst. See, in particular, Hardy and Ziliak, "Decomposing Trends in Income Volatility." They show that from 1980 on there has been significant growth in volatility at the bottom and top, in particular (and at other income levels, too, but less dramatically).

16.   Controlling for job changes reduces the CV of earnings from jobs by 33 percent; controlling for volatility in earnings within each job reduces the CV of earnings from jobs by 47 percent. These results exclude households with CV greater than 1.0, leaving a base sample size of 231 households.

17.   Farrell and Grieg, "Paychecks, Paydays, and the Online Platform Economy," 34.

18.   Canada, France, Germany, Italy, Japan, and the United Kingdom have recorded similar declines. See Bailey and Bosworth, "US Manufacturing."

19.   Data for the figure are from Lawrence Katz and Robert Margo, "Technical Change and the Relative Demand for Skilled Labor: The United States in Historical Perspective," table 1.6, panel A, via Autor, "Why Are There Still So Many Jobs?" Autor notes that the Katz and Margo table "is based upon the 1920 through 2000 Census of population IPUMS and 2010 American Community Survey." See also Bouston, Frydman, and Margo, *Human Capital in History*, 15–57.

20.   Autor and Dorn, "The Growth of Low-Skill Service Jobs and the Polarization of the U.S. Labor Market."

21.   Reich, *Beyond Outrage*.

22.   Bureau of Labor Statistics, "Union Members—2015."

23.   Desilver, "Job Categories Where Union Membership Has Fallen Off Most."

24.   One overview for general readers of the evolution of thinking in manufacturing during this time period is Womack, Jones, and Roos, *The Machine That Changed the World*.

25.   Production jobs means workers actually employed in the manufacturing process, as opposed to managers, and clerical positions in the sector. Nicholson, "An Update on Temporary Help in Manufacturing."

26.   For a detailed look at how jobs themselves have changed, see Kalleberg, *Good Jobs, Bad Jobs*.

27.   Comin, Groshen, and Rabin, "Turbulent Firms, Turbulent Wages?"

28.   Strain, "Do Volatile Firms Pay Volatile Earnings?"

29.   Bureau of Labor Statistics, "Characteristics of Minimum Wage Workers, 2015."

30.   Haley-Lock and Ewert, "Waiting for the Minimum"; Lambert, "Passing the Buck."

31.   Roughly equal shares of hourly and nonhourly workers had steady hours, 43 percent and 39 percent, respectively. Those employees typically worked forty to forty-four hours per week.

32.   Lambert, Fugiel, and Henly explore three dimensions of work schedules: (1) advance schedule notice, (2) fluctuating work hours, and (3) schedule control. While lack of control is a problem, evidence of steadiness can be good or bad. They note on page 13 that: "Limited advance schedule notice and hour fluctuations may be especially problematic for employees with limited say over the timing of their work schedules. When workers control their work schedules, variations in the number of hours worked may reflect employee-driven flexibility, a job quality highly valued by today's workers." On the other hand, steady hours may be a mixed blessing, sometimes reflecting "rigid job requirements that do not yield when personal matters require attention."

33.   The Ford Foundation summarizes this research on its Equals Change blog. Wann, "American Tipping Is Rooted in Slavery."

34.   Morrison and Gallagher Robbins, "Chartbook: The Women in the Low-Wage Workforce May Not Be Who You Think."

35. "Realizing the Dream."

36. Bureau of Labor Statistics, "Persons at Work in Nonagricultural Industries by Age, Sex, Race, Hispanic or Latino Ethnicity, Marital Status, and Usual Full or Part-Time Status."

37. Fox, "The Rise of the 1099 Economy."

38. "The Costs of Nonpayment."

39. Fox, "A College Degree Just Might Get You a Side Job."

40. Farrell and Grieg, "Paychecks, Paydays, and the Online Platform Economy."

41. Bureau of Labor Statistics, "Persons at Work in Nonagricultural Industries by Age, Sex, Race, Hispanic or Latino Ethnicity, Marital Status, and Usual Full or Part-Time Status."

42. We considered U.S. Financial Diaries households with two earners. We found that "the coefficient of variation of earnings from the primary earner is just 5 percent higher than that of the household, due to the labor income of the secondary earner, which indicates relatively little volatility-reduction from secondary workers on average." See Hannagan and Morduch, "Income Gains and Month-to-Month Income Volatility."

43. The Aspen Institute's EPIC program has published an overview of research on income volatility and its effects, which is a useful resource. Expanding Prosperity Impact Collaborative, "Income Volatility: A Primer."

44. Mullainathan and Shafir, *Scarcity.*

45. Henly and Lambert, "Unpredictable Work Timing in Retail Jobs."

46. Kantor, "Working Anything But 9 to 5."

47. Recent evidence shows that people who are more likely to face income uncertainty or to become liquidity constrained tend to be more risk averse. See Guiso and Paiella, "Risk Aversion, Wealth, and Background Risk."

48. Wolf et al., "Patterns of Income Instability among Low- and Middle-Income Households with Children."

49. Heckman, "The Economics and the Econometrics of Human Development."

50. Desmond, *Evicted.*

51. See Halliday, "Income Volatility and Health"; Smith, Stoddard, and Barnes, "Why the Poor Get Fat"; and Sanger-Katz, "The Big Problem with High Health Care Deductibles."

52. Orhun and Palazzolo, "Frugality Is Hard to Afford."

53. Lambert and Henly, "Double Jeopardy."

54. Ben-Ishai, "Volatile Job Schedules and Access to Public Benefits"; Lambert, Fugiel, and Henly, "Precarious Work Schedules among Early-Career Employees in the US."

55. Khullar, "How to Stop Bouncing between Insurance Programs under Obamacare."

Chapter 2: Spending

1. The median income in the United States was $52,280 in 2012 (the year we tracked the Johnsons' finances). In Sarah's area, the median family income was about $47,000. U.S. Census, http://quickfacts.census.gov.

2. The Johnsons also received occasional child support from Mathew's father and from the mother of Sam's daughter Anne; in our study year, those payments totaled $3,500. The couple also benefited from an income tax refund of another $3,500.

3. While the Johnsons' income was relatively steady from month to month, they had some months with larger inflows, mainly due to the receipt of student loan payments, timed to meet school expenses. They also received a tax refund in the spring. The Johnsons are unusual in having relatively steady income but variable expenses; in the Federal Reserve's 2015 survey, only 5 percent of households that reported steady income also had notably variable expenses (Board

of Governors of the Federal Reserve System, "Report on the Economic Well-Being of U.S. Households in 2015," 18).

4.   Sarah doesn't automate most of her bills, in order to have more control over which she pays when. Her payments depend on her priorities each month and how much cash she has on hand. Her paycheck arrives every two weeks, sometimes at the same time as Sam's, but not always. Two months a year, she receives an "extra" check because of when paydays fall. About half of the Diaries households share this pattern, with one member's paychecks arriving twice each month and the other's paychecks every other week. Sarah finds the months in which she and Sam are paid at different times to be much easier than the months in which checks pile up.

5.   Elizabeth Warren and Amelia Warren Tyagi describe this tension in their 2003 book, *The Two-Income Trap*. Based on an analysis of bankruptcy filings, they find that the rising costs of education, housing, and health care have outpaced the gains families have made by sending two workers into the workforce. People do not spend more proportionally on discretionary spending than they did in prior decades, yet they find themselves with less of a cushion between earnings and expenses. And because most families must have two earners in order to make ends meet, they spend more on child care, health care, and elder care and have more potential for financial challenges as a result of job losses.

6.   The Johnsons had just two automatically debited monthly payments: $7 for Netflix and $35 for a life insurance premium. (Sarah was careful not to commit to more.) The rest of their spending varied. They bought gas every few days, in $20 or $40 increments, rather than filling up the tank. In part to manage cash flow, they went to the grocery store to buy food almost every day, rather than shopping in bulk.

7.   During the Diaries interviews families often read directly from their bank or loan statements or receipts; however, not all of the recent household spending was easy for respondents to recall, and sometimes the spending of other family members was unknown. We estimate that the USFD data understate annual household spending, relative to annual household income, by approximately 10 percent for the average household. To avoid bias in the results, we checked the spending data against our other information about the household, asked the household follow-up questions if needed, tried to highlight only the largest instances of verifiable spending volatility, compared results across a variety of sample definitions, or else showed results that would only strengthen along the expected direction of bias.

8.   Households below the poverty line experienced an average of 2.2 months of unusually high spending (this is in addition to the month in which tax refunds arrive, which is typically also a month of unusually high spending). Households above the poverty line averaged 1.9 months with expense spikes.

9.   Board of Governors of the Federal Reserve System, "Report on the Economic Well-Being of U.S. Households in 2015," question I11, appendix C. The nationally representative survey included 5,642 respondents.

10.   The comparison of spending spikes and income spikes excludes months with tax refunds, but a similar result arises when months with tax refunds are included.

11.   The results on bill payment behavior should be considered suggestive, since data error could lead to unreported bill payments among Diaries households. Still, we find ample evidence of irregularity in bill payment in general, including changes in the part of the month in which bills are paid, instances of unusually large payments that would compensate for missed bill payment elsewhere, and reports of lateness, late fees, and threats of utilities disconnections or asset repossession.

12.   Pew documents that 60 percent of families experienced a major expense "shock" in a twelve-month period. Pew Charitable Trusts, "How Do Families Cope with Financial Shocks?" 5, figure 1.

13.   Board of Governors of the Federal Reserve System, "Report on the Economic Well-Being of U.S. Households in 2015." Data on medical expenses come from p. 153, question

E2-E2B, appendix C. The follow-up question on the average cost of the unexpected expense (1,349 observations) found that the mean was $2,782 and the median was $1,200. The follow-up question on unpaid bills and related debt (1,349 observations) found that 46 percent had an unpaid balance or owed money due to unexpected health expenses. Data on seeking medical care come from pp. 25–26 and figure 14.

14.   In a different analysis, we asked whether removing a big expense category might turn the spending spike into a normal spending month (within 25 percent of average). That was true for 44 percent of the spikes, so it remained that most of the time spikes had multiple causes.

15.   Hacker and O'Leary, *Shared Risk, Shared Responsibility*; Hacker, *The Great Risk Shift*, 3.

16.   The rate of growth is slowing and came down markedly in the three years after the Affordable Care Act. According to David I. Auerbach and Arthur L. Kellermann, "Health care expenditures, including insurance premiums, out-of-pocket expenditures, and taxes devoted to health care, nearly doubled between 1999 and 2009. This increase has substantially eroded what an average family has left to spend on everything else, leaving them with only $95 more per month than in 1999. Had health care costs tracked the rise in the Consumer Price Index, rather than outpacing it, an average American family would have had an additional $450 per month—more than $5,000 per year—to spend on other priorities" ("A Decade of Health Care Cost Growth Has Wiped Out Real Income Gains for an Average U.S. Family"). Also see S. Collins et al., "National Trends in the Cost of Employer Health Insurance Coverage, 2003–2013."

17.   Pew Charitable Trusts, "Household Expenditures and Income."

18.   Newberry, "Dodd-Frank Redlined America's Poorest Neighborhoods"; Salmon, "How One Small Company Is Saving the Homes of Poor Americans"; "American House Prices: Realty Check."

19.   National Center for Education Statistics, Fast Facts: http://nces.ed.gov/fastfacts/display .asp?id=76; Quinton, "The High Cost of Higher Education."

20.   These data are from the Center for Law and Social Policy (CLASP), "College Costs Rising Four Times Faster than Income, Two and a Half Times Faster than Pell." The report explains: "Financial aid has not filled the growing gap, and 'unmet financial need'—the share of college costs not covered by financial aid or what the family is expected to contribute—has risen sharply. According to data from the National Center for Education Statistics, half of community college students had unmet financial need in 2007–08, averaging $4,500 annually, as did 43 percent of students at public four-year colleges, with their unmet need averaging $6,400 per year."

21.   Mishel, Gould, and Bivens, "Wage Stagnation in Nine Charts"; Tankersley, "Middle Class Incomes Had Their Fastest Growth on Record Last Year."

22.   Data on changes in household median income are from table A-1 of Proctor, Semega, and Kollar, *Income and Poverty in the United States: 2015*, 23. The 2015 data showed a large jump, 5.2 percent improvement over 2014.

23.   Orman, *Suze Orman's Action Plan*, 106.

24.   Ibid., 107–12.

25.   Ibid., 113–14.

26.   The conflation of thrift with morality is a running theme in Horowitz, *The Morality of Spending*.

27.   Mishel, Gould, and Bivens, "Wage Stagnation in Nine Charts."

Chapter 3: Smoothing and Spiking

1.   The idea is associated with work by the economist Milton Friedman, and the theory that describes perfectly achieved, forward-looking smoothing is often described as the Permanent

Income Hypothesis. Friedman describes the issues and presents data in Friedman, *A Theory of the Consumption Function*. More recent work investigates precautionary motives for saving, liquidity constraints, and behavioral biases. See, for example, Carroll, "Buffer Stock Saving and the Life Cycle/Permanent Income Hypothesis" and Parker and Preston, "Precautionary Saving and Consumption Fluctuations."

2.   The data are from Board of Governors of the Federal Reserve System, "Report on the Economic Well-Being of U.S. Households in 2015," table 2, p. 8 (with our aggregation). The 76 million adults figure is from p. 7 of the report. Financial struggles are reported by 29 percent of white respondents, 39 percent of black (non-Hispanic) respondents, and 37 percent of Hispanic respondents.

3.   See the Consumer Financial Protection Bureau report "Financial Well-Being: The Goal of Financial Education." For a related view, see the work on "financial health" by the Center for Financial Services Innovation (CFSI). The broad point is that yearly income and spending are important, but they are important instrumentally. What we really care about is whether families are financially okay, which has both an objective component (Can they consume what they need when they need it?) and a subjective one (Do they feel financially secure and in control?) CFSI defines financial health to be when a person's day-to-day financial systems enable him or her to build resilience and to take advantage of opportunity. According to CFSI's Consumer Financial Health Study, approximately 57 percent of Americans lack financial health, including one-third of households with incomes greater than $60,000 per year, while one-third of households with incomes lower than $60,000 achieve financial health.

4.   Rising income inequality has been well documented, as has wage stagnation over the last decades. See Proctor, Semega, and Kollar, *Income and Poverty in the United States: 2015* and Mishel, Gould, and Bivens, "Wage Stagnation in Nine Charts."

5.   A 2015 analysis by William Emmons and Bryan Noeth of the Center for Household Financial Security at the Federal Reserve Bank of St. Louis investigates the disparities in wealth accumulation by age, education, and race, finding that about a quarter of the nation's households, generally those headed by someone who is middle-aged or older, white or Asian, and with a college degree alone or with a graduate or professional degree and who earns an above-average income, owns two-thirds of the economy's wealth. The remaining three-quarters of families are typically younger, less educated, and black or Hispanic. They earn average or below-average incomes, make less conservative financial choices, and have accumulated little or no wealth; they own just a third of the nation's total wealth. See Emmons and Noeth, "Race, Ethnicity, and Wealth."

6.   In 1996, 68 percent of poor families with children received assistance through the Temporary Assistance for Needy Families (TANF) program (often simply termed "welfare"), while by 2014, only 23 percent did; see Center for Budget and Policy Priorities, "Chart Book: TANF at 20." The deterioration of the safety net for the very poorest is described in Edin and Shaefer, *$2 a Day*. See also Hardy and Ziliak, "Decomposing Trends in Income Volatility" and Hardy, "Income Instability and the Response of the Safety Net." Hardy documents the instability reduction of government transfers but notes that "although the largest instability reductions occur among the poor, since 1980 the safety net appears less responsive to instability for the bottom income quintile, female-headed families, and black families."

7.   The numbers are from the 2015 Federal Deposit Insurance Corporation (FDIC), *Survey of Unbanked and Underbanked Households* (October 2016, https://www.fdic.gov/householdsur vey), which found that 7 percent of households in the United States were unbanked in 2015, or roughly 9 million households. Another 19.9 percent (24.5 million households) were "under-banked" in 2015, which means that they had a bank account but also used alternative financial services such as money orders, check cashers, or payday loans. Households with lower incomes, younger households, and black and Hispanic households consistently have higher unbanked rates than the overall population, and this remained true in 2015, in spite of declining rates among these groups. The most commonly cited reason for not having an account was "Do not

have enough money to keep in an account." Importantly, the 2015 survey added a new question about the "potential influence of income volatility on the ways households manage their finances." Those with income that "varied somewhat from month to month" had an unbanked rate of 8.7 percent, while those with income that "varied a lot from month to month" had an unbanked rate of 12.9 percent, compared to an unbanked rate of 5.7 percent among those with incomes that were "about the same each month."

8.   As in Figure 1.2, these results exclude four months spread across four households that were in the top 1 percent of spikes, which skew the result for the top income group. These four months have income spikes ranging from 448 to 569 percent of their households' average income. The results include all 235 households. The analysis here provides a simple way to visualize consumption smoothing. We also ran formal econometric tests of consumption smoothing based on linearized Euler equations. We found results similar in spirit to those in Figure 3.3. As we find here, the broader economics literature generally finds that households smooth consumption fairly well, but low-income households face liquidity constraints such that they still face considerable volatility of consumption. For a summary of the economic approach, see, for example, Jappelli and Pistaferri, "The Consumption Response to Income Changes." See also Deaton, *Understanding Consumption*.

9.   This question is asked on a series of surveys by different organizations, as is the question about having a rainy-day reserve. The Pew Charitable Trusts have a very useful collection of briefs on this topic ("The Role of Emergency Savings in Family Financial Security"); see especially "What Resources Do Families Have for Financial Emergencies?" We've also benefited from conversations with Pew's Clint Key. See also the excellent chapters collected in Collins, *A Fragile Balance*.

10.   The results are reported in Board of Governors of the Federal Reserve System, "Report on the Economic Well-Being of U.S. Households in 2015," 152. Survey of Household Economics and Decisionmaking question EF3 ("Suppose that you have an emergency expense that costs $400. Based on your current financial situation, how would you pay for this expense? If you would use more than one method to cover this expense, please select all that apply"). There were 5,642 respondents, and 1.1 percent refused to answer. These results are unweighted. When we obtained the raw data we generated results with sample weights to better approximate the population distribution. We found that 55 percent could handle the emergency with money on hand, 35 percent could come up with $400 with money on hand, and 10 percent said that there was just no way to come up with it.

11.   Authors' calculations of 2015 Federal Reserve Survey of Household Economics and Decisionmaking.

12.   The data here are from 2015, based on publicly available data, and weighted to be representative of the broader population using sample weights.

13.   Board of Governors of the Federal Reserve System, "Report on the Economic Well-Being of U.S. Households in 2015," 152. Survey of Household Economics and Decisionmaking question EF1 ("Have you set aside emergency or rainy day funds that would cover your expenses for 3 months in case of sickness, job loss, economic downturn, or other emergencies?"). There were 5,642 respondents, and 0.7 percent refused to answer.

14.   Board of Governors of the Federal Reserve System, "Report on the Economic Well-Being of U.S. Households in 2015," 152. Survey of Household Economics and Decisionmaking question EF2 ("If you were to lose your main source of income [e.g., job, government benefits], could you cover your expenses for 3 months by borrowing money, using savings, selling assets, or borrowing from friends/family?"). There were 2,931 respondents, and 0.9 percent refused to answer.

15.   The calculation of the 32 percent figure: 52 percent of households reported having inadequate saving, and, of those, 62 percent reported having no other means to come up with three months' worth of money. The calculation is 52 percent multiplied by 62 percent = 32.2.

The data here are from 2015, based on publicly available data, and weighted to be representative of the broader population using sample weights.

16.   Economists at Princeton and New York University estimate that about two-thirds of households living "hand to mouth" (their version of "paycheck to paycheck") are in fact relatively wealthy. These "wealthy hand-to-mouth" households are often young, and much of their asset holding is in illiquid forms (in housing and retirement accounts, for example), which keep the money out of easy reach. The study models broad trends using yearly longitudinal data from the University of Michigan Panel Study of Income Dynamics. It thus does not directly relate to the within-year patterns in the U.S. Financial Diaries data. From month to month, households may be able to save, borrow, and otherwise handle cash-flow imbalances, even if it is difficult to address the major year-to-year shocks that show up in the PSID data. See Kaplan, Violante, and Weidner, "The Wealthy Hand to Mouth."

17.   Some Diaries families reported more meaningful emergency savings balances than others when we asked them about it at one point during the study year. We found evidence that these households experienced smaller spending swings in months when their income spiked or dipped. But, importantly, families reporting zero emergency savings were also able to reduce the size of their spending swings during months with income spikes or dips. The implication would seem to be: having savings may help, but saving is not the only coping mechanism that households use. We can't say anything about causality here, however. Families with more emergency savings may smooth more of their income spikes and dips for reasons independent of their saving balances. They might, for example, be more disciplined in general or have fewer other demands on their resources. The clearer point is that a large pot of emergency savings does not appear necessary for achieving at least some smoothing. Having zero savings does not mean that families have no way to achieve greater security or are living paycheck to paycheck. Other tools, particularly borrowing, are important and often used.

18.   Studies establishing week-by-week and month-by-month illiquidity include Stephens, " '3rd of tha Month' "; Stephens, "Paycheque Receipt and the Timing of Consumption"; Mastrobuoni and Weinberg, "Heterogeneity in Intra-Monthly Consumption Patterns, Self-Control, and Savings at Retirement"; and Zhang, "Consumption Responses to Pay Frequency."

19.   The importance of the exact timing of paychecks can also be seen in the way that Sarah and Sam Johnson (introduced in chapter 2) managed their bills. Sarah had a straightforward system for paying their bills. Sam was paid twice monthly, on the first and the fifteenth of the month. Sarah allocated his first check to their mortgage and his second check to their car and insurance payments. She paid other bills with whatever was left over plus her own paycheck. Sarah's paycheck came every two weeks (rather than on the first and fifteenth), so sometimes it arrived at the same time as Sam's but other times not. (About half of the Diaries households share this pattern, with one member's job paying twice each month and the other's job paying every other week.) Sarah found that the months in which her paycheck alternated with Sam's were much easier to handle than the months when the checks piled up on top of each other, leaving wider spaces in between.

20.   Federal Reserve Survey of Household Economics and Decisionmaking question I12, appendix C. The question covered 3,069 respondents affected by income and expense volatility.

21.   Greene and Luo, "Consumers' Use of Credit Protection."

22.   This analysis is ongoing and draws on 118 households for which we have specific information on the timing of rent payments and income. While the Financial Diaries show that most families, even those with relatively low incomes, and little in savings balances, are able to pay most of the bills, most of the time, they also show that many families are coming up short at least some of the time. (As noted in the text, about a third reported a disconnection from utilities or cable, repossession of assets, or eviction, or a threat of one of these actions during the year.) That doesn't always mean that the families forgo needed consumption. Sometimes there are other ways, even when all other alternatives have been tapped, to shift spending. One

consumption need that is tough to forgo is heat in the winter. Recognizing the potential harm to low-income families, many states, including New York and Ohio, limit utilities from disconnecting service during winter months. Some households use these disconnection moratoriums as a spending safety valve, skipping a payment in these months. Beyond utility payments, we see households missing bills or paying bills late—often several months late—as a way to smooth consumption even when they can't come up with the money to spend. Missing a bill payment is a symptom of not being able to spend when needed. But it can also be a strategy to smooth consumption; it can be seen as an involuntary short-term loan from the company to the customer, another way for households to juggle money to insulate overall consumption from income spikes and dips or unexpected spending needs.

23. See Collins et al., *Portfolios of the Poor.*

24. The details are from email with Quinten Farmer, September 13, 2016. Farmer's quote and background on the birth of Even are from Giridharadas, "Want a Steady Income?"

25. Note that Even was part of the inaugural cohort of the Financial Solutions Lab, an incubator for financial technology innovators sponsored by the JPMorgan Chase Foundation and run by CFSI, where Schneider works. We have no financial interest in Even.

26. We have described Even's process as we understand it from public documents available in July 2016. We have also benefited from conversations with Jane Leibrock of Even. The app was not available to the public when the book was written and, given that it was still being tested, the app's features, rules, and processes may have changed by the time this book is published. Several important features of the app at the time of writing: the company never withdraws funds that would push users below their average earnings. If it withdraws funds for savings, the app prompts users to approve the amount to be saved. The extra money given in boosts is interest free, with no set timeline for repayment, although users can only get two boosts in a row before having to repay. Even, so far, is not set to work with everyone. While they presently review all applications, their terms of service state: "There are a few reasons we might not be able to let you use Even. These include: 1. If you earn too much, or too little money. 2. If you do not get paid by direct deposit. 3. If we aren't able to access enough of your income history to calculate your Even Pay. 4. If you just started a new job. 5. If your paychecks don't arrive on a regular schedule (like every other Friday, or the 1st and 15th of each month). 6. If you don't have a single employer that is the source of at least 50% of your income. 7. If your account is overdrawn at the time you sign up for Even, or was very recently overdrawn." More is available on Even's "frequently asked questions" page. https://even.com/terms and https://even.com/faq.

27. Jon Schlossberg connects the idea of the company to broader ideas in social science in "Why."

28. Ogden, "The IRS's Secret, Successful Low-Income Savings Program."

29. The possibilities provided by tax refunds were a common theme in the Financial Diaries. Households often filed their tax returns early in order to hasten the time until the refund check arrived. Often families had figured out how to spend the refund well before it was received. The ambitions (and conflicts) of 115 low-income respondents who received tax refunds are described in Halpern-Meekin et al., *It's Not Like I'm Poor.*

30. To add discipline, Janice opened a Christmas Club account at the bank, into which she deposited $15 a week from her paycheck. The account is limited so that withdrawals are available only during the Christmas season.

31. At the top of Janice's list is her monthly car payment ($345) and payment for the trailer she lives in ($390). After those bills get paid, she turns to electricity ($260 a month give or take, depending on the season) and $40 a week for gas money. Everything else comes afterward: cable, phone, water, and groceries.

Chapter 4: Saving

1.   CompStat, Week 8/15/2016—8/21/2016, vol. 23, no. 33.

2.   The annual sum is aggregated up from $11.25 an hour. In a 2015 interview, Robert reported a higher gross income because he'd received another raise since we last collected data from him.

3.   In 2013, the federal poverty line was $11,490 for a single adult; the SPM for a single adult renter in New York City was $13,384. See http://aspe.hhs.gov/poverty/13poverty.cfm#thresholds and http://www.census.gov/hhes/povmeas/methodology/supplemental/overview.html.

4.   These questions were taken from Lusardi and Mitchell, "Financial Literacy and Retirement Planning." For more on Lusardi's financial literacy research, see Dubner, "Are We a Nation of Financial Illiterates?"

5.   The analysis is from Lusardi and Mitchell, "The Economic Importance of Financial Literacy."

6.   Vanguard Funds, "The Power of Compounding."

7.   Ramsey, "How Teens Can Become Millionaires."

8.   The stock market increased about 13 percent per year between May 2010 and May 2015 as the economy climbed out of a recession, but going back twenty-five years, the average annual return was about 7 percent.

9.   Orman, "Suze Orman's Easy Money To-Do List."

10.   This section draws on conversations with Ray Boshara, Frank DeGiovanni, and Bob Friedman. Boshara and Michael Sherraden have written not only about the rationale for asset building but also about the politics and history of the asset-building movement, and we have benefited from their written insights. See Sherraden, *Assets and the Poor*; Sherraden, "From Research to Policy"; and Boshara, "From Asset Building to Balance Sheets."

11.   Bob Friedman first told us this story. It is also in Miller-Adams, *Owning Up*.

12.   The $1,000 asset limit was introduced in Ronald Reagan's first budget in 1981, and asset limits remain about $2,000–3,000 in most states. See Hamilton, "The Forgotten 1980s Rule That's Hurting Poor Families' Savings" and Ratcliffe et al., "Asset Limits, SNAP Participation, and Financial Stability." The Corporation for Enterprise Development has been a longstanding advocate for lifting asset limits.

13.   The distribution of tax subsidies is from Harris et al., "Tax Subsidies for Asset Development." The Corporation for Enterprise Development also provides useful analysis on who gets help saving and who doesn't.

14.   The American Dream Demonstration was funded by some of America's leading philanthropic organizations: the Ford Foundation, Charles Stewart Mott Foundation, Joyce Foundation, FB Heron Foundation, John D. and Catherine MacArthur Foundation, Citi Foundation, Fannie Mae Foundation, Levi Strauss Foundation, Ewing Marion Kauffman Foundation, Rockefeller Foundation, Metropolitan Life Foundation, and the Moriah Fund (Schreiner and Sherraden, *Can the Poor Save?* x–xi).

15.   The full list is: Fond Du Lac, Wisconsin; Ithaca, New York; Oakland, California; Washington, D.C.; Austin, Texas; Barre, Vermont; Tulsa, Oklahoma; Kansas City, Missouri; Portland, Oregon; Berea, Kentucky; Indianapolis, Indiana; and Chicago, Illinois. Details are from Schreiner and Sherraden, *Can the Poor Save?* chap. 3. A broad set of studies of the Demonstration can be found in McKernan and Sherraden, *Asset Building and Low-Income Families*.

16.   Most were women living in cities, between the ages of twenty and fifty; about half were African American. About 40 percent had attended at least some college. Only about half had incomes below the poverty line, but many were close to being poor. By design, all participants had jobs, at least at the start. Schreiner and Sherraden, *Can the Poor Save?* 82–89, 122.

17.   Data are from Schreiner and Sherraden, *Can the Poor Save?* 123–24. The study covered the time of enrollment in the IDA program through the end of 2001 (pp. 47, 82). The enrollment period ran from the middle of 1997 through December 1999, although seventeen extra enrollments happened in 2000 (p. 82). In part of the Tulsa site, data were collected through October 2003 (p. 47). No study was able to say much about the existence of a hypothesized "asset effect," with psychological and social changes flowing from becoming an asset holder, either positively or negatively. Some broader outcomes were found several years after the experiment ended, including outcomes on home repairs and education, especially for males; see Sherraden, "Asset Building Research and Policy."

18.   Schreiner and Sherraden, *Can the Poor Save?* 138.

19.   Ibid.

20.   Ibid., 138–39.

21.   Fellowes and Willemin, "The Retirement Breach in Defined Contribution Plans." See also Munnell and Webb, "The Impact of Leakages on 401(k)/IRA Assets," which proposes responding to leakage by making it even harder to withdraw from retirement accounts by limiting withdrawals to only truly "unpredictable" events and eliminating the ability to cash out when leaving a job.

22.   The quote is from Stephen P. Utkus, the director of retirement research at Vanguard, quoted in Lieber, "Combating a Flood of Early 401(k) Withdrawals."

23.   "Personal Saving Rate," U.S. Bureau of Economic Analysis, https://fred.stlouisfed.org /series/PSAVERT.

24.   See, for example, Morrissey, "The State of American Retirement."

25.   This is the definition of being "liquid asset poor" measured by the Corporation for Enterprise Development Asset Opportunity Scorecard. The national data align with the U.S. Financial Diaries data: nearly half of the families in the USFD sample have nothing put aside explicitly for emergencies.

26.   There's a chance that Robert will get his deposit back one day but only when he moves.

27.   The data cover all non-retirement bank accounts, notably checking and saving accounts. If we just focus on saving accounts, 80 percent of the funds were expected to be spent within three years. Two-thirds of the U.S. Financial Diaries core sample had no retirement account. Of the one-third of households with accounts, total retirement savings averaged $8,816. Some have zero dollar balances, and, excluding them, the average household's retirement holdings is $14,426.

28.   Deaton, *Understanding Consumption*. For a broad view, see Armendáriz and Morduch, *Economics of Microfinance*, 169–210.

29.   A New York City–sponsored savings program called $aveNYC, also offered at free tax preparation sites, was viewed as a terrific success. It hired enthusiastic, trained salespeople, included a $2 match for every $1 saved, and had take-up rates of 9 percent. $aveUSA, an expansion of $aveNYC, had take-up rates of 6 to 13 percent.

30.   Disclosure: CFSI, where Rachel Schneider works, is an investor in Core VC, which is an investor in Banking Up. We do not have a direct financial interest in any of the companies.

31.   One-third were single with dependents. And three-quarters had less than $5,000 in household savings and assets. Commonwealth was also managing to reach a population that could use help saving. Almost 40 percent said they had no other emergency savings, and 30 percent said they had less than $100. Almost a quarter of Rainy Day Reserve savers said that traditional savings methods had not worked for them in the past.

32.   Interview with Tim Flacke, March 12, 2015.

33.   Karlan and Linden, "Loose Knots."

34.   Brune et al., "Facilitating Savings for Agriculture."

35.   Dupas and Robinson, "Why Don't the Poor Save More?"

36.　By keeping part of his money with his mother, Robert may also be keeping it from the view of the government or creditors. Robert does not describe his strategy that way, but it is one motivation for saving workarounds.

37.　Participants increased their savings rates from 3.5 percent to 13.6 percent in under four years. We do not know whether participants withdraw from their retirement savings more or less often than non-participants. See Thaler and Benartzi, "Save More Tomorrow™."

38.　This idea is developed by Stuart Rutherford in *The Poor and Their Money*.

39.　See Morduch, Ogden, and Schneider, "Thriving But Still Vulnerable in the U.S."

40.　According to a 2016 survey, 24 percent of people with direct deposit split their payroll deposits between different bank accounts. National Automated Clearing House Association, "Beyond Simple and Safe."

41.　The Corporation for Enterprise Development website features a list of programs that handle tax-time savings at http://cfed.org/blog/inclusiveeconomy/building_financial_capability _at_tax_time/.

Chapter 5: Borrowing

1.　Pew Charitable Trusts, "Everything You Wanted to Know about Debt," tables 2 and 8. Also note: "Debt's relationship to the stability of American families' balance sheets is often unexpected. For the silent generation, those with the least debt are among the most financially secure; among Gen Xers and millennials, the most financially stable are also those with the most debt" (12).

2.　Graeber, *Debt*, 8–13.

3.　Maas, "Credit Scoring and the Credit-Underserved Population."

4.　The most common credit score is the FICO score, which uses a scale of 300–850. Above 720 is considered "excellent" and enables borrowers to access a wide range of credit products at lower interest rates. Below 600 is considered "poor" and leaves borrowers with far fewer, far more expensive credit options. Additional information on credit scores can be found on the Federal Information Commission website, https://www.consumer.ftc.gov/articles/0152-credit -scores.

5.　Pew Charitable Trusts, "The Complex Story of American Debt."

6.　Pew Research Center, "The Rising Cost of Not Going to College."

7.　Graeber, *Debt*, 40.

8.　"Consumer Credit Outstanding (Levels)," Historical Data, http://www.federalreserve .gov/releases/g19/HIST/cc_hist_mt_levels.html.

9.　Ibid.

10.　Lewis Nier, "The Shadow of Credit."

11.　See, for example, Armendáriz and Morduch, *Economics of Microfinance* and Collins et al., *Portfolios of the Poor*, chap. 6.

12.　Traub, "Discredited."

13.　Breevort, Grimm, and Kambara, "Data Point."

14.　The Federal Reserve's SHED found that 50 percent of credit card holders carried a balance at most once during the previous year. The data here are from 2015, based on publicly available data, and weighted to be representative of the population using sample weights. The Federal Reserve Board's Survey of Consumer Finances, conducted every three years, found in 2013 that 64 percent of credit card holders did not carry a balance. Board of Governors of the Federal Reserve System, "Changes in U.S. Family Finances from 2010 to 2013," table 5, p. 29.

15.   Thirty-two percent of SHED respondents in 2015 with income less than $25,000 a year, and carrying a balance on at least one credit card, paid the minimum most of the time. In contrast, only 17 percent of balance-carrying SHED respondents with income over $75,000 a year did the same. These figures are based on publicly available data, and weighted to be representative of the broader population using sample weights.

16.   "Waiving, Not Drowning."

17.   Flannery and Samolyk show that the loan loss rate is 59 percent for businesses older than four years and 86 percent for younger businesses. See Flannery and Samolyk, "Scale Economies at Payday Loan Stores," 3. Many sources have explored the financial model of payday lending. See also Caskey, "The Economics of Payday Lending" and Wolff, "The Cumulative Costs of Predatory Practices."

18.   Simon, "Mortgage Lenders Loosen Standards."

19.   For more information on how FICO scores are calculated, see http://www.myfico.com/crediteducation/whatsinyourscore.aspx.

20.   Other variables include the length of the borrower's credit history; his or her mix of credit cards, mortgage loans, and other forms of credit; and whether the borrower has opened several new accounts in a short period.

21.   The CARD Act of 2009 requires that credit card lenders disclose how long it will take to pay off current debt by making only the minimum payment, if ever. In practice this has meant that many lenders amortize the debt over eight years. Of course, if new debt is incurred, that can stretch out the length of time required to pay off the balance.

22.   Turner and Walker, "Predicting Financial Account Delinquencies with Utility and Telecom Payment Data."

23.   Using a framework that combines insights from psychology and economics, Ru and Schoar find that credit card issuers target less-educated customers with pitches like lower introductory interest rates but then charge higher late and over-limit fees. Better-educated customers are targeted with lower fees and somewhat higher interest rates. See Ru and Schoar, "Do Credit Card Companies Screen for Behavioral Biases?"

24.   Oak and Swamy, "Only Twice as Much."

25.   Ackerman, "Interest Rates and the Law"; Huddleston, "The Poorhouse."

26.   The initial framework endorsed by the G20 Finance Ministers and Central Bank Governors in 2011 can be found here: https://www.oecd.org/g20/topics/financial-sector-reform/48892010.pdf. It states: "Depending on the nature of the transaction and based on information primarily provided by customers, financial services providers should assess the financial capabilities, situation and needs of their customers before agreeing to provide them with a product, advice or service." The OECD Task Force on Financial Consumer Protection has sought to further explain what is meant by its framework, as well as offer examples of both "common" and "innovative/emerging" practice in line with the framework in later meetings and documents such as this one: https://www.oecd.org/finance/financial-education/G20EffectiveApproachesFCP.pdf. CFSI has also developed standards for the delivery of financial services and has applied those standards to small-dollar credit; see Brockland, "The Compass Guide to Small-Dollar Credit."

27.   The Consumer Financial Protection Bureau explains the ability to repay rule in mortgage lending here: http://www.consumerfinance.gov/askcfpb/1787/what-ability-repay-rule-why-it-important-me.html; the proposed payday rule is here: http://www.consumerfinance.gov/about-us/newsroom/consumer-financial-protection-bureau-proposes-rule-end-payday-debt-traps/.

28.   See our video, "Small Dollar Credit," for stories of two households' use of payday loans: http://www.usfinancialdiaries.org/small-dollar-vid.

Chapter 6: Sharing

1. The Institute for Justice interviewed over 750 street vendors nationwide and did a deep dive into the economics of vending in New York City. http://ij.org/wp-content/uploads /2015/10/upwardly-mobile-web-final.pdf.

2. Center for Urban Pedagogy, "Vendor Power."

3. New York City grants 2,800 citywide vendor permits, which are valid for a two-year period; 100 two-year citywide permits that are intended exclusively for disabled veterans, disabled persons, and non-disabled veterans; and 200 borough-specific permits. It also grants up to 50 two-year permits for each borough other than Manhattan, 1,000 seasonal permits for the period from April to October each year, and 1,000 permits for fruit and vegetable sellers. http:// www.nyc.gov/html/sbs/nycbiz/downloads/pdf/educational/sector_guides/street_vending.pdf.

4. In a 2006 report, the Street Vendors Project reported that there were 59,000 vending-related cases in New York City per year. Street Vendor Project, "Peddling Uphill."

5. These numbers are the maximum balances we recorded for each family. The numbers fluctuated throughout the year, as families spent down and then replenished their savings as described in chapter 3.

6. It can be difficult to tell a loan from a gift. However, most of the time we were able to see some repayment activity for the informal loans we documented, which gives us confidence that these are truly loans rather than gifts. Because of the small sample size of the USFD, we would caution against assuming that national numbers will be similar.

7. In the 2014 SHED, the question was only asked of those who reported going through financial hardship in the previous year, a sample size of 1,527 respondents. The data here are not weighted.

8. Sometimes a loan becomes a gift when financial circumstances change and vice versa. At the beginning of the Diaries year, Sarah reported owing her mom $6,000. During that year, her mom loaned her $850 for a car repair. But at the end of year, even though Sarah did not report making any payments to her mom, she said she owed her mother $4,000. It seems unlikely that she and her mom had a conversation about forgiving part of the loans. More likely, perhaps, is that Sarah and her mother are simply letting the loans go over time. Maybe her mother knows the money will never be paid back, but it is easier for everyone to refer to the funds as a loan rather than as a gift.

9. Their income based on SPM falls to about $37,000 after subtracting their year of expenses on health care and child support, positioning them at about 140 percent of the SPM poverty threshold.

10. Mills et al., "Evaluation of the American Dream Demonstration."

11. Stack, *All Our Kin*, 32.

12. At any given income level, households in the New York South Asian community had more emergency savings on average than households at other sites. The difference is statistically significant between the New York South Asian site and the seven other sites. It is not statistically significant for the difference between the New York South Asian site and the households outside of San Jose and in Brooklyn.

13. Demos and Winkler, "Online Lender Vouch Financial Shutting Down."

14. Information on Vouch's practices was gathered from their website in March 2016. The webpage that had information on lending rates is no longer available (https://vouchmoney .zendesk.com/hc/en-us).

15. Vouch's founder, Yee Lee, points out that they had only made $10 million in personal loans at the time, so it is not a large sample, and the loans were made during a credit-friendly environment. Nonetheless, Lee says they "demonstrated that meaningful enhancements can be made to lending results by incorporating social signals into underwriting. And with more

and more of the world connected in online social networks, that form of credit enhancement is becoming more and more accessible to people" (interview, November 1, 2016).

16. Federal Reserve, "Federal Fair Lending Regulations and Statutes: Overview," http://www.federalreserve.gov/boarddocs/supmanual/cch/fair_lend_over.pdf.

17. Rush, "Using Business Credit Scores to Graduate Borrowers."

18. Zelizer, *Economic Lives*, 90.

19. Zelizer, *The Social Meaning of Money*, 5. For a comparison of sociological and economic views on earmarking, drawing on examples from the U.S. Financial Diaries, see Morduch, "Economics and the Social Meaning of Money."

20. Zelizer points out that this idea of earmarking is related to mental accounting, which economists have explored, but it differs because, in her view, that idea "fails to acknowledge that social norms affect the definition of a specific earmark and the strength of the boundaries around it." Zelizer, "Special Monies."

21. The Mission Asset Fund in San Francisco has pioneered work along these lines.

Chapter 7: Sometimes Poor

1. We have benefited from comments from Ajay Chaudry, Frank DeGiovanni, Signe-Mary McKernan, Caroline Ratcliffe, and participants at a seminar on poverty and income volatility at the Center for the Study of Social Organization Seminar in the Department of Sociology at Princeton University, organized by Viviana Zelizer, in March 2016.

2. Becky and Jeremy's family income during the year was 42 percent above the federal poverty line, which makes no accommodation for regional price differences. See Meyer and Sullivan, "Identifying the Disadvantaged," for a discussion of competing poverty concepts. They describe the advantages of the SPM but note that it "uses a complex and convoluted way of determining changes in poverty over time" (112). A key issue is that the SPM framework does not judge well-being simply by income. Instead, the SPM framework modifies income to yield a measure of resources available to spend on food, clothing, shelter, and utilities. See Short, "The Supplemental Poverty Measure: 2014."

3. As described in chapter 3, Becky and Jeremy overwithheld taxes during the year, so their tax refund was larger than it otherwise would have been. Tax refunds for near-poor households like theirs were often bolstered by the earned income tax credit (EITC).

4. *The Other America* became part of the intellectual and moral armory that Lyndon Johnson drew on to formulate the War on Poverty in 1964. See Maurice Isserman, foreword to Harrington, *The Other America*. In his 1964 State of the Union address, Johnson declared that "our aim is not only to relieve the symptoms of poverty, but to cure it and, above all, to prevent it." See Matthews, "Everything You Need to Know about the War on Poverty." Johnson's legislative push produced initiatives that remain central to today's safety net: Head Start, Medicare and Medicaid, VISTA and other new job programs. The War on Poverty saw the expansion of food stamps too and, perhaps most important, the expansion of the Social Security system to retirees, widows, and the disabled.

5. The context for Harrington's book is described by Maurice Isserman in his 2012 foreword to *The Other America*. Isserman argues that while Harrington uses the language of a "culture of poverty" introduced by the anthropologist Oscar Lewis, his interpretation departs from Lewis's. Harrington focuses on the economic and social structures that reinforce poverty rather than psychological and cultural determinants.

6. In 1960, $3,000 was the equivalent of $24,135 in 2016 dollars. The federal poverty line for 2015 is from https://aspe.hhs.gov/2015-poverty-guidelines#threshholds. The poverty

comparison here uses the "official" federal poverty line, which shows that poverty rates fell since Harrington wrote. With the growth of the U.S. population, the 43 million people in poverty in 2015 translates to 13.5 percent of the population (rather than approximately one-quarter in Harrington's day). See Proctor, Semega, and Kollar, *Income and Poverty in the United States: 2015*. In most of this book, however, we use the census's SPM. Researchers have created a version of the SPM that can be used to compare poverty rates across time, called the anchored SPM. Estimating back to 1967, the anchored SPM shows a drop in poverty by 40 percent, driven by government policies rather than changes in the labor market. See Weimer et al., "Progress on Poverty?"

7.   Harrington, *The Other America*, 3.

8.   The list of books on poverty is now long. For a range of important perspectives, most highlighting entrenched poverty, see, for example, Danziger and Cancian, *Changing Poverty, Changing Policies*; Blank, *It Takes a Nation*; Edelman, *So Rich, So Poor*; Wilson, *The Truly Disadvantaged*; Jencks, *Rethinking Social Policy*; Abramsky, *The American Way of Poverty*; and Alexander, *The New Jim Crow*.

9.   Harrington's polemic differed greatly from other influential works like James Agee's deeply reported essays in Agee and Evans, *Let Us Now Praise Famous Men*. Contemporary ethnography has also provided rich portrayals of lives lived in poverty, including Desmond, *Evicted*; Edin and Shaefer, *$2 a Day*; and Newman, *No Shame in My Game*.

10.   The eligibility criteria for our sample required participating households to have a source of earned income, but 3 percent of our households spent the year without a job and surviving on public support. Household members lost the jobs they held between being recruited and the study beginning, and they did not find jobs during the time we followed them.

11.   Here we measure Taisha's annual sum as resources available to spend on FCSU as defined by the SPM poverty framework. Her annual total by SPM measures is $160 more than her net income. The SPM resource definition gives Taisha's capacity to spend on FCSU after accounting for government benefits received. The official poverty measure captures her capacity to spend on anything after accounting for government benefits received (but not in-kind benefits like SNAP). Taisha's net income (which we use to measure income volatility) captures her capacity to spend on anything that was not paid for via paycheck deductions, also after accounting for government benefits received.

12.   The notion that poor people cannot save is rebutted by McKernan, Ratcliffe, and Shanks, "Is Poverty Incompatible with Asset Accumulation?"

13.   For the near-poor (those with incomes between the poverty line but no more than 1.5 times above it), for example, the average was 2.3 spikes and 2.3 dips. For this group, instability was a problem, but a less acute one. As we discussed in chapter 1, bank account data collected by the JPMorgan Chase Institute, as well as the Federal Reserve's household data, also showed this pattern of income volatility. Measurement error is always a problem when viewing the ups and downs of the poorest families. What looks like a rapid drop in income could be the result of a careless transcription error by researchers or a forgotten income source by respondents. By following just 235 households, rather than thousands, the Financial Diaries are small enough in scale that we could diagnose and correct measurement error household by household. We spent most of a year verifying data after we collected it. Still, the process was not perfect, especially when collecting spending data, and here the small scale can work against us; every data problem weighs more heavily since each household is a larger fraction of the whole (one of 235 rather than one of, say, 5,000). The problem worsens when looking at particular regions or when dividing into income groups. Our findings, though, align broadly with those of other studies using alternative approaches and data sets.

14.   The connection between instability and poverty was prominent in the earlier financial diaries collected in India, Bangladesh, and South Africa that formed the basis of the book *Portfolios of the Poor*. There, the authors described a "triple whammy" to capture the condition of

poverty. The three elements are (1) low income, (2) instability, and (3) a lack of mechanisms to cope with the instability. The triple whammy describes many poor households we saw in the United States. The connection between poverty and instability in the original financial diaries is also described by Morduch in "Notre façon de voir la pauvreté." Related ideas are described in the context of year-to-year instability in India in Morduch, "Poverty and Vulnerability." The analysis of spikes and dips in the book deliberately departs from the SPM framework used to measure poverty; most important, we track income without subtracting out-of-pocket spending for medical necessities.

15.   Hardy and Ziliak use the U.S. Current Population Survey, a national survey used to calculate the U.S. poverty rate ("Decomposing Trends in Income Volatility"). Hardy and Ziliak measure poverty using the official poverty line.

16.   The data stretch from the SIPP 1984 panel to the 2008 panel. The SIPP provides a window on month-to-month income volatility (as measured by the coefficient of variation), and the researchers narrowed their focus to households with children. See Morris et al., "Income Volatility in U.S. Households with Children." They find that the increase in month-to-month income volatility for poor households is mainly from unearned income (not job income), suggesting that the changes may be bound up with changes in the availability of public transfers. The changes do not seem to be due to changes in the racial or ethnic composition of the poorest households.

17.   The SIPP shows that volatility for the richest group fell, while the Current Population Survey shows an increase. Part of the difference may be due to month-to-month income volatility (measured by the SIPP) and year-to-year volatility (measured by the Current Population Survey).

18.   This analysis draws on Morduch and Siwicki, "In and Out of Poverty." The paper includes analyses of the impacts of government transfer programs for Diaries households, showing that most programs do more to raise their incomes overall than to reduce the variability of income. The length of time under the poverty line was calculated using the SPM definitions. To conservatively address measurement error, we dropped data on all months in which reported income or spending was under $100. The data on months spent below the line are conditional on spending at least one month below the line. (The census definition of a poverty spell, in contrast, is a minimum of two months.) The patterns in the Financial Diaries are clear, but this is a place where we need to be especially careful in extrapolating to the broader population. The households are not statistically representative of the American population, and, apart from putting households into buckets by income, Figure 7.1 does not control for how close households are to the poverty line on average.

19.   This analysis excludes household-month observations where spending or income was below $100. Monthly spending figures in this analysis are also adjusted to exclude the spending categories that are excluded from the SPM-adjusted income.

20.   Duncan, Hofferth, and Stafford, "Evolution and Change in Family Income, Wealth, and Health."

21.   The data for 2009–11 are from the Survey of Income and Program Participation, as reported by Ashley Edwards ("Dynamics of Economic Well-Being"). Even though the SIPP is a representative sample, it is an unrepresentative period in American economic life, coming so soon after the Great Recession of 2007–8. Still, Edwards shows that the basic shape of the evidence lines up with data from earlier periods. Between 2005 and 2007, 27.1 percent of Americans experienced at least two months of poverty (versus 31.6 percent between 2009 and 2011). The rate of chronic, persistent poverty was 3.5 percent in 2009–11 and 3 percent in 2005–7. Most studies of episodic poverty focus on spells of at least two months in a row. Given the relatively short time frame of the Diaries (most households were observed for a year only), we instead focus on spells as short as one month in the analysis of the Diaries experience.

22. Researchers have written much on poverty dynamics and intergenerational poverty. An overview is provided by McKernan et al., "Transitioning in and out of Poverty." They find that slightly more than half of the U.S. population (focusing on adults ages twenty and older) experiences an episode of poverty at some point before age sixty-five. In analyzing long-term poverty, they find that about half of those who exit poverty will become poor again within five years.

23. Proctor, Semega, and Kollar, *Income and Poverty in the United States: 2015*. Using SPM poverty lines (and resource definitions), rather than the official poverty line, 103 million people, 32 percent of the U.S. population, had household resources that placed them above the SPM poverty line but below twice the line. See Short, "The Supplemental Poverty Measure: 2014."

24. Data are from Bane and Ellwood, "Slipping into and out of Poverty," 11.

25. Bane and Ellwood found that in the 1980s entrances to poverty were often associated with major shocks to households—events like divorce, a departing household member, or a health crisis. Their evidence suggested that we should spend less time focused on the spikes and dips of earnings and more on the structural challenges of families. Nearly half the time, they found, it was family structure and life-cycle events that marked the start of an episode of poverty. The discussion is from Bane and Ellwood, "Slipping into and out of Poverty," 11. Their work has been extended to 1987 by Stevens, "The Dynamics of Poverty Spells."

26. O'Brien and Pedulla, "Beyond the Poverty Line."

27. The data for 2011 are from the Survey of Income and Program Participation, as reported by Ashley Edwards ("Dynamics of Economic Well-Being"). The percentages in poverty are our calculations using figures from appendix tables A-2, A-4, and A-6.

28. The federal poverty line has been debated and adjusted over time, particularly in the 1970s. The details here are from Fischer, "The Development of the Orshansky Poverty Thresholds."

29. The Financial Diaries show the importance of measurement issues. The biggest challenges of collecting household financial data arise when transactions are small and frequent, and thus easy to forget, and in cash so there is often no record of the transaction. Cash wasn't a big factor in terms of income. The median household in our study received just 4 percent of inflows in cash (often help from family members), though there were a few families that received a much larger percentage in cash, so that the sample average was 19 percent. By contrast, nearly half of all transactions were in cash, making up 35 percent of the spending by value of the median household (42 percent for the average). Moreover, the cash purchases were small: half were $10 or under, and 84 percent under $50. The recall of cash is exacerbated by time. Our field researchers sought to meet with households every two weeks, but the gaps between meetings typically stretched to three to five weeks because of busy schedules and irregular work hours. When households had to try to remember smaller transactions from more than two weeks in the past, the quality and quantity of spending data fell. Similar issues arise in large national surveys. As a comparison, the Federal Reserve of Boston collects representative data on modes of consumer payments. In 2013 they found that 26.3 percent of transactions were in cash. Schuh and Stavins, "The 2013 Survey of Consumer Payment Choice."

30. Most poorer countries base poverty measurement on spending data, which is easier to collect than income when large shares of workers are employed in informal labor markets, especially in farming and other forms of self-employment. It also has the advantage of accounting for consumption smoothing. Meyer and Sullivan, ("Identifying the Disadvantaged") argue that consumption data for the poorest households tend similarly to be more accurate than income data in the United States.

31. See Meyer and Sullivan, "Winning the War" and Meyer and Sullivan, "Identifying the Disadvantaged."

32.   Spending in the Diaries study tends to be underreported relative to income. This increases the number of months that households appear to be in consumption poverty. Across the full year, we observed households in consumption poverty roughly as frequently as they were in income poverty. Despite this bias, we still saw the average household avoid consumption poverty when in income-poor months.

33.   Massey and Fischer, "The Geography of Inequality in the United States, 1950–2000."

34.   The withering of the safety net since the late 1990s is documented in Edin and Shaefer, *$2 a Day*. Ife Floyd writes that "by 2014, TANF provided a temporary safety net in the form of cash benefits to only 23 families with children for every 100 families in poverty, down substantially from 68 assisted families in 1996." Floyd, "Our Safety Net Misses the Poorest."

35.   Propel, a start-up designed to make applying for benefits much easier, provides one model.

36.   Corporation for Enterprise Development, "Asset Limits in Public Benefit Programs."

37.   See Ratcliffe et al., "Asset Limits, SNAP Participation, and Financial Stability."

38.   See Ben-Ishai, "Volatile Job Schedules and Access to Public Benefits." The data about how much pain this actually causes are sparse because they require a state-by-state analysis of the rules. TANF in practice adjusts to some of these labor market realities by allowing many TANF recipients to meet their "work" requirement in supported activities like a "job club." If a TANF recipient has a job where the hours fluctuate from week to week, then the number of hours of participation in the job club could be adjusted to meet the number of total required hours. A reduction in work hours alone would not then negatively affect eligibility. We appreciate insights from Caroline Ratcliffe and Heather Hahn of the Urban Institute.

Chapter 8: Secure and in Control

1.   The Aspen Institute Initiative on the Future of Work has explored these ideas specifically in relationship to gig economy workers, with the needs of independent contractors in mind, but they apply just as well to part-time workers and those with irregular schedules; see "Common Ground for Independent Workers."

2.   For more about San Francisco's Retail Workers Bill of Rights, see http://retailworker rights.com. Similar bills have been offered in ten other states, as well as Washington, D.C. See DePillis, "The Next Labor Fight Is over When You Work, Not How Much You Make."

3.   Lambert, "The Limits of Voluntary Employer Action for Improving Low-Level Jobs."

4.   Walmart has taken steps in this direction as well, as described in Irwin, "How Did Walmart Get Cleaner Stores and Higher Sales?"

5.   The argument to redirect the tax system to help poor and low-income families save is developed in Sherraden, *Assets and the Poor*. As we note in chapter 3, Sherraden's Individual Development Account proposal is one attempt to shift incentives to help a broader part of the population. The Diaries suggest that families need a broader range of saving services, but Sherraden's diagnosis of the federal subsidy and tax system still has currency.

6.   The Retirement Savings Contribution Credit, or "saver's credit," was enacted as part of the Bush administration's 2001 tax plan to promote retirement savings for moderate- and low-income workers. It allows tax filers to reduce their federal income tax liability by making eligible contributions. Because it is "nonrefundable," it can reduce a taxpayer's federal income tax liability to zero, but it cannot result in a tax refund. Mark Ivry has written extensively about the potential benefit of a broader, refundable saver's credit. See also Alicia Munnell's contribution to Hacker and O'Leary, *Shared Responsibility, Shared Risk*. Rather than expanding the existing saver's credit, or creating a new credit, another route would be to expand the EITC, as

described by Halpern-Meekin et al., *It's Not Like I'm Poor*. A further proposal is to allow house-holds to receive a tax credit in the first part of the year in order to provide families with a boost to their short-term savings, acting as a near-term emergency savings account and providing a buffer against near-term economic shocks.

7. See Jones, "Information, Preferences, and Public Benefit Participation."

8. Note that Digit was part of the inaugural cohort of the Financial Solutions Lab, an incubator for financial technology innovators sponsored by the JPMorgan Chase Foundation and run by CFSI, where Schneider works. The authors have no financial interest in Digit.

9. Cowley, "New Payday Options for Making Ends Meet." See also Knope, "All the Ways Uber and Lyft Drivers Can Get Paid Instantly." CFSI notes that a trend among financial technology start-ups has been to seek to partner with employers as a distribution channel. They highlight DoubleNetPay, a company that integrated with prominent payroll provider ADP in order to enable workers to schedule payments around their paycheck cycles and deduct planned fixed expenses ahead of time. They say that "by pulling fixed expenses out, consumers can focus on managing their discretionary spending." Falvey et al., "Financial Solutions Lab Snapshot," 4.

Companies could also time workers' pay to when they need the money most, just as some bill payees allow customers to choose payment dates. Katherine Lopez, the nonprofit worker in California, spent time and attention deciding which bills to pay with the first paycheck of the month and which to pay with the second. Imagine if employers paid workers just enough in that first paycheck to cover what they'd calculated as critical, "must-pay" bills. Katherine and Sarah could then count on being able to put all of their second paycheck toward other needs. Employers could do this across an annual cycle, too. For example, they could offer the option of a "thirteenth month" of earnings or a bonus, which employees could access at any time during the year at their discretion. Presumably, workers would receive less in other paychecks, but they might value the opportunity to access their pay in a more flexible way.

10. "The 2013 Federal Reserve Payments Study."

11. For discussion of this idea, see John, "Making Retirement Saving Even More Valuable by Adding Automatic Emergency Savings."

12. Information about the myRA account from the U.S. Department of the Treasury can be found at https://myra.gov.

13. Clarity and control are also important when it comes to work schedules and government benefits. If workers had more certainty and transparency around how much work is coming and when they'll be needed, and how much government support they can expect and when it will arrive, some of their financial difficulties would be eased.

14. Theodos et al. "An Evaluation of the Impacts of Two 'Rules of Thumb' for Credit Card Revolvers."

15. Simple's description of Safe-to-Spend can be found at https://www.simple.com/help/articles/getting-started/safe-to-spend.

Bibliography

Abramsky, Sasha. *The American Way of Poverty: How the Other Half Still Lives*. New York: Perseus/Nation, 2013.

Ackerman, James M. "Interest Rates and the Law: A History of Usury." *Arizona State Law Journal* (1981): 61–110.

Agee, James, and Walker Evans. *Let Us Now Praise Famous Men*. New York: Houghton Mifflin, 1939.

Alexander, Michelle. *The New Jim Crow: Mass Incarceration in the Age of Colorblindness*. New York: The New Press, 2010.

"American House Prices: Realty Check." *Economist*, August 24, 2016. http://www.economist.com/blogs/graphicdetail/2015/11/daily -chart-0.

Armendáriz, Beatriz, and Jonathan Morduch. *The Economics of Micro-finance*. Cambridge, MA: MIT Press, 2010.

Auerbach, David I., and Arthur L. Kellermann. "A Decade of Health Care Cost Growth Has Wiped Out Real Income Gains for an Average U.S. Family." *Health Affairs* 30, no. 9 (September 2011): 1630–36.

Autor, David H. "Why Are There Still So Many Jobs? The History and Future of Workplace Automation." *Journal of Economic Perspectives* 29, no. 3 (Summer 2015): 3–30.

Autor, David H., and David Dorn. "The Growth of Low-Skill Service Jobs and the Polarization of the US Labor Market." *American Economic Review* 103, no. 5 (2013): 1553–97.

Bailey, Martin Neil, and Barry Bosworth. "US Manufacturing: Understanding Its Past and Its Potential Future." *Journal of Economic Perspectives* 28, no. 1 (2014): 3–26.

Bane, Mary Jo, and David Ellwood. "Slipping into and out of Pov-
    erty: The Dynamics of Spells." *Journal of Human Resources* 21,
    no. 1 (Winter 1986): 1–23.
Ben-Ishai, Liz. "Volatile Job Schedules and Access to Public Bene-
    fits." Center for Law and Social Policy, 2015. http://www.clasp.org
    /resources-and-publications/publication-1/2015.09.16-Scheduling
    -Volatility-and-Benefits-FINAL.pdf.
"Beyond Simple and Safe: Opportunities to Expand the Use of
    Direct Deposit via ACH for Payroll." Javelin Strategy & Research
    on behalf of NACHA—The Electronic Payments Association.
    April 2016. https://www.nacha.org/system/files/resources/NACHA
    _Javelin_Direct_Deposit_Survey_Report_2015.pdf.
Blank, Rebecca. *It Takes a Nation: A New Agenda for Fighting Poverty*.
    Princeton: Princeton University Press, 1997.
Board of Governors of the Federal Reserve System. "Changes in U.S.
    Family Finances from 2010 to 2013: Evidence from the Survey
    of Consumer Finances." *Federal Reserve Bulletin* 100, no. 4 (2014).
    https://www.federalreserve.gov/pubs/bulletin/2014/pdf/scf14.pdf.
———. "Report on the Economic Well-Being of U.S. Households
    in 2013." 2014. https://www.federalreserve.gov/econresdata/2013
    -report-economic-well-being-us-households-201407.pdf.
———. "Report on the Economic Well-Being of U.S. Households
    in 2014." 2015. https://www.federalreserve.gov/econresdata/2014
    -report-economic-well-being-us-households-201505.pdf.
———. "Report on the Economic Well-Being of US Households in
    2015." 2016. http://www.federalreserve.gov/2015-report-economic
    -well-being-us-households-201605.pdf.
———. "Survey of Consumer Finances." 2013. http://www.federal
    reserve.gov/pubs/bulletin/2014/pdf/scf14.pdf.
Boshara, Ray. "From Asset Building to Balance Sheets: A Reflection
    on the First and Next 20 Years of Federal Assets Policy." CSD
    Perspective, no. 12-24. St. Louis: Center for Social Development,
    George Warren School of Social Work, Washington University,
    2012.
Bourdieu, Pierre. *Acts of Resistance: Against the New Myths of Our
    Time*. Trans. Richard Nice. Cambridge: Polity Press, 1998.

Bouston, Leah Platt, Carola Frydman, and Robert Margo, eds. *Human Capital in History: The American Record*. Chicago: University of Chicago Press, 2014.

Breevort, Kenneth P., Philipp Grimm, and Michelle Kambara. "Data Point: Credit Invisibles." Consumer Financial Protection Bureau, May 2015. http://files.consumerfinance.gov/f/201505_cfpb_data-point-credit-invisibles.pdf.

Brockland, Beth. "The Compass Guide to Small-Dollar Credit." Center for Financial Services Innovation, November 24, 2014. http://www.cfsinnovation.com/Document-Library/The-Compass-Guide-to-Small-Dollar-Credit.

Brodkin, Evelyn, and Gregory Marston, eds. *Street-Level Organizations and Workfare Politics*. Washington, DC: Georgetown University Press, 2013.

Brumberg, Richard, and Franco Modigliani. "Utility Analysis and the Consumption Function: An Interpretation of Cross-Section Data." In *Post-Keynesian Economics*, ed. Kenneth K. Kurihara, 388–436. New Brunswick, NJ: Rutgers University Press, 1954.

Brune, Lasse, Xavier Giné, Jessica Goldberg, and Dean Yang. "Facilitating Savings for Agriculture: Field Experimental Evidence from Malawi." *Economic Development and Cultural Change* 64, no. 2 (2016): 187–220. http://www.journals.uchicago.edu/doi/full/10.1086/684014.

Bureau of Labor Statistics. "Characteristics of Minimum Wage Workers, 2015." Current Population Survey, U.S. Department of Labor, April 2016.

———. "Persons at Work in Nonagricultural Industries by Age, Sex, Race, Hispanic or Latino Ethnicity, Marital Status, and Usual Full or Part-Time Status." Current Population Survey, U.S. Department of Labor, 2015.

———. "Union Members—2015." Current Population Survey, U.S. Department of Labor, 2016.

Carpenter, Dick M., II. "Upwardly Mobile: Street Vending and the American Dream." Institute for Justice, September 2015. http://ij.org/wp-content/uploads/2015/10/upwardly-mobile-web-final.pdf.

Carroll, Christopher D. "Buffer Stock Saving and the Life Cycle/ Permanent Income Hypothesis." *Quarterly Journal of Economics* 112, no. 1 (1997): 1–56.

Caskey, John. "The Economics of Payday Lending." Madison: Filene Research Institute, University of Wisconsin, 2002.

Center for Budget and Policy Priorities. "Chartbook: TANF at 20." August 5, 2015. http://www.cbpp.org/sites/default/files/atoms /files/8-22-12tanf_0.pdf.

Choi, Laura, David Erickson, Kate Griffin, Andrea Levere, and Ellen Seidman, eds. *What It's Worth: Strengthening the Financial Future of Families, Communities and the Nation*. Federal Reserve Bank of San Francisco, the Corporation for Enterprise Development, and the Citi Foundation, 2015. http://www.strongfinancialfuture.org /the-book/.

"College Costs Rising Four Times Faster than Income, Two and a Half Times Faster than Pell." Center for Law and Social Policy blog, 2013. http://www.clasp.org/issues/postsecondary/did-you -know/college-costs-rising-four-times-faster-than-income-two-and -a-half-times-faster-than-pell.

Collins, Daryl, Jonathan Morduch, Stuart Rutherford, and Orlanda Ruthven. *Portfolios of the Poor: How the World's Poor Live on $2 a Day*. Princeton: Princeton University Press, 2009.

Collins, J. Michael, ed. *A Fragile Balance: Emergency Savings and Liquid Resources for Low-Income Consumers*. New York: Palgrave MacMillan, 2015.

Collins, Sara R., David C. Radley, Cathy Schoen, and Sophie Beutel. "National Trends in the Cost of Employer Health Insurance Coverage, 2003–2013." Commonwealth Fund. December 2014. http:// www.commonwealthfund.org/~/media/files/publications/issue -brief/2014/dec/1793_collins_nat_premium_trends_2003_2013 .pdf.

Comin, Diego A., Erica L. Groshen, and Bess Rabin. "Turbulent Firms, Turbulent Wages?" *Journal of Monetary Economics* 56, no. 1 (2009): 102–33.

"Common Ground for Independent Workers: Principles for Delivering a Stable and Flexible Safety Net for All Types of Work." Ed. Portable Benefits. What's the Future of Work? November 10,

2015. https://medium.com/the-wtf-economy/common-ground -for-independent-workers-83f3fbcf548f#.yjppqgcd5.

Corporation for Enterprise Development. "Asset Limits in Public Benefit Programs." http://scorecard.assetsandopportunity.org /latest/measure/asset-limits-in-public-benefit-programs.

"The Costs of Nonpayment: A Study of Non-Payment and Late Payment in the Freelance Workforce." Freelancers Union, 2015. https://d3q437fqezjn6j.cloudfront.net/content/advocacy/uploads /resources/FU_NonpaymentReport_r3.pdf.

Cowley, Stacy. "New Payday Options for Making Ends Meet." *New York Times*, July 4, 2016. http://www.nytimes.com/2016/07/05 /business/dealbook/new-payday-options-for-making-ends-meet .html?_r=0.

"Credit Scores." Federal Trade Commission, September 2013. https:// www.consumer.ftc.gov/articles/0152-credit-scores.

Dahl, Molly, Thomas DeLeire, and Jonathan A. Schwabish. "Estimates of Year-to-Year Volatility in Earnings and in Household Incomes from Administrative, Survey, and Matched Data." *Journal of Human Resources* 46, no. 4 (2011): 750–74.

Danziger, Sheldon, and Maria Cancian, eds. *Changing Poverty, Changing Policies*. New York: Russell Sage, 2009.

Deaton, Angus. *Understanding Consumption*. Clarendon Lectures. Oxford: Oxford University Press, 1992.

Demos, Telis, and Rolfe Winkler. "Online Lender Vouch Financial Shutting Down." *Wall Street Journal*, June 5, 2016. http://www .wsj.com/articles/online-lender-vouch-financial-shutting-down -sources-1465148253.

DePillis, Lydia. "The Next Labor Fight Is over When You Work, Not How Much You Make." *Washington Post*, May 8, 2015. https://www .washingtonpost.com/news/wonk/wp/2015/05/08/the-next-labor -fight-is-over-when-you-work-not-how-much-you-make/.

Desilver, Drew. "Job Categories Where Union Membership Has Fallen Off Most." Pew Research Center FactTank blog, April 27, 2015. http://www.pewresearch.org/fact-tank/2015/04/27/union -membership/.

Desmond, Matthew. *Evicted: Poverty and Profit in the American City*. New York: Crown, 2016.

Dubner, Stephen J. "Are We a Nation of Financial Illiterates?" Freak-onomics blog, July 21, 2008. http://freakonomics.com/2008/07/21/are-we-a-nation-of-financial-illiterates/.

Duncan, Greg J. "The PSID and Me." In *Landmark Studies of the 20th Century in the US*, ed. Erin Phelps, Frank F. Furstenburg Jr., and Anne Colby, 133–66. New York: Russell Sage, 2002.

———. *Years of Poverty, Years of Plenty: The Changing Economic Fortunes of American Workers and Families*. Ann Arbor: University of Michigan Institute for Social Research, 1984.

Duncan, Greg J., Sandra L. Hofferth, and Frank P. Stafford. "Evolution and Change in Family Income, Wealth, and Health: The Panel Study of Income Dynamics, 1968–2000." In *A Telescope on Society: Survey Research and Social Science at the University of Michigan and Beyond*, ed. James S. House, F. Thomas Juster, Robert L. Kahn, Howard Schuman, and Eleanor Singer, 156–93. Ann Arbor: University of Michigan Press, 2004.

Dupas, Pascaline, and Jonathan Robinson. "Why Don't the Poor Save More? Evidence from Health Savings Experiments." *American Economic Review* 103, no. 4 (2013): 1138–71.

Dynan, Karen, Douglas Elmendorf, and Daniel Sichel. "The Evolution of Household Income Volatility." *BE Journal of Economic Analysis and Policy* 12, no. 2 (2012): 1–42.

Edelman, Peter. *So Rich, So Poor: Why It's So Hard to End Poverty in America*. New York: New Press, 2012.

Edin, Kathryn, and H. Luke Shaefer. *$2 a Day: Living on Almost Nothing in America*. New York: Houghton Mifflin Harcourt, 2015.

Edwards, Ashley N. "Dynamics of Economic Well-Being: Poverty, 2009–2011." *Current Population Reports*. Washington, DC: U.S. Census Bureau, 2014.

Emmons, William, and Bryan Noeth. "Race, Ethnicity, and Wealth." Essay No. 1 in *The Demographics of Wealth: How Age, Education and Race Separate Thrivers from Strugglers in Today's Economy*, ed. Ray Boshara, William Emmons, and Brian Noeth. St. Louis: Center for Household Financial Stability, Federal Reserve Bank of St. Louis, 2015.

Expanding Prosperity Impact Collaborative. "Income Volatility: A Primer." Aspen Institute, May 2016. https://assets.aspeninstitute

.org/content/uploads/files/content/docs/pubs/EPIC+Volatility
+Primer+(May).pdf.

Falvey, Ryan, Sohrab Kohli, Asad Ramzanali, and Eva Wokowitz.
"Financial Solutions Lab Snapshot: Solutions to Manage Household Cash Flow." Center for Financial Services Innovation. September 10, 2015. http://www.cfsinnovation.com/Document
-Library/Financial-Solutions-Lab-Snapshot-Solutions-to-Mana.

Farrell, Diana, and Fiona Grieg. "Paychecks, Paydays and the Online
Platform Economy." JPMorgan Chase Institute, 2016. https://
www.jpmorganchase.com/corporate/institute/document/jpmc
-institute-volatility-2-report.pdf.

———. "Weathering Volatility: Big Data on the Financial Ups and
Downs of U.S. Individuals." JPMorgan Chase Institute, 2015.
https://www.jpmorganchase.com/corporate/institute/document
/54918-jpmc-institute-report-2015-aw5.pdf.

"Federal Fair Lending Regulations and Statutes: Overview." Federal
Reserve, September 1, 2016. http://www.federalreserve.gov/board
docs/supmanual/cch/fair_lend_over.pdf.

Fellowes, Matt, and Katy Willemin. "The Retirement Breach in Defined Contribution Plans: Size, Causes, and Solutions." Hello
Wallet, January 2013. http://info.hellowallet.com/rs/hellowallet
/images/HelloWallet_The%20RetirementBreachInDefined
ContributionPlans.pdf.

"Financial Well-Being: The Goal of Financial Education." Consumer
Financial Protection Bureau, January 2015. http://files.consumer
finance.gov/f/201501_cfpb_report_financial-well-being.pdf.

Fischer, Gordon M. "The Development of the Orshansky Poverty
Thresholds and Their Subsequent History as the Official U.S.
Poverty Measure." U.S. Census Bureau, 1992. https://www.census
.gov/hhes/povmeas/publications/orshansky.html.

Flannery, Mark, and Katherine Samolyk. "Scale Economies at Payday Loan Stores." *Proceedings of the Federal Reserve Bank of Chicago's 43rd Annual Conference on Bank Structure and Competition*
(May 2007): 233–59.

Floyd, Ife. "Our Safety Net Misses the Poorest." Real Clear Policy
blog, September 28, 2015. http://www.realclearpolicy.com/blog
/2015/09/28/our_safety_net_misses_the_poorest_1429.html.

Fox, Justin. "A College Degree Just Might Get You a Side Job." *Bloomberg View*, August 3, 2016. https://www.bloomberg.com/view /articles/2016–08–03/a-college-degree-just-might-get-you-a-side -job.

———. "The Rise of the 1099 Economy." *Bloomberg View*, December 11, 2015. https://www.bloomberg.com/view/articles/2015–12 –11/the-gig-economy-is-showing-up-in-irs-s-1099-forms.

"Frequently Asked Questions." Even. https://even.com/terms and https://even.com/faq.

"Frequently Asked Questions." Street Vendor Project, sponsored by the Urban Justice Center. http://streetvendor.org/faq/.

Friedman, Milton. *A Theory of the Consumption Function*. Princeton: Princeton University Press, 1957.

"From Upside Down to Right-Side Up: Redeploying $540 Billion in Federal Spending to Help All Families Save, Invest, and Build Wealth." Corporation for Enterprise Development, 2014. http:// cfed.org/assets/pdfs/Upside_Down_to_Right-Side_Up_2014.pdf.

Garfinkel, Irwin, Sara McLanahan, and Christopher Wimer. *Children of the Great Recession*. New York: Russell Sage Foundation, 2016.

Garon, Thea, Alicia Gutman, Jeanne Hogarth, and Rachel Schneider. "Understanding and Improving Consumer Financial Health in America." Center for Financial Services Innovation. March 24, 2015. http://www.cfsinnovation.com/Document-Library/Under standing-Consumer-Financial-Health.

Giridharadas, Anand. "Want a Steady Income? There's an App for That: A Silicon Valley Start-up Wants to Put Workers on an Even Keel." *New York Times Magazine*, May 3, 2015. http://www.nytimes .com/2015/05/03/magazine/want-a-steady-income-theres-an-app -for-that.html.

Gosselin, Peter. *High Wire: The Precarious Financial Lives of American Families*. New York: Basic Books, 2008.

Gottschalk, Peter, and Robert Moffit. "The Rising Instability of U.S. Earnings." *Journal of Economic Perspectives* 23, no. 4 (2009): 3–24.

Graeber, David. *Debt: The First 5,000 Years*. New York: Melville House, 2012.

Greene, Claire, and Mi Luo. "Consumers' Use of Credit Protection." Federal Reserve Bank of Boston, Research Report 15-8, November 2015.

Guiso, Luigi, and Monica Paiella. "Risk Aversion, Wealth, and Background Risk." *Journal of the European Economic Association* 6, no. 6 (2008): 1109–50.

Hacker, Jacob. *The Great Risk Shift: The Assault on American Jobs, Families, and Health Care—And How You Can Fight Back*. New York: Basic Books, 2006.

———. "The New Economic Insecurity—And What Can Be Done About It." *Harvard Law and Policy Review* 1 (2007): 111–26.

Hacker, Jacob, and Ann O'Leary, eds. *Shared Responsibility, Shared Risk: Government, Markets and Social Policy in the Twenty-First Century*. New York: Oxford University Press, 2013.

Haley-Lock, Anna, and Stephanie Ewert. "Waiting for the Minimum: US State Wage Laws, Firm Strategy, and Chain-Restaurant Job Quality." *Journal of Industrial Relations* 53, no. 1 (2011): 31–48.

Halliday, Timothy. "Income Volatility and Health." Working Paper No. 200729, University of Hawaii at Manoa, Department of Economics, 2007.

Halpern-Meekin, Sarah, Kathryn Edin, Laura Tach, and Jennifer Sykes. *It's Not Like I'm Poor: How Working Families Make Ends Meet in a Post-Welfare World*. Berkeley: University of California Press, 2015.

Hamilton, Leah. "The Forgotten 1980s Rule That's Hurting Poor Families' Savings." *Atlantic*, March 11, 2015. http://www.the atlantic.com/business/archive/2015/03/the-forgotten-1980s-rule -thats-hurting-poor-families-savings/387373/.

Hannagan, Anthony, and Jonathan Morduch. "Income Gains and Month-to-Month Income Volatility: Household Evidence from the US Financial Diaries." Federal Reserve System Community Development Research Conference: Economic Mobility, Washington, DC, April 2–3, 2015. Revised June 29, 2015.

Hardy, Bradley. "Income Instability and the Response of the Safety Net." *Contemporary Economic Policy*, June 2016. https://spea .indiana.edu/doc/research/finance-conference/hardy_income -instability.pdf.

Hardy, Bradley, and James Ziliak. "Decomposing Trends in Income Volatility: The 'Wild Ride' at the Top and Bottom." *Economic Inquiry* 52, no. 1 (2014): 459–76.

Harrington, Michael. *The Other America*. New York: Scribner, 1962.

Harris, Benjamin H., Eugene C. Steuerle, Signe-Mary McKernan, Caleb Quakenbush, and Caroline Ratcliffe. "Tax Subsidies for Asset Development: An Overview and Distributional Analysis." Tax Policy Center, Urban Institute and Brookings Institution, February 2014. https://www.brookings.edu/wp-content/uploads /2016/06/taxsubsidiesforassetdevelopment.pdf.

Heckman, James. "The Economics and the Econometrics of Human Development." Econometric Society Presidential Address, Allied Social Sciences Association Meetings, Philadelphia, January 2, 2014.

Henly, Julia R., and Susan J. Lambert. "Unpredictable Work Timing in Retail Jobs: Implications for Employee Work-Life Conflict." *Industrial & Labor Relations Review* 67, no. 3 (July 2014): 986–1016.

"The History of Usury." Americans for Fairness in Lending. https:// americansforfairnessinlending.wordpress.com/the-history-of -usury/.

Horowitz, Daniel. *The Morality of Spending: Attitudes toward the Consumer Society in America, 1875–1940*. Baltimore: Johns Hopkins University Press, 1985.

House, James S., F. Thomas Juster, Robert L. Kahn, Howard Schuman, and Eleanor Singer, eds. *A Telescope on Society: Survey Research and Social Science at the University of Michigan and Beyond*. Ann Arbor: University of Michigan Press, 2004.

Huddleston, Diane M. "The Poorhouse: Industrialization of the Poor." Western Oregon University, Department of History Capstone paper, 2012.

Irwin, Neil. "How Did Walmart Get Cleaner Stores and Higher Sales? It Paid Its People More." *New York Times*, October 15, 2016. http://www.nytimes.com/2016/10/16/upshot/how-did-walmart-get -cleaner-stores-and-higher-sales-it-paid-its-people-more.html?_r=1.

Jappelli, Tullio, and Luigi Pistaferri. "The Consumption Response to Income Changes." *Annual Review of Economics* 2, no. 1 (2010): 479–506.

Jencks, Christopher. *Rethinking Social Policy: Race, Poverty, and the Underclass*. New York: HarperCollins, 1992.

Jensen, Shane T., and Stephen H. Shore. "Semiparametric Bayesian Modeling of Income Volatility Heterogeneity." *Journal of the American Statistical Association* 106, issue 496 (2011): 1280–90.

John, David. "Making Retirement Saving Even More Valuable by Adding Automatic Emergency Savings." AARP Policy Thinking blog, July 13, 2015. http://blog.aarp.org/2015/07/13/making-retirement-saving-even-more-valuable-by-adding-automatic-emergency-savings/.

Joliffe, Dean, and James Ziliak, eds. *Income Volatility and Food Assistance in the United States*. Kalamazoo, MI: W. E. Upjohn Institute for Employment Research, 2008.

Jones, Damon. "Information, Preferences, and Public Benefit Participation: Experimental Evidence from the Advance EITC and 401(k) Savings." *American Economic Journal: Applied Economics* 2 (April 2010): 147–63.

Kahnemann, Daniel. *Thinking Fast and Slow*. New York: Farrar, Straus and Giroux, 2011.

Kalleberg, Arne L. *Good Jobs, Bad Jobs: The Rise of Polarized and Precarious Employment Systems in the United States, 1970s to 2000s*. New York: Russell Sage, 2013.

Kantor, Jody. "Working Anything But 9 to 5." *New York Times*, August 13, 2014. http://www.nytimes.com/interactive/2014/08/13/us/starbucks-workers-scheduling-hours.html.

Kaplan, Greg, Giovanni L. Violante, and Justin Weidner. "The Wealthy Hand to Mouth." *Brookings Papers on Economic Activity* (Spring 2014): 77–138.

Karlan, Dean, and Leigh Linden. "Loose Knots: Strong versus Weak Commitments to Save for Education in Uganda." Yale University Economic Growth Center Discussion Paper no. 1037, April 1, 2016. http://ssrn.com/abstract=2379594.

Khullar, Dhruv. "How to Stop Bouncing between Insurance Programs under ObamaCare." *New York Times*, March 23, 2016. http://www.nytimes.com/2016/03/24/upshot/how-to-stop-the-bouncing-between-insurance-plans-under-obamacare.html.

Knope, Jonathan. "All the Ways Uber and Lyft Drivers Can Get Paid Instantly." *The Rideshare Guy*. April 15, 2016. http://therideshareguy.com/all-the-ways-rideshare-drivers-can-get-paid-instantly/.

Kurihara, Kenneth K., ed. *Post-Keynesian Economics*. New Brunswick, NJ: Rutgers University Press, 1954.

Lambert, Susan J. "The Limits of Voluntary Employer Action for Improving Low-Level Jobs." In *Working and Living in the Shadow of Economic Fragility*, ed. Marion Crain and Michael Sherraden, 120–39. New York: Oxford University Press, 2014.

———. "Passing the Buck: Labor Flexibility Practices That Transfer Risk onto Hourly Workers." *Human Relations* 61, no. 9 (2008): 1203–27.

Lambert, Susan J., Peter J. Fugiel, and Julia R. Henly. "Precarious Work Schedules among Early-Career Employees in the U.S.: A National Snapshot." Employment Instability, Family Well-being, and Social Policy Network at the University of Chicago, August 2014. https://ssascholars.uchicago.edu/sites/default/files /work-scheduling-study/files/lambert.fugiel.henly_.precarious _work_schedules.august2014_0.pdf.

Lambert, Susan J., and Julia R. Henly. "Double Jeopardy: The Misfit between Welfare to Work Requirements and Job Realities." In *Work and the Welfare State*, ed. Evelyn Z. Brodkin and Gregory Marston, 69–84. Washington, DC: Georgetown University Press, 2013.

Latner, Jonathan. "Income Volatility and Social Stratification." Working paper, University of Wisconsin–Madison, 2014.

Lewis Nier, Charles, III. "The Shadow of Credit: The Historical Origins of Racial Predatory Lending and Its Impact upon African American Wealth Accumulation." *University of Pennsylvania Journal of Law and Social Change* 11, no. 2 (2007–8): 131–94.

Lieber, Ron. "Combating a Flood of Early 401(k) Withdrawals." *New York Times*, October 5, 2014. http://www.nytimes.com/2014 /10/25/your-money/401ks-and-similar-plans/combating-a-flood -of-early-401-k-withdrawals.html.

Lower-Basch, Elizabeth. "Opportunity at Work: Improving Job Quality." Center for Law and Social Policy, Policy Paper: Opportunity at Work Series, No. 1, September 2007. http://www.clasp .org/issues/body/0374.pdf.

Lusardi, Annamaria, and Olivia S. Mitchell. "The Economic Importance of Financial Literacy: Theory and Evidence." *Journal of Economic Literature* 52, no. 1 (2014): 5–44.

———. "Financial Literacy and Retirement Planning: New Evidence from the Rand American Life Panel." Michigan Retirement Research Center Research Paper 6, October 2007.

Lynch, Mamie, Jennifer Engle, and Jose L. Cruz. "Lifting the Fog on

Inequitable Financial Aid Policies." The Education Trust, 2011. http://edtrust.org/wp-content/uploads/2013/10/Lifting-the-Fog -FINAL.pdf.

Maas, Ericca. "Credit Scoring and the Credit-Underserved Population." Federal Reserve Bank of Minneapolis, May 1, 2008. https:// www.minneapolisfed.org/publications/community-dividend /credit-scoring-and-the-creditunderserved-population.

Mangan, Dan. "Job Health Insurance Costs Rising Faster than Wages." CNBC, December 9, 2014. http://www.cnbc.com/2014 /12/08/job-health-insurance-costs-rising-faster-than-wages.html.

Massey, Douglas, and Mary Fischer. "The Geography of Inequality in the United States, 1950–2000." Brookings-Wharton Papers on Urban Affairs, 2003.

Mastrobuoni, Giovanni, and Matthew Weinberg. "Heterogeneity in Intra-Monthly Consumption Patterns, Self-Control, and Savings at Retirement." *American Economic Journal: Economic Policy* 1, no. 2 (2009): 163–89.

Matthews, Dylan. "Wonkblog: Everything You Need to Know about the War on Poverty." *Washington Post*, January 8, 2014. https://www .washingtonpost.com/news/wonk/wp/2014/01/08/everything-you -need-to-know-about-the-war-on-poverty/.

McKernan, Signe-Mary, Caroline Ratcliffe, and Stephanie Riegg Cellini. "Transitioning in and out of Poverty." The Urban Institute, September 2009. http://www.urban.org/url.cfm?ID=411956.

McKernan, Signe-Mary, Caroline Ratcliffe, and Trina Shanks. "Is Poverty Incompatible with Asset Accumulation?" In *Oxford Handbook of the Economics of Poverty*, ed. Philip N. Jefferson, 463–93. Oxford: Oxford University Press, 2012.

McKernan, Signe-Mary, and Michael Sherraden, eds. *Asset Building and Low-Income Families*. Washington, DC: Urban Institute Press, 2008.

Meyer, Bruce, and James Sullivan. "Identifying the Disadvantaged: Official Poverty, Consumption Poverty, and the New Supplemental Poverty Measure." *Journal of Economic Perspectives* 26, no. 3 (Summer 2012): 111–36.

———. "Winning the War: Poverty from the Great Society to the Great Recession." *Brookings Papers on Economic Activity* (Fall 2012): 133–83.

Miller-Adams, Michelle. *Owning Up: Poverty, Assets, and the American Dream*. Washington, DC: Brookings Institution, 2002.

Mills, Gregory, Rhiannon Patterson, Larry Orr, and Donna DeMarco. "Evaluation of the American Dream Demonstration: Final Evaluation Report." Abt Associates Inc., 2004. http://www.usc.edu/dept/chepa/IDApays/publications/abt%20ADD%20final.pdf.

Mishel, Lawrence, Elise Gould, and Josh Bivens. "Wage Stagnation in Nine Charts." Economic Policy Institute, January 2015. http://www.epi.org/publication/charting-wage-stagnation/.

Montezemolo, Susanna. "Payday Lending Abuses and Predatory Practices." Center for Responsible Lending, 2013. http://www.responsiblelending.org/state-of-lending/reports/10-Payday-Loans.pdf.

Morduch, Jonathan. "Economics and the Social Meaning of Money." In *Money Talks*, ed. Nina Bandelj, Frederick F. Wherry, and Viviana Zelizer. Princeton: Princeton University Press, 2017.

———. "Notre façon de voir la pauvreté" [How we see poverty]. *FACTS*, special issue 4 (Lutte contre la pauvreté) (January 2012): 14–19.

———. "Poverty and Vulnerability." *American Economic Review* (AEA Papers and Proceedings) 84, no. 2 (May 1994): 221–25.

Morduch, Jonathan, Timothy Ogden, and Rachel Schneider. "Thriving But Still Vulnerable in the U.S." U.S. Financial Diaries Household Profile. http://www.usfinancialdiaries.org/house10-ny.

Morduch, Jonathan, and Rachel Schneider. "Spikes and Dips: How Income Uncertainty Affects Households." U.S. Financial Diaries Issue Brief, October 2013. http://www.usfinancialdiaries.org/issue1-spikes/.

Morduch, Jonathan, and Julie Siwicki. "In and Out of Poverty: Poverty Spells and Income Volatility in the U.S. Financial Diaries." Working paper, U.S. Financial Diaries, September 2016.

Morris, Pamela, Heather Hill, Lisa Gennetian, Chris Rodrigues, and Sharon Wolff. "Income Volatility in U.S. Households with Children: Another Growing Disparity between the Rich and the Poor?" IRP discussion paper, University of Wisconsin Institute for Research on Poverty, 2015.

Morrison, Anne, and Katherine Gallagher Robbins. "Chartbook: The Women in the Low-Wage Workforce May Not Be Who You Think." National Women's Law Center, September 15, 2015. https:// nwlc.org/resources/chart-book-women-low-wage-workforce-may -not-be-who-you-think/.

Morrissey, Monique. "The State of American Retirement: How 401(k)s Have Failed Most American Workers." Economic Policy Institute, March 3, 2016. http://www.epi.org/publication/retire ment-in-america/.

Mullainathan, Sendhil, and Eldar Shafir. *Scarcity: Why Having Too Little Means So Much*. New York: Times Books, Henry Holt, 2013.

Munnell, Alicia H., and Anthony Webb. "The Impact of Leakages on 401(k)/IRA Assets." Center for Retirement Research at Boston College, no. 15–2, February 2015. http://crr.bc.edu/wp-content /uploads/2015/01/IB_15-2.pdf.

"Neshoba County African-American Heritage Driving Tour." Pamphlet. Philadelphia Coalition. http://www.neshobajustice.com /documents/RootsofStruggle.pdf.

Newberry, Jorge. "Dodd-Frank Redlined America's Poorest Neighborhoods." *Huffington Post*, June 15, 2016. http://www.huffington post.com/jorge-newbery/dodd-frank-redlined-ameri_b_10484242 .html.

Newman, Katherine. *No Shame in My Game: The Working Poor and the Inner City*. New York: Knopf and Russell Sage Foundation, 1999.

Nicholson, Jessica R. "An Update on Temporary Help in Manufacturing." ESA Issue Brief 02-15, U.S. Department of Commerce, Economics and Statistics Administration, April 29, 2015.

Oak, Mandar, and Anand Swamy. "Only Twice as Much: A Rule for Regulating Lenders." *Economic Development and Cultural Change* 58, no. 4 (July 2010): 775–803.

O'Brien, Rourke, and David Pedulla. "Beyond the Poverty Line." *Stanford Social Innovation Review* 8, no. 4 (Fall 2010): 30–35.

Ogden, Timothy. "The IRS's Secret, Successful Low-Income Savings Program." *Stanford Social Innovation Review*, April 15, 2015. https:// ssir.org/articles/entry/the_irss_secret_successful_low_income _savings_program.

Orhun, A. Yesim, and Mike Palazzolo. "Frugality Is Hard to Afford." Nielsen Dataset Paper Series 2-031, Kilts Center for Marketing at the University of Chicago, March 20, 2016.

Orman, Suze. *Suze Orman's Action Plan: New Rules for New Times.* New York: Spiegel and Grau, 2010.

———. "Suze Orman's Easy Money To-Do List." CNN, January 6, 2010. http://www.cnn.com/2010/LIVING/personal/01/06/o.orman .easy.money.list/.

Parker, Jonathan, and Bruce Preston. "Precautionary Saving and Consumption Fluctuations." *American Economic Review* 95, no. 4 (2005): 1119–43.

"Peddling Uphill: A Report on the Conditions of Street Vendors in New York City." Street Vendor Project, Urban Justice Center, 2006. https://www.scribd.com/document/18948529/Peddling-Uphill.

Pew Charitable Trusts. "Americans' Financial Security: Perception and Reality." March 2015. http://www.pewtrusts.org/~/media /assets/2015/02/fsm-poll-results-issue-brief_artfinal_v3.pdf.

———. "The Complex Story of American Debt." July 2015. http:// www.pewtrusts.org/~/media/assets/2015/07/reach-of-debt-report _artfinal.pdf.

———. "Household Expenditures and Income." Research and Analysis blog, March 30, 2016. http://www.pewtrusts.org/en/research -and-analysis/issue-briefs/2016/03/household-expenditures-and -income.

———. "How Do Families Cope with Financial Shocks?" October 2015. http://www.pewtrusts.org/~/media/assets/2015/10 /emergency-savings-report-1_artfinal.pdf.

———. "The Precarious State of Family Balance Sheets." Research and Analysis blog, January 29, 2015. http://www.pewtrusts.org /en/research-and-analysis/reports/2015/01/the-precarious-state -of-family-balance-sheets.

———. "What Resources Do Families Have for Financial Emergencies?" November 2015. http://www.pewtrusts.org/~/media/assets /2015/11/emergencysavingsreportnov2015.pdf.

Phelps, Erin, Frank F. Furstenberg, and Anne Colby, eds. *Looking at Lives: American Longitudinal Studies of the Twentieth Century.* New York: Russell Sage, 2002.

"The Power of Compounding." Vanguard Funds. https://investor
.vanguard.com/investing/how-to-invest/risk-reward-compounding.

"Preparing for Retirement in America." Employee Benefit Research
Institute and Greenwald & Associates, 2016. https://www.ebri
.org/pdf/surveys/rcs/2015/RCS15.FS-3.Preps.pdf.

Price, Stephen. "Why Does America Still Write Checks?" *Payments
Journal: Industry Blogs*, July 10, 2015. http://www.paymentsjournal
.com/Blog.aspx?id=26434.

Proctor, Bernadette D., Jessica L. Semega, and Melissa A. Kollar.
Income and Poverty in the United States: 2015. U.S. Census Bureau,
Current Population Reports, P60-256. Washington, DC: U.S.
GPO, 2016.

Putre, Laura. "Counting Temporary Workers Could Give Manufacturing a Boost." *IndustryWeek*, May 11, 2015. http://www.industry
week.com/temp-data.

Quinton, Sophie. "The High Cost of Higher Education." Pew Charitable Trusts Research and Analysis blog, January 25, 2016. http://
www.pewtrusts.org/en/research-and-analysis/blogs/stateline/2016
/01/25/the-high-cost-of-higher-education.

Ramsey, Dave. "How Teens Can Become Millionaires: Disciplined
Saving Early in Life Will Reap Millions . . . Literally!" Dave Ramsey blog, March 12, 2010. http://www.daveramsey.com/article
/how-teens-can-become-millionaires/lifeandmoney_kidsand
money/.

Ratcliffe, Caroline, Signe-Mary McKernan, Laura Wheaton, Emma
Kalish, Catherine Ruggles, Sara Armstrong, and Christina Ober-
lin. "Asset Limits, SNAP Participation, and Financial Stability."
Urban Institute Research Report, 2016. http://www.urban.org
/research/publication/asset-limits-snap-participation-and-financial
-stability/view/full_report.

"Realizing the Dream: How the Minimum Wage Impacts Racial
Equity in the Restaurant Industry and in America." Restaurant
Opportunities Centers United, June 19, 2013. http://rocunited
.org/wp-content/uploads/2014/02/report_realizing-the-dream.pdf.

Reich, Robert. *Beyond Outrage: Expanded Edition: What Has Gone
Wrong with Our Economy and Our Democracy, and How to Fix It*.
New York: Vintage, 2012.

"Resource Guide: Lifting Asset Limits in Public Benefit Programs." Corporation for Enterprise Development, 2013. http://cfed.org /assets/scorecard/2013/rg_AssetLimits_2013.pdf.

"The Rising Cost of Not Going to College." Pew Research Center Social and Demographic Trends blog, February 11, 2014. http:// www.pewsocialtrends.org/2014/02/11/the-rising-cost-of-not-going -to-college/.

Rosebush, Fran. "Building Financial Capability at Tax Time." Corporation for Enterprise Development's Inclusive Economy blog, April 13, 2015. http://cfed.org/blog/inclusiveeconomy/building _financial_capability_at_tax_time/.

Ru, Hong, and Antoinette Schoar. "Do Credit Card Companies Screen for Behavioral Biases?" Working Paper 22360, National Bureau of Economic Research, June 2016.

Rush, Suzanna. "Using Business Credit Scores to Graduate Borrowers." Kiva blog, June 9, 2016. https://borrow.kiva.org/blogs.

Rutherford, Stuart. *The Poor and Their Money*. Delhi: Oxford University Press, 1998.

Salmon, Felix. "How One Small Company Is Saving the Homes of Poor Americans." Fusion, July 29, 2016. http://fusion.net/story /331313/financial-crisis-housing-ahp-financing/.

Sanger-Katz, Margot. "The Big Problem with High Health Care Deductibles." *New York Times*, February 5, 2016. http://www.nytimes .com/2016/02/07/upshot/the-big-problem-with-high-health-care -deductibles.html.

Schlossberg, Jon. "Why." *Medium*, January 3, 2015. https://medium .com/@jschloss/why-69a9d8193075#.1wltm8wa1.

Schmitt, Mark. "Michael Sherraden's Compounding Interest." *Washington Monthly*, July/August 2012. http://washingtonmonthly.com /magazine/julyaugust-2012/michael-sherraddens-compounding -interest/.

Schreiner, Mark, and Michael Sherraden. *Can the Poor Save? Saving and Asset Building in Individual Development Accounts*. New Brunswick, NJ: Transaction, 2007.

Schuh, Scott, and Joanna Stavins. "The 2013 Survey of Consumer Payment Choice: Summary Results." Federal Reserve Bank of Boston Research Data Report 15-4, November 2015.

Sherraden, Michael. *Assets and the Poor: A New American Welfare Policy.* New York: M. E. Sharpe, 1991.

———. "Asset Building Research and Policy: Pathways, Progress, and Potential of a Social Innovation." In *The Assets Perspective: The Rise of Asset Building and Its Impact on Social Policy*, ed. R. Cramer and T. R. Williams Shanks, 263–84. London: Palgrave MacMillan.

———. "From Research to Policy: Lessons from Individual Accounts." *Journal of Consumer Affairs* 34, no. 2 (2000): 159–81.

Short, Kathleen. "The Supplemental Poverty Measure: 2014." U.S. Census Bureau, 2015. https://www.census.gov/content/dam/Census/library/publications/2015/demo/p60-254.pdf.

Simon, Ruth. "Mortgage Lenders Loosen Standards." *Wall Street Journal*, July 6, 2005. http://www.wsj.com/articles/SB112234272837695744.

Smith, Trenton G., Christiana Stoddard, and Michael G. Barnes. "Why the Poor Get Fat: Weight Gain and Economic Insecurity." Working Paper No. 2007-16, Washington State University, School of Economic Sciences, 2007.

Stack, Carol. *All Our Kin.* New York: Basic Books, 1974.

Stephens, Melvin, Jr. "Paycheque Receipt and the Timing of Consumption." *Economic Journal* 116, no. 513 (July 2006): 680–701.

———. " '3rd of tha Month': Do Social Security Recipients Smooth Consumption between Checks?" *American Economic Review* 93, no. 1 (March 2003): 406–22.

Stevens, Ann Huff. "Climbing out of Poverty, Falling Back in: Measuring the Persistence of Poverty over Multiple Spells." *Journal of Human Resources* 34, no. 3 (1999): 557–88.

———. "The Dynamics of Poverty Spells: Updating Bane and Ellwood." *American Economic Review* 84, no. 2 (May 1994): 34–37.

Strain, Michael. "Do Volatile Firms Pay Volatile Earnings? Evidence Using Linked Worker-Firm Data." Working Paper No. 2013-01, American Enterprise Institute, March 2013.

"Street Vending." New York City Department of Consumer Affairs, 2010. http://www.nyc.gov/html/sbs/nycbiz/downloads/pdf/educational/sector_guides/street_vending.pdf?epi-content=GENERIC.

Sunstein, Cass, and Richard Thaler. *Nudge.* New Haven: Yale University Press, 2008.

Tankersley, Jim. "Middle Class Incomes Had Their Fastest Growth on Record Last Year." *Washington Post*, September 13, 2016. https://www.washingtonpost.com/news/wonk/wp/2016/09/13/the-middle-class-and-the-poor-just-had-the-best-year-since-the-end-of-the-great-recession/.

Thaler, Richard, and Shlomo Benartzi. "Save More Tomorrow™: Using Behavioral Economics to Increase Employee Saving." *Journal of Political Economy* 112, no. 1, pt. 2 (2004): S164–S187.

Theodos, Brett, Christina Plerhoples Stacy, Margaret Simms, Katya Abazajian, Rebecca Daniels, Devlin Hanson, Amanda Hahnel, and Joanna Smith-Ramani. "An Evaluation of the Impacts of Two 'Rules of Thumb' for Credit Card Revolvers." Urban Institute, September 8, 2016. http://www.urban.org/research/publication/evaluation-impacts-two-rules-thumb-credit-card-revolvers-0.

Thomas, Hannah, Janet Boguslaw, Sara Chaganti, Alicia Atkinson, and Thomas Shapiro. "Employment Capital: How Work Builds and Protects Family Wealth and Security." Institute on Assets and Social Policy, December 2013. http://iasp.brandeis.edu/pdfs/2013/Employment.pdf.

Ton, Zeynep. *The Good Jobs Strategy: How the Smartest Companies Invest in Employees to Lower Costs and Boost Profits*. Boston: Houghton Mifflin, 2014.

"Too Much Month at the End of the Money." Performed by Billy Hill, written by Dennis Robbins, Bob DiPiero, and John Scott Sherrill. *I Am Just a Rebel*. Reprise Records, CD, 1989.

Traub, Amy. "Discredited: How Employment Credit Checks Keep Qualified Workers Out of a Job." *Demos*, March 2013. http://www.demos.org/discredited-how-employment-credit-checks-keep-qualified-workers-out-job.

Turner, Michael A., and Patrick Walker. "Predicting Financial Account Delinquencies with Utility and Telecom Payment Data." Property and Environment Research Center, May 2015. http://www.perc.net/wp-content/uploads/2015/05/Alt-Data-and-Traditional-Accounts.pdf.

"The 2013 Federal Reserve Payments Study: Recent and Long-Term Trends in the United States, 2003–2012." Federal Reserve, July 2014. http://docplayer.net/4215453-The-2013-federal-reserve-payments-study.html.

"Vendor Power! A Guide to Street Vending in New York City." Center for Urban Pedagogy, 2009. http://welcometocup.org/file_col umns/0000/0012/vp-mpp.pdf.

"Waiving, Not Drowning." *Economist*, July 3, 2008. http://www .economist.com/node/11671060.

Wann, Elizabeth. "American Tipping Is Rooted in Slavery—And It Still Hurts Workers Today." Ford Foundation's Equals Change blog, February 18, 2016. http://www.fordfoundation.org/ideas /equals-change-blog/posts/american-tipping-is-rooted-in-slavery -and-it-still-hurts-workers-today/.

Warren, Elizabeth, and Amelia Warren Tyagi. *The Two-Income Trap: Why Middle Class Parents Are Going Broke*. New York: Basic Books, 2003.

Weimer, Christopher, Liana Fox, Irv Garfinkel, Neeraj Kaushal, and Jane Waldfogel. "Progress on Poverty? New Estimates of Historical Trends Using an Anchored Supplemental Poverty Measure." *Demography* (electronic publication ahead of print, June 28, 2016).

Wilson, William Julius. *The Truly Disadvantaged: The Inner City, the Underclass, and Public Policy*. Chicago: University of Chicago Press, 1987.

Wolf, Sharon, Lisa Gennetian, Pamela Morris, and Heather D. Hill. "Patterns of Income Instability among Low- and Middle-Income Households with Children." *Family Relations* 63, no. 3 (2014): 397–410.

Wolff, Sarah. "The Cumulative Costs of Predatory Practices." Center for Responsible Lending, 2015. http://www.responsiblelending .org/state-of-lending/reports/13-Cumulative-Impact.pdf.

Womack, James, Daniel Jones, and Daniel Roos. *The Machine That Changed the World*. New York: Free Press, 1990.

Zelizer, Viviana. *Economic Lives: How Culture Shapes the Economy*. Princeton: Princeton University Press, 2010.

———. *The Social Meaning of Money: Pin Money, Paychecks, Poor Relief, and Other Currencies*. Princeton: Princeton University Press, 1994.

———. "The Social Meaning of Money: 'Special Monies.'" *American Journal of Sociology* 95, no. 2 (September 1989): 342–77.

Zhang, C. Yiwei. "Consumption Responses to Pay Frequency: Evidence from 'Extra' Paychecks." Draft manuscript, Wharton School, University of Pennsylvania, November 7, 2013.

Index

A page number in *italics* refers to a figure or table.